DISCARD

AMERICAN MANIA

American

MANIA

When More Is Not Enough

Peter C. Whybrow

W. W. NORTON & COMPANY

NEW YORK   LONDON

For information about permission to reproduce selections from this book, write to
Permissions, W. W. Norton & Company, Inc., 500 Fifth Avenue, New York, NY 10110

Manufacturing by R. R. Donnelley, Harrisonburg
Book design by Lovedog Studio
Production manager: Amanda Morrison

LIBRARY OF CONGRESS CATALOGING-IN-PUBLICATION DATA

Whybrow, Peter C.
American mania : when more is not enough / Peter C. Whybrow.— 1st ed.
          p. cm.
Includes bibliographical references and index.
ISBN 0-393-05994-4 (hardcover)
1. Social values—United States. 2. Wealth—Social aspects—United States.
3. Consumption (Economics)—Health aspects—United States.
4. Self-interest—United States. 5. Social ethics—United States. 6. Happiness.
7. National characteristics, American—History. I. Title.
HN90.M6W55 2005
301'.0973—dc22

                                                              2004018699

W. W. Norton & Company, Inc., 500 Fifth Avenue, New York, N.Y. 10110
www.wwnorton.com

W. W. Norton & Company Ltd., Castle House, 75/76 Wells Street, London W1T 3QT

2 3 4 5 6 7 8 9 0

For my brother,
John William Whybrow

The doctrine of self-interest properly understood does not inspire great sacrifices, but every day it prompts some small ones; by itself it cannot make a man virtuous, but its discipline shapes a lot of orderly, temperate, moderate, careful, and self controlled citizens. If it does not lead to virtue, it establishes habits which unconsciously turn it that way.

Providence did not make mankind entirely free or completely enslaved. Providence has, in truth, drawn a predestined circle around each man beyond which he cannot pass; but within those vast limits man is strong and free, and so are peoples.

Alexis de Tocqueville
Democracy in America, 1835

CONTENTS

ACKNOWLEDGMENTS

THIS BOOK BEGAN IN conversation with friends and colleagues, during those frenzied years of the stock-market bubble in the late 1990s. At times our discussions were spirited, even rancorous. Just what was happening in America and to American culture? we asked. Frequently there were as many opinions as there were people around the table. But it is to those friendly arguments that I now owe gratitude, for they forced reflection on my experience as a migrant in America and triggered my investigation of what we can learn about ourselves from these revolutionary times.

It is impossible to thank individually each of those who have contributed to the facts, insights, and opinions that I express in these pages, but there are some who were particularly tolerant as I tested my emerging ideas. First, I thank Nancy Main for her partnership, love, and forbearance. David Gregory, Pam Cummins, Brad Lovette, and Paula Golden have been stalwart in their support and in their contributions to content, while the gracious hospitality of Anna and Hans Wirz, and the Tuscan solitude of the Villa di Monte, helped guide the initial creative process. My special thanks go to Gordon and Fern Wilder and to all those who enthusiastically gave of their time in contributing personal stories to these pages. Also Lynn Fairbanks, Nga Mai, Susan Goldy, Sasha Bystritsky, Pierre Caland, Peter Loge, Eva Redei, Andy Leuchter, and Bob Stein were especially generous in sharing their experience and in critiquing parts of the manuscript during preparation.

In the research department, Pam Crespin, anthropologist, and Maureen Silos, sociologist, provided able assistance, advice, and friendship while quietly filling in the blank spaces that I discovered in my own education. Sally Arteseros and Helen Whybrow, as in the past, offered indispensable editorial guidance and consistent encouragement. And in that latter regard I owe thanks to Zoe Pagnamenta, a friend who believed in the project from the beginning. I am indebted to Michelle Tessler at the Carlisle Agency for her gentle care and counsel, to Gill Coleridge for her sage advice, and to Don Lamm, who was there when I needed him. But it was Angela Von der Lippe, truly an angel, who with the able assistance of Alessandra Bastagli and the extraordinary team that is W. W. Norton turned this book into a reality. For Angela's intelligence, kindness, and efficient editorial leadership, I am deeply grateful.

Finally, without the help of my colleagues at UCLA's Neuropsychiatric Institute, this book probably would not exist. My many friends there have taught me many things and I thank them all. But I am especially grateful for the affection of Fawzy Fawzy and of Sharon Chavez, who together made it possible for me to secure the necessary time to complete the project. Theirs was an essential gift.

Introduction

THE MANIC SOCIETY

America was set apart in a special way . . .
It was put here between the oceans
To be found by a certain kind of people . . .
A beacon of hope to the rest of the world.

Ronald Reagan
"A Time for Choosing," 1964

AMERICANS HAVE AN ASTONISHING appetite for life. As the nation of bold ideas, big cars, fast food, sky-thrusting cities, and unparalleled military power, America is a monument to the ambition and industry of its people. In the brief span of a few generations the citizens of the United States have created a culture of unprecedented affluence. The Pharaohs were wealthy, as were many citizens of Rome, but neither empire achieved the broad distribution of riches and the seductive prosperity that exist in America today. In fact, the material wealth and the abundant choice available in contemporary U.S. society are unique in human experience. Never before in the history of our species have so many enjoyed so much.

This extraordinary accomplishment has brought America to the leading edge of an unusual human experiment. Building on a philosophical foundation of unbridled self-interest and commercial freedom, and supercharged now by a revolution in information technology, we have built a dynamic society of tantalizing appeal. But the resulting mix of technology, affluence, and competitive social challenge that we have created for ourselves is radically different from the natural world in which our species rose to dominance some two hundred thousand years ago. That radical difference in social habitat has fostered a craving and an acquisitive behavior in America that are now testing the limits of our ancestral biology—in mind and in body—and eroding the foundations of our community. In short, in our compulsive drive for more, we are making ourselves sick. How through knowledge of the brain sciences we may better understand our acquisitive craving and its impact on the health and happiness of individual citizens, why such an addictive environment should have emerged first in America, and why in seeking a balanced civil society we must revisit the economic principles that now shape the material focus of our yearning are the subjects of this book.

TO WANT more is a basic human instinct, one that has been essential to our survival. It was our hunger for better things, and the intelligence to imagine them, that gave us mastery over the dangerous and depriving environment in which we evolved, and it was that same hunger that first propelled us forward in the search for a promised land. Having achieved something akin to El Dorado in contemporary American society, however, we now find ourselves in the confusing position of falling victim to our own acquisitive ambition.

This confusion became painfully obvious during the economic boom of the late 1990s, when our appetite for riches and material comfort triggered a competitive frenzy of greed and shortsighted speculation. In the words of George Carlin, the comedian and satirist, America became a land of puzzling contradictions, a nation of "bigger houses but smaller families; more conveniences but less time; wider freeways but narrower viewpoints; taller buildings but shorter tempers; more knowledge but less judgment." In our relentless search for material wealth, Carlin suggests, Americans have embraced a culture where steep profits and shallow relationships have multiplied our possessions but reduced our social values.

My natural inclination is to dismiss such polemical ramblings, but Carlin's caricature of contemporary American life contains some disturbing truths. For the majority of Americans the nation's dramatic increase in material wealth has not been translated into a subjective sense of enhanced well-being. The evidence for such disenchantment is pervasive and readily available. From the character of the struggles that my patients report; from the subject matter of newspaper and magazine articles; from talk shows and the concerns expressed during chance conversations with strangers; and from discussions with colleagues, friends, and family, it is clear to me that many Americans are experiencing a discomfort for which they have little explanation. For a year or so after 9/11, the threat of random terror gave cruel focus to America's troubled state of mind, but alone those events and the military actions that followed offer no lasting explanation for our deepening discomfort. Indeed, it is evident that our uneasiness as a nation was already percolating when the World Trade Center and the Pentagon were struck. A variety of surveys conducted during the 1980s and 1990s recorded a declining satisfaction with life in America. Why, for example, does nearly one-third of the U.S. population now struggle with the complications of obesity? And why, amid our drive for wealth and self-improvement, are the best-selling drugs on the American market those prescribed for the stress-related diseases of ulcer, depression, and high blood pressure? In our demand-driven, debt-saturated culture many families find themselves too pressured to enjoy, even to notice, their affluence. Time is chronically in short supply and the "free moments" that once balanced a busy life have all but disappeared. The demands of securing and maintaining material wealth in a rapidly shifting economic climate—particularly for Americans who shoulder considerable debt—have created an accelerated, competitive lifestyle that steals away sleep and kindles anxiety, threatening the intimate social webs that sustain family and community. For many Americans the hallowed search for happiness has been hijacked by a discomforting and frenzied activity.

As a practicing psychiatrist I find much in this frenetic chase that is reminiscent of mania, a dysfunctional state of mind that begins with a joyous sense of excitement and high productivity but escalates into reckless pursuit, irritability, and confusion, before cycling down into depression. In the continuum of human emotion, mania is the close cousin and polar opposite of depression. Whereas in profound depression, energy and positive thinking shrink and contract, in mania they accelerate and expand, magnifying and caricaturing the normal experience of happiness through a distorting aggrandizement of the self. Thus, in psychiatric parlance, mania is the *dysphoric* state of activity—from the Greek *dusphoria* meaning "discomfort"—that begins with happiness *but lies beyond it* in a tumult of anxiety, competition, and social disruption. By analogy, one can look on America's increasing frenzy as evidence of a nation stumbling into something akin to this dysphoric state. Unwittingly, in our relentless pursuit of happiness we have overshot the target and spawned a manic society with an insatiable appetite for more. America's dream of a Utopian social order—fueled from the beginning by the twin beliefs that material success equates with personal satisfaction (a notion that is embellished now by a commercially contrived illusion of infinite opportunity) and that technical advance is the key to social progress—has become mired in a confusing mix of manic desire and depressive discomfort.

There are those who will quickly dismiss my analogy to the illness of manic depression, protesting that I misinterpret in my examination of America's malaise the aggressive pursuit required to further the nation's commercial self-interest. After all, as the world's leading trader—at a time when globalization is proceeding apace—is it not appropriate that America is in the vanguard of the race for market domination? And is it not inevitable that when locked in such vital international competition, there will be winners and losers at home? The frenzied discomfort that many Americans are now experiencing merely reflects a time-limited period of adjustment, the predictable response to an evolving economic challenge. As the market forces of globalization play out, America will find a new social balance, the dysphoria will subside, and all will be well.

Unfortunately, while appealing in its simplicity, such an analysis falls short when it comes to helping individual Americans understand what is happening to them. As I will describe (and about which many books have already been written), globalization and changing economic conditions are an essential part of the conundrum that is America's mania. But the economy alone is not a sufficient explanation for the sea change that many Americans are now forced to navigate; nor is it one for the obesity, the growing anxiety, and the corporate greed (each a topic about which there is also a growing literature) that increasingly plague the conduct of everyday life in our nation. No, what you will discover in subsequent chapters—as I explore the lives of individual Americans through their personal stories and reference them back to what we know about human behavior and how the brain works—is that these seemingly distinct manifestations of ill health are parts of a larger sickness. From the vantage point of neurobiology, given the daring temperament of the American people and the conditions in which we now find ourselves, the damaging frenzy that now engulfs our nation was predictable and is treatable.

Let me elaborate. In practicing psychiatry one learns early that self-destructive behaviors are commonly the result of conflict among opposing forces, only some of which are within conscious awareness. Usually these forces are deeply rooted in both biology and experience, and in finding an effective remedy for the dysfunctional behavior, it is essential both to identify those roots and to respect them. And that is how I will proceed in my exploration of America's mania. To solve the puzzle and to accurately diagnose the frenzy that now grips America—and, most importantly, to diminish its corrosive impact—we must look beneath the singular explanation of a changing economy. We must seek to understand the roots of the growing conflict that exists in American culture between our instinctual striving for more and the reward system of the affluent society that we have built for ourselves.

The human brain, the organ that acts as the transducer in interpreting daily experience and the lens through which we view the world, was programmed long ago to keep us safe from harm. Thus, by nature, humans are curiosity-driven, reward-seeking, and harm-avoiding creatures. Having evolved in circumstances of danger and privation, these instincts of self-preservation remain the vital force behind much of our behavior. These ancient drives motivate us to get out of bed each morning and to tackle the challenges of the day. And, contrary to what we would like to believe about ourselves, each day our astonishing intelligence functions largely as servant to this passionate self-interest.

The countervailing force to this self-indulgence, which is weak by comparison and depends on social learning, draws its strength from our deep attachment to others. Our intelligence aids here too. Skilled in complex communication, we are intensely social creatures and find comfort in living together in stable social hierarchies. Loyal to those we love and in whom we trust, and aggressive and punitive toward those who may threaten us, we learn quickly from personal experience and from others.

Hence, in simple terms, it is the dynamic tension between innate desire and social learning that determines individual behavior and underpins the extraordinary complexity of the myths and social agreements that we call *human culture*. And because of this tension we rarely exercise the basic instincts of self-preservation as solitary animals but rather do so in competitive collaboration with others. The give-and-take of a market economy may be understood within such a conceptual framework as a natural by-product of human social evolution, one where competitive collaboration is exploited as a collective benefit. Thus, with the adoption of a few rules—such as honesty in competition, respect for private property, and the ability to exchange goods for money—a market culture is essentially an ordering of human instinct and competition by those traditional cooperative, sharing practices that our forebears found to be fruitful and successful. Through the give-and-take of social interaction, and through the internalization of the conventions and customs it promotes, instinctual self-interest is liberated and molded to the common good. The capitalist enterprise is founded on this dynamic premise.

Such was the insight of Adam Smith—the Scottish philosopher and the patron saint of American capitalism—who in the latter part of the eighteenth century and during the nascent days of the American Republic championed the social value of harnessing the instinctual drives of curiosity and self-interest within the framework of the marketplace to create a self-regulating economic order. The Founding Fathers, in their eager quest for commercial independence, took Smith's vision seriously, and in America today we still prefer to satisfy the nation's social and economic needs through market mechanisms. But in recent decades we have placed Adam Smith's original texts aside, as we have done with many patron saints. That is unfortunate, for as I will detail in later pages, Smith's economic philosophy was predicated on a dynamic balance between commercial liberty and a set of social structures that are rapidly eroding in America. Smith worried in his writings, as did many other thinkers of the time, that human envy and our tendency toward compulsive craving, if left unchecked, would destroy the empathic feeling and neighborly concerns that are essential to his economic model and a free market's successful operation. In searching for the necessary counterbalance to this natural human avarice, Smith took comfort in the fellowship and social constraint that he considered inherent in the tightly knit communities characteristic of the eighteenth century.

Given the social conditions that prevailed during his lifetime, Adam Smith was prescient in his judgment. Experience tells us that small markets do produce their own constraint and rational order, founded as they are on an interlocking system of self-interested exchange. However, Smith lived before the invention of the megacorporation, before instant communication with a global reach, and before the double cheeseburger and stock options. In America, living with such an abundance of choice, we have discovered some disturbing facts about human behavior—facts that from knowledge of modern neurobiology are predictable and that confirm Smith's worst fears. In times of material affluence, when desire is no longer constrained by limited resources, the evidence from our contemporary American experiment suggests that we humans have trouble setting limits to our instinctual craving. This comes as little surprise to the behavioral neuroscientist, for it is now well established that under certain contingencies it is possible to "overload" the reward circuits of the brain, triggering craving and insatiable desire. As the quintessential reward-driven culture, America bears witness to this truth, for there is considerable evidence suggesting that unchecked consumption fosters our social malaise, eroding self-constraint and pulling the cultural pendulum toward excessive indulgence and greed.

Compounding this erosion of self-constraint is an increasing globalization, consolidating the commercial power of a few megacompanies of international reach. In such organizations the traditional checks and balances of the marketplace are removed from the communities they serve, threatening the wellspring of the social mores—neighborliness and empathy—that Adam Smith in his economic theory had relied on as the major bridle for our instinctual passions. Another consequence of the increasing consolidation of commerce and the destruction of small community-based markets is that the distribution of wealth in America is becoming badly skewed. This trend, and it shows little sign of abating, fosters the envy, the debt accumulation, and the demand-driven work environments that fuel the discomforting frenzy experienced by many American families. The result—again predictable from knowledge of the dynamics of human behavior—is that the delicate balance between individual desire and social responsibility—the bedrock of a healthy society—is increasingly threatened.

But why has this potentially damaging cultural climate—a malignant social mania that fosters envy over empathy—emerged first in America, among the many wealthy nations in the world? Key to fitting this particular piece of the puzzle into the whole is an understanding of the American temperament—the roots of which are to be found in the immigrant history of the United States—and how America's laissez-faire commercial culture is uniquely driven by the migrant mind-set.

America is an unusual nation—it is in many ways a genetic experiment as much as it is a social one—in that the temperament of the migrant has played a unique role. Most Americans, or the forebears of most Americans within a generation or two, came to this country because they chose to do so. For three centuries and longer, America has been a lure for those of the migrant disposition, "a certain kind of people" for whom a love of competition, curiosity, and a willingness to take risks are instinctual and enduring talents. Migrants are by temperament restless and ingenious and the United States represents the largest single collection of such individuals in the world today.

The aggressive migrant temperament has always been a feature of American life. Alexis de Tocqueville, that astute eyewitness of American habits and culture, observed as much when he visited in 1831. The Americans, he wrote in *Democracy in America*, approach life "like a game of chance . . . or the day of a battle." Although Tocqueville had in mind the first generations of European immigrants who then populated the states of the eastern seaboard, his observations serve equally well to explain the competitive success of the diverse peoples who subsequently migrated to the Union's fifty states. In California, where I live amid the restless energy and ethnic diversity of Los Angeles, it is plain to see that America is held together not by race, color, or creed but by the migrant's burning ambition and the ancient skills essential to human survival. Migrants approach life with extraordinary resolve: self-selected in their search for betterment and shaped further by the challenge of their journey, the migrant's principal goal is one of individual achievement.

The migrant's heightened ambition and love of competition serve to reinforce the self-interest that is so essential to success in a free-market society. This is the second important piece in the puzzle of understanding our American mania. It also helps explain the dominance of the market ideology in American culture and why we have become such a successful commercial nation. The competitive ambitions of the migrant have found unusual opportunity in America's embrace of laissez-faire commerce and in the vast natural resources of the North American continent. Whereas much of the cultural cohesion of Europe is drawn from a communal sense of place and history, America's national identity is held together by dreams of individual freedom, property, and material betterment. Successive immigrant waves have infused America with new energy and fresh ideas, and with this commercial advantage the nation is now undisputed as the world's economic leader.

Perhaps the key piece in solving our puzzle, however, and the immediate stimulus to America's increasing frenzy, is the advent of the information age. Only with that revolution, and with the dramatic changes that it has spawned in America's social and economic environment, did our manic predisposition come to full flower. Previously the marketplace has always had its natural constraints. For the first two centuries of the nation's existence, even the most insatiable American citizen was significantly leashed by the checks and balances inherent in a closely knit community, by geography, by the elements of weather, or, in some cases, by religious practice. Then toward the end of the twentieth century, two important events revolutionized capital markets across the world. The Soviet Union collapsed—and with it the competing economic philosophy of communism—leaving capitalism supreme. And almost simultaneously an information technology capable of leaping the barriers of time and space became broadly available. Operating in a world of instant communication with minimal social tethers, America's engines of commerce and desire became turbocharged. The constraints of time and space that have dictated the fundamental rhythms of human existence throughout our evolution—the great oceans, the mountains, and the planetary cycles of light and dark—were no longer significant impediments to America's commercial enterprise. With the coming of the information age, the restless migrant spirit of America was unleashed on a new global frontier, and in the excitement of that moment our mania blossomed.

Americans have fallen back from the pinnacle of manic activity that characterized the late 1990s, and in the period of depressive rumination that inevitably follows, we have begun to survey as a nation the personal and social damage wrought by our excess. But the reality remains. We have invented a new demand-driven environment for ourselves—a "Fast New World"—where data, money, and ideas circle the globe with dizzying dispatch. Globalization now offers American business a commercial environment without limits, one where entrepreneurs of manic predisposition may work around the clock. Vast stores of information are now available at the touch of a button. With the nomadic tools of telephone and laptop we have immediate access to friends, family, business associates, news, personal banking services, stock trading, and navigational aids regardless of where we happen to be—and so, too, do others have immediate access to us.

It is the resonance between this accelerated social and economic environment and the competitive, workaholic ways of the migrant temperament that now spurs America's manic pursuit. But this resonance alone does not explain the growing personal discomfort felt by many Americans. There is another vital element to be considered—and it is one easily forgotten, given that as humans we prefer to think of ourselves above the animal herd. While we are fascinated by the novelties of the Fast New World, as evolved creatures of our planet we are physiologically ill equipped for the turbocharged lifestyle that they promote. Simply put, the strain of unbridled manic pursuit, whether we enjoy it or not, is damaging to both health and happiness.

For many Americans the sense of exhilaration and the reward-laden opportunities afforded by the manic society are compelling, indeed even habit forming. But for those mentally unprepared or unwilling to impose personal constraint, there are dangers in such a demand-driven, helter-skelter existence. As any individual who has suffered mania knows, despite the seductive quality of the initial phases of the condition, life at the manic edge is impossible to sustain in any coherent fashion. So it is, by analogy, when one revels in the affluence and immediacy of the Fast New World. Initially the excitement of the competition and the lure of the potential payoff are so energizing that concerns about health are forgotten or swept aside. But such denial ignores that our instincts are those of an ancient brain that evolved over many thousands of years, and that the human body is tuned for optimum function under conditions radically different from those that we enjoy in America today. Hence, our ingenuity in creating novel environments—such as the competitive opportunities of a global commerce that never sleeps, or an infinite supply of high-calorie food—rather than enhancing well-being may actually disrupt the ancient mechanisms that sustain our physical and mental balance. Such is the potential danger of the social and economic environment developing in America today.

The individual of migrant temperament, quick witted and vigilant, is particularly well equipped to deal with the challenge and physical risk of frontier life. Thus it is an odd twist of fate that the same curiosity, hard work, and intelligence that first enabled the migrant to shape these United States have now invented a lifestyle that can be physiologically and mentally disabling. Inadvertently, through the choices we have made, we have created an imbalance—a mismatch—between the demands of our time-sensitive commercial culture and the biology that we have inherited. Indeed, the anxiety and much of the ill health from which Americans now suffer can be traced to the strain of this growing cultural-biological mismatch. Predictably, by the way in which we have chosen to conduct our lives, we are making ourselves sick.

So what is to be done? States of health and illness reflect a complex interaction between the individual and the social and environmental circumstances under which that individual must live. When the interaction proceeds in relative harmony, health is sustained, and when the balance is lost, the result is illness. Only in considering both sides of the equation—the role of individual behavior and the demands of the environment—can the potential outcome of the interaction be clearly understood. We accept that tobacco smoke in the air that we breathe, for example, or chemicals in the water that we drink can be toxic to individual health, and we adapt our behaviors and social laws accordingly. But we have difficulty employing a similar logic when evaluating the food we eat or the social distribution of economic wealth, both of which are important determinants of health and happiness. For most individuals living in postindustrial, information-driven societies—of which the United States is the exemplar—the stress of daily life is now tied not to physical toxins but to the toxic demand of a world that never sleeps, and to how we think and feel about our material circumstances. Today it is no longer the threat of physical harm but the uncertainty of an unpredictable workplace, the loss of intimacy associated with an unstable marriage, or a perceived change in social status that seeds our smoldering discomfort, with declining harmony and mounting anxiety. In the frenzy of America's affluent society, the individual state of mind determined by the balance we strike between choice and opportunity is what decides health and illness.

If as Americans we are to enjoy the benefits of the Fast New World and to avoid its pitfalls, we must first control the mania that it induces. We live in a culture in which our acquisitive cravings have been promoted beyond our needs, and the demand and strain, which that craving now inflicts on mind and body, are beginning to exceed the flexibility inherent in our biological heritage. Thus do we promote our own sickness. Protection against such a sickness comes through knowledge of the assets and liabilities of our migrant culture and from an understanding of the physiological and behavioral limits imposed on us by our evolutionary past. It is my goal in writing this book to help the reader achieve that understanding and improve self-awareness in these complex times, thus enhancing the conscious life choices that can mitigate the strain of our American mania.

THE BOOK is divided into three approximately equal parts, each with three chapters. In Part I, The American Temperament: A Mania for Prosperity, I begin by describing how America's freedoms and poorly distributed affluence have spawned a competitive consumerism, where in our envy and migrant yearning—aided and abetted by merchants and politicians who recognize that it is more popular and more profitable to satisfy desire than to limit it—we have accumulated a mountain of personal debt. This debt, which in a time of diminished economic activity is increasingly difficult to service, now burdens the average American family and helps drive our treadmill-like existence. In the new cultural reality of expanding commercial dominance in parallel with shrinking personal priority setting, time has become the constraining variable. The social balance is shifting: the more time we spend at work, the less time there is for the family; the more people with whom we interact, the less attention each of them receives; and the greater the distance that we travel, the thinner is our appreciation of the neighbor who lives next door. As never before, whether we like it or not, commerce has become a relentless intruder into the private life of every American citizen. And in consequence the challenges that beset us each day and the choices that we make are driven largely by the demands of the workplace, to the detriment of family and community.

The compelling attraction of laissez-faire commerce is that it harnesses the competitive human instincts for self-preservation, particularly curiosity and self-reward, and promotes through a division of labor those who are innovative in their adaptation to market forces. This is the truth that Adam Smith recognized in his economic philosophy a century or so before Darwin published his theory of evolution, founded on similar ideas about competition and survival. Hence, after describing the instinctual roots of Smith's philosophy, I draw together these elements to explain why competition in the marketplace is especially attractive to the survival instincts of the migrant temperament, and how in consequence the migrant's aggressive striving has shaped the American cultural experiment. Instinctual imperatives continue to have a powerful influence on human behavior. Despite our planetary dominance and sophisticated intelligence, science reminds us that we remain creatures tethered to an ancient past, as will become clear when I explain the bonds we share with our primate cousins. Finally, in concluding the first part of the book, I explore, through the stories and experiences of three Americans who live life at the manic edge, how the culture of the American workplace changed in the closing decades of the twentieth century and how the entrepreneurial spirit that is now central to America's commercial success is fostered by the reward-driven neurobiology and the love of risk that comprise the migrant temperament.

In Part II, Over the Top: Prosperity's Paradox, I describe some of the contradictory consequences of our American mania and the challenges to the nation's physical and moral health that the Fast New World has induced. While for a select few life in America has never been more privileged, many citizens now live in a state of chronic stress. A surfeit of choice and material goods, an abundance of fast food, fragmented sleep and rapid travel across time zones, and the relentless competitive demand of an unstable marketplace are all novel in the annals of human experience. We did not evolve in such a world, where every waking moment carries its own microemergency. Prolonged exposure to such conditions tends to confuse our ancient protective mechanisms, exhausting the body's stress-arousal systems and lowering resistance to disease.

And yet despite these warning signs, we press on. Drawn forward by debt, desire, or both, Americans are emerging as the first addicts of the technological age, driven still by some ancient instinct for self-preservation that in our time of affluence is misplaced. Ironically, we are better tuned physiologically to face the privations and dangers inherent in an unexpected terrorist attack than we are to endure the relentless propositions and stressful abundance of our consumer society. It is in this blind pursuit of material prosperity that Americans have begun to push the boundaries of human adaptation, as is evidenced by rising levels of greed, anxiety, and obesity.

In the final part of the book, More is not Enough: Prosperity Reconsidered, I outline the principles that we must employ if we are to bridle our manic craving. First, I turn to Europe to explore—and to learn from—the mixed reaction to America's changing social agenda and to our strident dominance in international commerce and political affairs. I suggest that in the marketing of American culture, the ideals of the Enlightenment—the ideals of individual freedom and unalienable rights that form the foundation of the American system of economic democracy—have been caricatured to mean the "pleasure" of material possession. It is this "pop" culture of self-desire—together with its rampant consumerism and treadmill-like demand—that is now equated in many minds with the American "way of life." In consequence, not all peoples on the world stage are happy with America's growing supremacy. Some fear that in its global dominance our market enterprise and military might threaten to overwhelm, perhaps even to extinguish, other cultures. In fact, with globalization we have come full circle to a new mercantilism—to something reminiscent of the commercial hegemony that Adam Smith so stridently opposed, and that drove his philosophy of economic liberty—where multinational corporations control most of the world trade, potentially bending individuals and democracy to their will.

At home America's mania for more is shifting the vital equilibrium— where the liberties of the individual and community life are balanced to mutual advantage—that promotes human happiness and sustains a civil society. Because of this shift, enabled by a laissez-faire political doctrine, America's social infrastructure has been inadvertently weakened through a potentially addictive intertwining of self-interest–driven craving that is reinforced by relentless commercial competition for consumer markets. Thus I return to the philosophy of Adam Smith, who believed that it is society that transforms people into moral beings. For Smith social liberty was not freedom from all social control, but rather freedom as an individual to control one's own passions and to channel that energy toward socially beneficial behavior within a local market structure. While with careful thought and changes in lifestyle—the principles of which I review—the more fortunate among us can accommodate the immediate challenges of America's Fast New World, in the longer view we must refine and reaffirm Smith's social vision if we are to curb our individual cravings and nurture the health of our civil society. The established roots of human meaning and the cornerstones of any democracy—freedom, honesty, caring relationships, a belief in the next generation—derive their power from the mutual respect of individuals and from an investment in community at home and abroad. The ancient truth remains. It is through the empathic intimacy of human relationships, not in the accumulation of material goods, that true prosperity is secured.

IN MANY of the human stories that illustrate *American Mania* I have drawn on my experience and practice as a psychiatrist, and in drawing inference from those stories I have relied heavily on my knowledge as a behavioral neuroscientist. I have also benefited in my analysis from discussion with many colleagues and friends, some of whom are mentioned in these pages. I will introduce you, for example, to Peanut, the New Hampshire fish farmer who through ingenuity and hard work swims against the tide of big business, and to Americans who thrive in the Fast New World and to some who do not: to Marcel, who began his adult life as a competitive athlete, later to find a comfortable balance in the business world; to Tom, who in his success recognized the seeds of his own destruction but regained his balance; to Kim, an immigrant, who despite growing anxiety and briefly loosing her balance continues to pursue her dream—and to the many others from whom, in their generosity, I have learned about life at the manic edge.

But the stories I tell are also informed by my own experience as a migrant, for like so many Americans I am of a wandering spirit. Why such a restless soul should have settled on me is unclear. My father's forebears spent several centuries in the English county of Essex, where there are gravestones to prove it, while my mother's family—the Abbotts—lived for generations on London's East Side. Careful inspection of the family archives, however, reveals hints of restlessness. Just after the First World War my father's elder brother disappeared into a logging camp in western Canada. And later, when I was a boy, a maternal uncle's tales of his African adventures enthralled me. But it was in the union of these two families that the taste for the journey truly declared itself. My brother John, to whom this book is dedicated, lives the nomadic existence of an international merchant, while my own professional responsibilities have led me steadily westward to the University of California and to the city of Los Angeles.

Los Angeles—the dream-making capital of the world—serves as the backdrop for a number of the stories I recount. Some readers who cut their teeth in the urban centers of Europe or on the East Coast of America may prefer to dismiss what happens in Los Angeles as from a place apart, the aberrations of a migrant's city within a migrant land. Such sentiments are understandable. Awash in the solar energy of a subtropical paradise, Los Angelinos engage life in the moment. The pace is fast, the music loud, and money is on display. Part of me, too, would prefer to dismiss such an existence as a mythmaker's parody. But the place is real. In its immediacy and in its magnification of the familiar, Los Angeles creates its own reality and in so doing offers a "fast-forward" simulation of our collective future as a migrant culture.

As Americans we must now decide whether such a future is of our choice, and whether it is sustainable. In the pages that follow, it is my goal to help inform that choice. Will we learn as a people to constructively channel the opportunities and individual enticements of the Fast New World toward an equitable social order, as Adam Smith had envisioned, or will the material demand for economic growth continue to erode the microcultures and intimate social bonds that are the hallmark of our humanity and the keys to health and personal happiness? Have the goals of America's original social experiment been hijacked by its commercial success, threatening the delicate dance between individual desire and social responsibility, or will the nation in its migrant wisdom effectively apply its market and military dominance to remain a "beacon of hope," enhancing the well-being of all the world's peoples? This is a critical time in America, a time for careful thought and diligent action, for we have discovered in our commercial success that in an open society the real enemy is the self-interest that begins with a healthy appetite for life and mushrooms into manic excess during affluent times. Americans are again in the vanguard of human experience, and the world is watching.

It is again a time for choosing.

PART I

THE AMERICAN TEMPERAMENT: A MANIA FOR PROSPERITY

It is odd to watch with what feverish ardor the Americans pursue prosperity. Millions of men are all marching together toward the same point on the horizon; their languages, religions, and mores are different, but they have one common aim. They have been told that fortune is to be found somewhere toward the west, and they hasten to seek it.

Alexis de Tocqueville
Democracy in America, 1835

Chapter One

ADAM SMITH'S AMERICAN DREAM: OF DESIRE AND DEBT

A spacious hive well stock't with bees
That liv'd in luxury and ease
Millions endeavoring to supply
Each other's lust and vanity . . .

Every part was full of vice
Yet the whole mass a paradise
Envy itself and vanity,
Were ministers of industry.

Bernard de Mandeville
The Fable of the Bees, 1723

AN OLD MOON RETREATS before a December dawn. My taxi lurches forward, across the eight lanes of Wilshire Boulevard, and heads west. We pass the picture windows of LA Fitness and the rows of glistening bodies that run in place, preparing for the mental treadmill of the day ahead. The taxi driver, my instant friend from Odessa, lapses into animated Russian as his dispatcher calls. Cradling the phone at his ear, he speeds through two amber lights. Swiftly we are up the ramp and onto the freeway, nosing into the glare of the rising sun. Ahead is a changing river of blinking color, as vehicles brake and weave. Without a moment's hesitation we join the flow. The traffic is heavy, even in this predawn, which comes as no surprise. America is the global nation and night and day Los Angeles is on the move. The flatness of the passing city is broken as a billboard looms into view and a smiling Santa offers an invitation. "Visit Disneyland, the happiest place on earth." Today that's not for me. This taxi to the airport, plus an early-morning flight to New York, will be my only rides.

My plane east is delayed in its arrival from Tokyo. It's just days before Christmas and the wave of seasonal travel is cresting. After running the gauntlet of security, I take refuge in the executive lounge and dose fitfully amid the jingle and buzz of cell phones. Men and women in little cubicles are bent over the luminous screens of laptops. Coffee is in great demand. Through the lounge window I can see the bustle of the runway, choreographed in deceptive silence. It's 6:30 A.M. and the sky has been repainted Californian blue.

Across from me sits an executive who has put aside her business chores for the moment and is speaking on a cell phone with her young daughter. It's a wake-up call. I'm struck, not for the first time, with how at ease we have become in airing private thoughts in public places. With technology running ahead of public decorum, I'm now a confidant to the intimate details of this stranger's family life. The daughter is unhappy. She doesn't want to go to school. The mother's voice is firm and reassuring, although from my privileged seat the furrowed brow and trembling lip that signal her discomfort are readily apparent. It is the promise of special gifts and a magical holiday that finally proves convincing. Finishing the call, the mother sighs to herself and turns to reading. Presumably to better scrutinize some detail, she holds up her magazine to the sunlight that is now flooding through the window. An advertisement on the back cover catches my attention. It's for a luxury car and the photographs highlight the vehicle's interior, a rich brown leather interior. "Think of it as chocolate, as another sweet spot in your life," is the drift of the spin doctor's advice. Another sweet spot? I'm still only half-awake. Which magazine is this that blends appetites so freely? Intrigued, I shift my position to better decipher the lettering above the elegant Yuletide wreath that adorns the title page. It is a magazine of the good life— *Martha Stewart Living*—a special edition to bring delight at the holiday season. I'm prompted to ponder my neighbor's life beyond the business suit: her dreams, her personal passions, the waiting family, and how she fits them all together in the world of turbocapitalism. How does she balance the competing priorities, I wonder. But my musing is interrupted as a flight is called and the magazine disappears, along with the phone and the laptop, into a black attaché case. For the moment the executive is back, as a harried mother heads home to bestow seasonal joy.

IN AMERICA the central message is that each of us is free to write our own story. A polyglot nation of prodigious energy, we are held together by dreams of material progress. Seventy-eight percent of Americans still believe that anybody in America can become rich and live the good life. All it takes is desire, hard work, a little luck, and the right timing. The fable of wealth for the 1990s was telecommunications and the "new economy" of the Internet. But throughout the nation's history there have been similar stories of riches won and lost—in the westward migration of the nineteenth century, in the excesses of the Gilded Age that closed it, in the champagne bubble of the 1920s before the Great Depression, and during the deficit spending spree of the 1980s—stories that reflect the hopeful striving of a daring people. It is because of this bounding optimism that America is an amazing and seductive place to live, something that continues to be affirmed each day by the battalions of migrants that scramble ashore in the risky pursuit of happiness. Thus the dream endures.

But now, for millions of Americans, the magic of the dream is tarnished. Something is not right and an alien sense of discomfort grips the dreamer. Despite the excitement and promise that heralded globalization, American business seems frenzied and fickle. Many Fortune 500 companies, once considered havens of lifetime employment, have transformed themselves into profit-driven workaholic cults. The scramble for "the dream" demands a lengthened workday, diminished sleep, continuous learning, unusual energy, and a high tolerance for financial insecurity. To be "successful" is to be a multitasking dynamo. We rise early and burn the lights late. We exercise to CNN at breakfast and telephone while driving, for there's not a moment to lose. At dinner we graze on snacks and fast food, but with a laptop computer as the preferred companion. In the culture of global commerce, which is etched most visibly on the face of America but increasingly apparent in Europe and other industrialized nations, the quest for economic prosperity has become a competitive high-speed game. For some the pursuit is seductive—as when I rise at dawn in Los Angeles to dine at dusk in New York—and it offers a mask of accomplishment and purpose. But for those snarled in traffic jams and crowded airport lounges, and for the lonely children who do not understand, America's accelerated lifestyle is increasingly a source of anxiety and frustration.

Thus the young executive-mother whom I encountered at the LA airport is not alone. From general conversation with colleagues and patients, and with relatives and friends, I know her discomfort to be mirrored in the lives of many Americans, and in their families, for in the lexicon of America's Fast New World the word *technology* has replaced *tranquility*. For some it is an experience they must struggle to define: a vague but pervasive sense of unease, despite affluence and opportunity. For others it is an uncomfortable irritability, and a ready anger when juggling the daily demands of family and workplace. But for the majority it is the distinct awareness of a declining satisfaction with life, of being perpetually off balance with too many demands to meet and with too little time in which to meet them. Indeed, it is my experience that even those most upbeat and successful acknowledge that life is moving too fast, as do I in those moments when honesty prevails. Despite our nation's extraordinary achievements and our technological wizardry—at the millennium the average hour of American effort was approximately twenty-five times more productive than it had been in 1850—numerous surveys make it clear that Americans are working longer hours, giving less time to their families, and plowing ever deeper into debt.

That the pace of the treadmill driving us at home seems to accelerate in step with America's growing dominance in the world abroad just adds confusion to our discomfort. Not since ancient Rome has a single nation so towered above the international order. America's military superiority is unquestioned. Our weapons are without parallel and are backed by a military budget that is larger than that of all other nations combined. Similarly, American corporations are the most powerful on earth and dominate an economy of global reach. American aircraft connect the world's cities, while the Internet and American software link the world's citizens. American satellites facilitate international communication; Hollywood provides the canned entertainment; patties of American beef feed those in a hurry and Coca-Cola is everywhere. The world is dancing to a distinctly American beat.

In little more than two centuries America has emerged as the richest nation the world has ever seen. During the last decade of the twentieth century Americans enjoyed the longest period of wealth creation in the nation's economic history. Productivity—the goods and services produced per hour worked—grew at a steady rate of somewhere between 2 and 3 percent each year. According to the U.S. Census Bureau, between 1992 and 1997 the median income of married couples in America, when adjusted for inflation, rose from $48,008 to $51,681. During the Internet boom of the late 1990s unemployment fell to around 4 percent, the lowest in thirty years. America's appetite for material things expanded in tune with this rising affluence. The mania kindled. There was no tomorrow. Throughout America, larger became better. Warehouse-sized shopping malls mushroomed across the land. In what Patrick J. Kiger has dubbed the "gulp culture of excess" the 12-inch dinner plate, the 32-ounce soda, and the 64-inch TV screen became the norm. The homes of the wealthy rivaled cathedrals: at the century's turn even the median size of a newly constructed American house exceeded two thousand square feet, a 25 percent increase in just two decades. Similarly, the family car underwent an elephantine metamorphosis until it had much in common with an armored personnel carrier.

The time and money required to sustain this affluent lifestyle, however, have plunged the nation into an orgy of debt. For the majority of American families, debt has become a burden of staggering proportions. Whereas government borrowing launched the economic boom of the 1980s—and spiked again after 2001 with the recession, the tax cuts, and President Bush's war on terror—during the gala decade of the 1990s America's consumer-driven economy was fueled by runaway personal debt. By 1997 the combined indebtedness of the nation's households had reached an unparalleled 89 percent of total household income. Debt climbed from 95 percent of disposable household income early in the 1990s to 124 percent in the last quarter of the year 2000. The average rate of personal savings fell to zero over the same time period and by 2001 was firmly in negative territory, at minus 6 percent—something not seen since the darkest days of the Great Depression when 25 percent of America's workforce was unemployed. The American dream is now heavily mortgaged.

So what went wrong? Why do we live this way in this land where we are free to choose? What drives our mania for material things? As citizens of the richest nation in the world, why do we not choose to simply enjoy what we have, to slow down, to save more, and to spend more time with those we love—as we say we wish to do?

Economists tend to squabble about the answers to such questions, or to avoid them. Listening to the classicists of the free-market persuasion, for example, one would be forced to conclude that our profligate spending is an issue of moral weakness—that Americans who stagger under a heavy burden of debt have nobody to blame but themselves. Humans, the argument goes, are intelligent "utility-maximizing" creatures, which in rough translation means that in our economic planning we are rational beings and make decisions appropriate to our needs. In a market society, wealth creation—seeking and owning material things—demands money, which in turn requires work. Hence, these economists argue, when an individual borrows against future wages in order to purchase some desired object, that is a rational act. Well-informed shoppers are independent of outside influence and are consistent in the choices they make, based on need. In the absence of need, the rational shopper saves her money and buys savings bonds. Debt is a matter of personal choice.

While neat and tidy, such theorizing falls short in accounting for the American debtor. So says Juliet Schor, an economics professor at Boston College, in her book *The Overworked American* and in its companion volume, *The Overspent American*. In America's turbocharged commercial culture, argues Schor, there is little about the shopping experience that promotes rational conduct. That is why Americans lead the industrialized world when it comes to the amount of personal debt they carry. (The cumulative personal debt in the United States in 2002 was equal to the gross national product of Great Britain and Russia combined.) If shopping behavior were a rational process, and our choices were influenced only by need, then brand-name T-shirts would sell no better than other shirts of equal quality. And that is certainly not the case. In reality, many shopping decisions are biased by the merchant's advertising campaign or distorted by the desire to satisfy some competitive urge or to reward some emotional need. (I am reminded of the "sweet spot" advertisement for the luxury car, designed to catch the eye of the weary traveler, or the promise of Disney happiness offered to those fighting the dismal congestion of a Los Angeles freeway.) Relentless corporate promotion, says Schor, that is specifically designed to increase market share and a media that glamorizes profligate spending—fostering social inequality, envy, and intense rivalry—are what drive our personal debt. The American consumer is a victim of corporate exploitation.

As a psychiatrist and behavioral scientist, I find both explanations incomplete. Certainly, the immediate cause of our treadmill-like pursuit is clear enough. By embracing the merchants' Faustian invitation during those giddy days of the 1990s, when money seemed in infinite supply, many Americans have entered a vicious cycle of work and spend. By loading ourselves with massive personal debt—that we now struggle to repay in a postparty economy—we have become enslaved to the work-place, the chastened, time-starved prisoners of our own material dreams. But what lies at the root of America's romance with the mer-chant? To my mind, whether we label the immediate cause of the debt burden we carry *moral turpitude* or *victimization* doesn't really matter, for our indebtedness is symptomatic of a deeper problem. In an affluent society such as in the United States, it is not need but unbridled desire that drives debt. So it is the genesis of our *desire*—our *craving*—for material things that we must better understand, and why it is that dur-ing the time of America's affluence that craving has become rampant. In seeking that understanding we can learn something from history and from the neurobiology of behavior, for the economic philosophy that is the foundation of our market economy grew first from a thoughtful enquiry into human instinct.

IT BEGAN almost three centuries ago. The engines of America's extraordinary material success have their origin in the philosophy of the Enlightenment, a period of history that culminated in American inde-pendence from Britain and in the French Revolution. During the seven-teenth and eighteenth centuries the Roman Church, which for a millennium had been the dominant social power in Europe, was in decline. With the Protestant Reformation there emerged a new faith in human reason. Voyages of international discovery brought to European attention vast lands that offered seductive opportunities for settlement, trade, and conquest. For the adventurous, especially Europeans who colonized the American continent, it was a time of expanding horizons. Against this backdrop of opportunity and "enlightened" reasoning, a Scottish professor of moral philosophy named Adam Smith put forth a set of simple principles designed to free the self-interest of the average workingman from the taxes and tariffs of government-controlled mer-cantilism and to achieve "universal opulence" (Smith's quaint eighteenth-century term for widespread affluence). Smith's writings were to become the guiding philosophy of the capitalist enterprise and the bedrock of America's economic success. Thus knowledge of the time in which Smith lived and in which he formulated his ideas, and the behavioral principles on which those ideas are rested, is essential to understanding the growing discomfort that we now experience in contemporary American society.

Most important is to recognize that Adam Smith's theory of economics is firmly grounded in the biology of human behavior. His major contribution as a philosopher is that he was the first to rationalize human instinctual desire within the practical economic framework of the marketplace. Smith believed that the "behavior of multitudes" is the sum of individual desires and that it is the collective drive for self-preservation that shapes the activities of the market. Thus, Smith argued, when appropriately balanced within a free market, the universal human drive for self-love and our instinctual curiosity can be the engines of social improvement, to the benefit of the community at large.

Born in 1723 in the small seaport of Kirkcaldy, Scotland, and educated in Glasgow and Oxford, Smith was a careful student of human behavior throughout his life. He was also a thinker well ahead of his time. For example, anchored as it is in the competitive nature of human instinct, Smith's economic philosophy has much in common with Charles Darwin's theory of the evolution of species, which was first published almost a century later. Indeed, there is evidence that Darwin developed his ideas about natural selection in part through an interest in economics, and from knowledge of Smith's assertion that the economy of an ordered society is best achieved through the struggle for personal gain. We know from Darwin's diaries that in 1839 he was reading Smith's treatise on human psychology, *The Theory of Moral Sentiments*, which had been first published in 1759. Darwin was particularly impressed by the dynamic nature of Smith's argument that individuals, in their self-interest, sought to maximize their place in the world. Darwin had learned from his own financial investments—made in the early years of the Industrial Revolution—that competition among manufacturers and merchants for the sale of their products fostered technical innovation and the development of new markets. Drawing on that experience, he saw in the struggle for the creation of wealth a parallel with the competition for resources that occurred among species. In part through his knowledge of Smith's thinking, Darwin recognized that in their evolution, market economies and the natural selection of species obey similar dynamic laws. Thus free-market economics and evolution, disciplines of thought that today may seem distinct, in fact have a common conceptual root.

In the natural struggle for survival, Smith asserted in his writings, *self-love*—what we call *self-interest* today—was God's "incomprehensible remedy" through which human society could achieve a balanced ordering. It was also *enlightened* self-love—the desire to preserve kin and those closest to us from harm—that created human decency. Motivated by this desire of self-preservation and the need for loving attachment, most humans are ingenious and hard-working, keeping the promises they make and willing to exchange the fruits of their labor with those of other individuals to great social benefit. Therefore, Smith argued, when appropriately shaped by the dynamic give-and-take of the market, such self-interest made possible a society where the products of individual labor are fairly traded, placing a decent life within the reach of all. "Give me that which I want, and you shall have this which you want," quipped Smith. "It is not from the benevolence of the butcher, the brewer, or the baker, that we expect our dinner, but from their regard to their own interest."

Smith considered *instinctual curiosity*—the inquisitiveness that drives the urge to explore new places, seeds invention, and sparks novel ideas—as the essential complement to this innate self-interest. In *The Theory of Moral Sentiments* he discusses the curiosity we have with the working of machines and our obsessive desire to achieve the "proper fitness"—the perfection—of things. Smith writes on the subject of the pocket watch, for example, an instrument that was in rapid evolution during his lifetime. Substitute in your mind the cell phone or the latest laptop computer and you will find that he is describing behavior that is familiar. "A watch," Smith notes, "that falls behind above two minutes in a day, is despised by one curious in watches. He sells it perhaps for a couple of guineas, and purchases another at fifty, which will not lose above a minute in a fortnight. The sole use of watches however is to tell us what o'clock it is, and to hinder us from breaking any engagement. . . . But the person [with the more accurate watch] . . . will not always be found more scrupulously punctual than other men . . . or concerned to know precisely what time of day it is. What interests him is not so much the attainment of . . . this knowledge, as the perfection of the machine that serves to attain it."

Slipping momentarily into rebuke, Smith asks, "What pleases these lovers of toys? How many people ruin themselves by laying out money on trinkets of frivolous utility?" But, he adds hastily, it is this same curiosity that prompts our species "to cultivate the ground, to build houses, to found cities and commonwealths . . . to invent the sciences . . . [and to] . . . change the whole face of the globe." Our easy titillation by novelty and invention, Smith believed, is what "keeps in continual motion the industry of mankind," promoting risky investments, foolish adventures, and all "feverish work beyond that which is necessary to provide for basic physical need." History supports Smith's assertion. In market societies financial speculation generally crests during periods of technical innovation when curiosity and the thrill of uncertainty heighten the desire for self-gain. (The perfect contemporary example, of course, is the mania that exploded in America during the 1990s around information technology and the Internet.)

In Smith's theory, driving these twin economic engines of self-interest and curiosity is *ambition*—the competitive human drive for social betterment. "Mankind is disposed to make parade of our riches and conceal our poverty," wrote Smith in an early chapter of *Moral Sentiments*, when musing on "the origins of ambition and of the distinction of ranks." "Nothing is so mortifying," he continued, "as to be obliged to expose our distress to the view of the public. For what purpose is all the toil and bustle of this world? What is the end of avarice and ambition, of the pursuit of wealth, of power and pre-eminence? Is it to supply the necessities of nature? The wages of the meanest laborer can supply them. Do they [the rich] imagine that their stomach is better or their sleep sounder in a palace rather than in a cottage? The rich man glories in his riches because he feels that they naturally draw upon him the attention of the world. The poor man, on the contrary, is ashamed of his poverty."

Smith recognized, however, that the economic engines of curiosity and self-interest only run smoothly when individuals have the *freedom* to express their ambition. Thus, Smith argued, individual liberty and democratic rights are essential to a successful market society. Only by ensuring the freedom and dignity of its laboring citizens can a nation secure its true economic wealth. Without such fundamental privileges, curiosity and ambition are eclipsed by the more powerful survival instinct of fear. And because human dignity flows from the independent command of one's own labor, *all* citizens must be considered part of the market enterprise. It is not through the accumulation of money—of the silver and gold sought by the European kingdoms during the mercantile era—but by the assurance that each citizen may freely enjoy the fruits of his or her labor that a government ensures social prosperity. Thus, inevitably, in a thriving market-based economy there is a division of labor: we all work for each other, with no individual providing for himself or herself alone. A poor man in a rich country therefore, Smith asserted, is better off than a rich man in a poor country, and offered by way of illustration his famous example of the coat worn by the day laborer—a simple article of clothing and yet one where "the number of people whose industry . . . has been employed in procuring him this accommodation, exceeds all computation." It is this divided responsibility and codependence, together with the innate propensity of humans to "truck, barter, and exchange"—behaviors that one might summarize as "competitive collaboration"—that makes a market-based democracy possible.

Thus, in Adam Smith's analysis, the instinctual strivings of self-interest, curiosity, and social ambition expressed in a love of market competition and material gain are the keys to social improvement. In his day Smith found a ready history to support his thesis in the economic cycles of the nascent London stock market, which had emerged as a social institution at the end of the seventeenth century. Following the

"Glorious Revolution" of 1688, when the Protestant William of Orange snatched the English throne from his Catholic father-in-law, James II, the merchants of England were prospering and had money to spare. With the need to finance the ongoing hostilities with France, guaranteed government loans were floated, and by 1694 the Bank of England was founded with the permission to circulate paper money. As the opportunities for private investment in new businesses grew, the number of inventions seeking a market mushroomed. One of the first technical devices to spark the public imagination was the diving bell, a simple iron cone designed to trap air within its shell when immersed underwater, thus facilitating exploration of the seabed. A mania for such devices developed after speculators investing in the salvage of a Spanish vessel wrecked off Hispaniola had become extraordinarily rich. With an excitement reminiscent of Americans' giddy fascination with information technology three hundred years later, a profusion of copycat patents appeared and fledgling companies began offering stock with the promise of riches.

For a while the market for such devices "bubbled" happily, but in 1697 when the crash came, 70 percent of the speculative companies failed. That was a lesson learned, but more importantly it was an early demonstration that market freedom and unleashing self-interest stimulated individual creativity and economic growth. A similar but larger speculative bubble occurred around the time of Adam Smith's birth, in the 1720s, when the South Sea Company, established to foster trade in the Americas, caught the public's imagination. When the king and the British Parliament began actively championing the South Sea scheme, speculative fever was not far behind. The company's shares rose rapidly until South Sea stock was trading at one thousand pounds, an extraordinary sum in those days and some six or seven times its original value. But again, as the bubble burst, many of the English elite who had invested were caught in their folly, including Sir Isaac Newton, then Master of the Mint, who lost twenty thousand pounds. "I can calculate the motions of the heavenly bodies," Newton is said to have complained in a mood of bitter reflection, "but not the madness of people."

To Smith and his contemporaries this potential "madness of people" was the most troubling aspect of any proposition that promoting self-interest within a market framework could have broad social value. Thus when *An Inquiry into the Nature and Causes of the Wealth of Nations* was published in 1776, it was a thesis considered suspect at first, particularly by the established church. While there was ready agreement that self-interest and the opportunity for personal profit fostered market growth and entrepreneurial endeavor, the important question arose as to what would contain the juggernaut? Did a system of free enterprise have any natural brakes? What was to prevent those caught up in their own success from running away to greed? What was the counterweight to self-interest that would ensure virtue and social balance? The pursuit of profit in classical Christian theology was considered a close cousin to the sins of avarice, lechery, and self-indulgence (all termed *luxuria* by the church) and thus damaging to virtuous behavior.

Smith, however, was an optimist when it came to human reason. He accepted the bleak forecast of Thomas Hobbes, the influential English philosopher who wrote in 1651 that mankind is by nature self-absorbed and aggressive, but believed this to be an unfair assessment of the human passions. As a serious student of moral philosophy, he acknowledged that God had not gifted the human animal with absolute goodness, but he also rejected the argument that we are irretrievably evil and totally given to excess. (Although in his writing, Smith did take pains not to irritate his theological friends by avoiding the word *luxury*, substituting for it instead the rather grandiose term *universal opulence*.) As a student Smith had been deeply influenced in his optimism by Francis Hutcheson, the professor of moral philosophy at Glasgow College, which in the eighteenth century was an acknowledged center of the European Enlightenment. Smith had been particularly impressed by Hutcheson's belief that human desire and self-interest are balanced by a need to be loved by others and by the need for social acceptance. Later Smith adopted these tenets as a cornerstone of his economic philosophy, asserting that in the give-and-take of a free-market society the instincts for survival and self-preservation—self-interest, curiosity, and ambition—are balanced by the powerful need to seek and obtain the sympathetic support of others for one's enterprise. In Smith's optimistic and passionate belief, therefore, greed and similarly undesirable behaviors would be held in check by the powerful human need for peer recognition and neighborly social acceptance. "The man whom we naturally love the most," Smith wrote in *The Theory of Moral Sentiments*—the book that established his reputation as a thinker—"is he who joins to . . . his own original and selfish feelings, the most exquisite sensibility . . . and sympathetic feelings of others." Thus in Smith's opinion it was the *dynamic balance* between healthy ambition and individual desire and an individual's empathic, observing conscience—what Smith referred to as the "impartial spectator"—that provided the prescription for positive social change in a free-market economy, ensuring a stable civil order and an equitable distribution of wealth.

As Adam Smith was emerging as a leading philosopher in England, a fledgling America was contemplating its independence. Smith's dream of a market-driven humanitarian culture had enormous appeal to the American colonists and became integral to the vision of the Founding Fathers. The enlightened European thinkers of the eighteenth century—including Joseph Addison, Jonathan Swift, and later David Hume—championed political and economic reform at home. But it was in America, where the likes of Benjamin Franklin, Thomas Jefferson, and Thomas Paine argued for an end to the constraints of British tradition, for justice, and for the liberty to pursue their own entrepreneurial endeavors with a minimum of government interference, that Smith's ideas found their highest practical application. The intent in the founding of America, still exalted today on the back of each dollar bill, was to build *novus ordo seclorum*, a "New Order of the Ages." The vision was of a prosperous future for all mankind, replacing feudalism—when a few land barons and a hierarchy of privileged churchmen and aristocrats dominated the husbandry of life—with the ideal of a free market and an enduring people's democracy. The American experiment was to be unique in the history of mankind.

FOR TWO centuries America has pursued Adam Smith's dream of universal opulence, with great material success. Whether the old philosopher and our enlightened forefathers would recognize themselves as the architects of the competitive, supercharged culture of desire in which we live today, however, is questionable. Their experience, after all, was of an agrarian and mercantile economy. Adam Smith was writing before the Industrial Revolution. Within the close-knit towns and rural villages of eighteenth-century Britain and of colonial America there was a social intimacy that has almost completely disappeared from American life. Two centuries ago the market systems that Smith championed were embedded in the industry of the local people. Businesses reflected local capital investment, and to be solicitous of one's neighbor was prudent insurance against future personal need. Thus the economic goal for most individuals was both private advancement *and* the social welfare of the community, which helps give perspective to Smith's faith in the social gyroscope of an "impartial spectator."

But today, when the American dream is magnified through the commercially tinted lens of a globalized, technology-driven culture, the neighborly impulse to serve the social good has little practical value and offers even less opportunity for economic reward. The accumulation of material wealth is now America's yardstick of social success. In the race to "get ahead" and to triumph as an individual, competitive struggle and conspicuous consumption dominate our daily experience. The cultural and economic landscape in which we live has shifted dramatically, and the interplay between social concern and individual desire has shifted with it, endangering the vital balance that Adam Smith considered essential to a civil society.

The psychic discomforts and physical disabilities that many Americans are now experiencing are rooted in this shift. Intoxicated by the Fast New World that we have created, in our craving for personal success we are neglecting our personal health and the infrastructure of the civil society—the New Order of the Ages—that it had first been our intention to build. Adam Smith did not foresee (nor, I suspect, did he even imagine) such an outcome. And yet, from the perspective of neurobiology, such social neglect is the predictable consequence of envy and affluent circumstance. Selfish behaviors are reward driven and innate, wired deeply into the survival mechanisms of the primitive brain, and when consistently reinforced, they will run away to greed, with its associated craving for money, food, or power. On the other hand, the self-restraint and the empathy for others that are so important in fostering physical and mental health are learned behaviors—largely functions of the new human cortex and thus culturally dependent. These social behaviors are fragile and learned by imitation, much as we learn language. To be sustained across generations they must be carefully nurtured by extended families and viable communities. Inadvertently, in our frenzied search for profit and economic efficiency we have built a consumer society dominated by centralized megamarkets that magnifies desire and minimizes collective responsibility, eroding the small market-based economies that once provided stable and meaningful employment. Our ill health and growing discomfort are in step with these social trends.

THE CULTURAL SHIFT toward the self and away from community began slowly in America, but accelerated with the coming of the information age. By the late 1990s, after the triumph of laissez-faire capitalism over communism, Adam Smith's twin engines of economic growth—self-interest and curiosity—were in high gear. In this deregulated economic environment personal ambition became focused increasingly on the competitive enhancement of material gain and a collective mania was kindled.

Predictably under such circumstances, although technical innovation has flourished, so has social inequality. Particularly evident is that the rich have grown richer. The resulting disparity in income directly contributes to the rising social discomfort of which many Americans now complain. Since the 1970s the gap between the wealthiest Americans and everyone else has been widening and is now greater than in any other industrialized nation. Despite the booming economy between

1977 and 1999, income after taxes—adjusted for inflation—actually decreased for over 50 percent of American households, with those in the bottom quarter of the population experiencing a genuine decline in their purchasing power. Over the same two decades (but at the other end of the social spectrum), spurred on in part by Wall Street exuberance, stock options, and greed, the average annual compensation of a chief executive at a large American company—as reported by the Institute for Policy Studies in Washington—rose approximately 500 percent, from $1.8 million to $10.6 million per annum. This income is 419 times the earnings of a typical production worker.

Thus at the century's turn the richest 1 percent of the population— the 2.7 million Americans who were the most affluent—had as many after-tax dollars to spend each year as did the bottom 100 million citizens combined. And they have been spending it. Extravagance by wealthy Americans began in the 1980s and, after a slowdown in the early 1990s, increased exponentially during the boom years that followed. Thanks to persistent marketing of the good life on television and in magazines, the average American has become intensely aware of the physical comforts of the affluent lifestyle and yearns to live similarly. But given the growing disparity of income in America's "champagne glass" society, the material comfort achieved by the middle-class family consistently falls short of that portrayed as desirable by the media and the merchant. Thus a survey conducted in the late 1990s found that the level of income considered necessary by the average American "to fulfill one's dreams" was approximately twice the nation's median household income at the time.

We see here an example of how desire, if continuously reinforced, will kindle envy and outstrip reason. But before blaming the merchant, think again. For the merchant it is satisfying desire, not thwarting it, that brings profit. That is their mandate in a market society, and as a free people we must also take responsibility for the shift that has occurred. As America's commercial hegemony has increased and our social networks have eroded, we have lost any meaningful reference as to how rich we really are, especially in comparison to other nations. Shrink the population of the world to a village of one hundred people, for example, and eighty would be living in poor housing. Approximately one-third of the villagers would never have made a telephone call and half would be undernourished. Just six individuals would control most of the wealth and all six would be American. Indeed in 1998, as the Internet boom was reaching its stride, a report from the United Nations Development Program estimated that the combined fortune of America's then three richest citizens exceeded that of the entire combined gross national product of the world's poorest countries and their 600 million inhabitants.

In reality the reciting of such statistics has little impact on our behavior. We guide our lives not by reason, but by immediate comparison: by the exemplar rather than by the rule. And hence, just as the merchant has steadfastly raised our expectations for the good life, so have we escalated the comparisons we make, regardless of the money we earn. While with the exercise of diligent effort most citizens living in America today can enjoy physical comfort and economic success, our dreams are modeled elsewhere, in the media and through the promises of the billboard. Personal pride in the product of one's labor and the love and gratitude of others are no longer satisfying goals. No, we wish to be a Donald Trump or a Julia Roberts. It is here where we find the roots of envy. The shared mythology in America is that we can each enjoy fame and fortune and live in opulence at the top of the social pyramid. Under relentless market pressure the American dream has become an illusion worthy of Charles Ponzi—that all can be first, and all can be wealthy.

For those not fortunate enough to live on the lip of the champagne glass, the accumulation of debt fills the financial gap between reality and these dreams of material opulence. The households of America's rich have insignificant liabilities compared to their total worth. In 1998 debt was 3.3 percent of assets for these families, a decline from 5.9 percent in 1983. Similarly, the poorest people in America have little or no debt simply because there are few bankers who will lend them money. The heaviest liabilities are to be found among families who dream of living a middle-class or upper-middle-class existence, the categories to which most Americans think of themselves belonging. For these "average"

American families, debt has been increasing steadily, rising as a percentage of net worth from 37.4 percent in the 1980s to 51.8 percent in 1998.

In all market societies borrowing increases during boom times as individuals relax their guard and take advantage of the opportunities presented to them, and slows during periods of economic recession. But Americans—virtually regardless of the prevailing economy—consistently save less and borrow more than those living in other wealthy industrialized societies. Thus, factoring in debt, half of America's households have a net worth of $17,800 or less, and two-thirds of Americans save nothing in a typical year. Furthermore, only 30 percent of Americans—those who are most affluent—pay off their credit cards each month, with the other 70 percent carrying an average unpaid balance of $7,000 and increasing. In our debt-driven consumer economy these habits are fostered early. College students, for example, are particular targets of credit card companies. Thus, 77 percent of full-time students at four-year colleges have credit card debt. Indeed, schools are encouraged in soliciting the students to establish credit—and get perks from the credit card industry for doing so—such that some 40 percent of students graduate with a credit card debt of $3,000 or more. For the majority of Americans, debt has become a way of life.

THE PROMOTION of personal debt as an engine of economic growth has a long history in America. Indeed, buying dreams on credit is an American invention. Large-scale financing of mass consumption through debt became popular during the flapper years of the 1920s—a period of social mania comparable to the 1990s—when the average American first grew giddy with the nation's exploding wealth. In the aftermath of the First World War, new federal laws helped contain the social inequities so commonplace during America's early industrialization, and a new and growing middle class emerged. Being from frugal pioneering stock intent on security and survival, however, such individuals were suspicious of borrowing and tended to keep their money in the bank or under the mattress. Notwithstanding, clever merchants eager to grow prosperous recognized in the nation's accumulating wealth an opportunity for commercial expansion and invented the principle of "buying on time." The goal was to create the public illusion that the lifestyle of the rich, and those products once considered luxuries, were now necessities for all citizens.

Caught in this illusionary web of material happiness, Americans have had difficulty extricating themselves. This is in part because, as Thorstein Veblen caricatured in his book *The Theory of the Leisure Class*, material possessions are particularly important in defining social position in America's immigrant culture, where traditional social hierarchies and family loyalties are weakened. During Veblen's time, in the late nineteenth century, the ultimate social distinction was of the English model—to be a gentleman of means who did not work at all or who did not admit to doing so, but who spent lavishly "on apparel and architecture . . . [and] manly beverages and trinkets." Similarly, today, the social competition inherent in America's achievement-oriented culture fosters the purchase of nonessential items or brand-name products—an oversized vehicle, the latest television technology, or the most diminutive cell phone—as a conspicuous means of burnishing one's self-image. With such purchases we make a social statement: we display something other than the merchandise itself. Buying Ralph Lauren shirts enables me to enter the social class of my dreams, even if I cannot afford a house in Bel Air or the Hamptons. Self-anointed doyennes such as Martha Stewart can help too: if I display appropriate manners and cultural taste, then my place in the social hierarchy is secure. Here we see ambition, Adam Smith's driving force of social change, diligently at work.

When Veblen was writing, the robber barons of the Gilded Age were spending freely enough, but they were few in number. During the 1920s, however, the number of Americans indulging their desire grew rapidly, as advertising boomed and the merchants' "buy-now, pay-later" strategy became popular. Sixty percent of the household furniture bought during that decade was purchased on credit. The number of cars on the road rose from 8 million to 23 million. With Hollywood on its way to becoming a world power—as the motion picture industry launched its unprecedented mission to redefine reality—the glitz of new money and celebrity became an intoxicating lure for all Americans, whether they were farmers or factory workers. No longer were Americans working to meet basic needs but instead labored to satisfy their newly discovered thirst for novelty and luxury goods. F. Scott Fitzgerald caught the essence of this national intoxication in *The Great Gatsby*. As Fitzgerald described it, America had seen the "green light," and a firm belief in the "orgiastic future that year by year recedes before us" had been established.

Such optimism and boundless desire were roughly bridled during the years of America's Great Depression. As the practical value of personal prudence and neighborly interdependence became painfully apparent, the pendulum swung once again toward community concerns and the importance of sustaining a social balance. It was a cautionary experience for all Americans, one that is not entirely forgotten even today. Nonetheless, when a boom economy returned after World War II, the majority of Americans were quick to return to their embrace of debt financing as the preferred path to dreamland. The boom years of the 1950s and the 1960s, however, were also years of stable and predictable employment in America. Despite the cold war with communism, a patriotic sense of future had been restored, which made debt accumulation feel relatively safe. But today, in the changing job market of America's Fast New World, for those lured along the debtor's path, Scott Fitzgerald's vision of an "orgiastic future" is but a cruel reminder of the mistakes they have made.

The cruelty is that for a brief moment in the 1990s, during the Internet boom, it seemed to most Americans that such an orgiastic future was within the national grasp. But with the bursting of the bubble and the recession that followed—compounded by the rise of international terrorism—such optimism has drained away. Americans were caught unawares: for the average worker the debt remains, but the world in which we live has changed. In the interests of efficiency in a global market, the labor force of many U.S.-based companies is now internationally distributed. America's Fast New World has adopted what Harris Collingwood has described as the "sink-or-swim" economy, where despite respectable economic growth, wages are stagnant and the unemployment rate is rising.

Americans are now the world's traders. But the manufacturing base in the United States has been declining, and as many businesses go offshore, the creation of full-time jobs has slowed. This fosters market economy, cheap imports, and commercial flexibility—it's easier to cut jobs selectively when they are distributed around the world—but it does little for local communities, driving out small merchants and destabilizing the job market until the hourly wage earner, in search of his or her next meal, is reduced to a frenetic, nonstop pursuit. So is primed the treadmill of our ill health and social discomfort. By measures such as the gross national product, the economy appears stable. But in reality it is capricious: at one end of the social scale individuals are making money faster than they can spend it, while at the other end individuals are counting every penny. Economists call this "idiosyncratic volatility," and it is becoming the hallmark of our economic age.

As a result of this volatility, predictable full-time employment within any community—once considered the cornerstone of a stable middle-class family—is fast becoming the dinosaur of American commerce. Hence a 1999 study found that only 21 percent of California workers had been in their jobs for more than ten years. Carrying an excessive burden of debt is financially risky at any time, but without job security it can be crippling. Thus even during the affluence of the 1990s the number of bankruptcies declared in America continued to set new records, rising from 800,000 in 1994 to over 1.4 million in 1998. The decades after World War II, when Americans enjoyed remarkable economic growth and steady employment, are unlikely to return. Lifelong competition has replaced lifetime security, and a new age of fiscal uncertainty has fallen on the average American family.

In America's debt-driven economy, especially during times of market downturn, this uncertainty magnifies the stress of maintaining an upper-middle-class standard of living. Many families who walk the financial tightrope between high expenses and low savings live from paycheck to paycheck, and for them maximizing the family income in a highly competitive workplace is a constant source of discomfort and strain. Between 2001 and 2003, approximately 3 million jobs were lost from the American economy, many from manufacturing. Ironically the temporary jobs that sometimes replaced them—and on which so many young families now depend—were initially stimulated by the giddy consumption of personal goods and services that began during the bubble years of the 1990s. Women, including women with young children, make up the majority of the temporary workers in America, often with deleterious effects on family cohesion. In 1960, 70 percent of American families had at least one parent who stayed at home. By 2000, the figures had switched: 70 percent of families had two parents employed outside the home or were headed by a single working parent. This shift places a particular burden on young women. In 1999, 62 percent of all American women with children under six living with their husbands were in the workforce (approximately 17 percent of the total number of women who worked outside the home) as opposed to just 18 percent in 1960. And of these, two-thirds were working forty hours a week or more, although relatively few enjoyed job security or social benefits such as retirement annuities and comprehensive health insurance.

All of this brings back to mind the young executive at the LA airport whom I observed trying to comfort her daughter while simultaneously preparing for the last leg of her homeward red-eye journey. For such professional women a traditional family structure has virtually disappeared. Priorities are not easily set. Whether to aggressively pursue a career becomes an issue not only of talent but also of conscience as child care shifts to hired assistants. Inevitably, these young mothers face the emotional challenge of abandoning close family ties if they are to compete in a helter-skelter working world. (And as I heard that morning, it is often with gifts and material reward that the parent strives uncomfortably to ease that sense of neglect.) A steady erosion of the tax-based social infrastructure on which many young families depend has compounded the dilemma. With the championing of deregulated capital markets that began in the 1980s, and the slashing of social services during the economic recession that began in 2001, the investment of public capital in schools, day-care centers, and other family amenities has diminished. Now there is a need for families to replace essential social services in the private sector. This further increases the financial demand placed on young households already burdened with debt. The labor of both parents must be sold in the workplace to finance the cost of child care, in addition to buying the private schooling, the designer clothes, and the utility vehicle that signal continued social success.

In sustaining this treadmill existence, the ultimate limitation is time. There are only twenty-four hours in each day. As deadlines mount, last-minute planning, cell phones, reduced sleep, and fast food become the essential strategies of survival. Recently a patient of mine, a newly widowed older man, decided to accept an invitation to live with his daughter's family. To his surprise he quickly learned that the family never sat down together for dinner. The children ate in relays, usually directly from the fridge. It was, he reported, like living at a fast-food restaurant. In an effort to bring some routine to the household, he began cooking a regular evening meal, but few members of the family were ever there to eat it. After two months he decided to move out. In my experience this story is no longer unusual. Small wonder, therefore, that the latest cultural innovation being championed by those at America's manic edge— perhaps in an effort to realign with reality—is the twenty-four-hour, seven-day-a-week (24/7) work schedule. Compared to those living in other industrialized countries, we Americans are workaholics, tied to our jobs for more hours each day—adding up to between six to eight additional workweeks each year—and taking on average only thirteen days of annual vacation. That is less than half the standard for Japan and a mere third of the holidays enjoyed by our European neighbors.

SO WHAT drives America's relentless pursuit? Why such workaholic ways? While with globalization, rapidly advancing technology, and the information revolution life has quickened in every industrialized nation, America is decidedly ahead of the pack when it comes to the frenzied quest for material affluence. I believe the major factor in determining this leadership and our restless striving is America's migrant heritage. We are the quintessential immigrant nation. Americans, at the bone, are a self-selected group of hard-working opportunists with an insatiable hunger for self-improvement. Even the average American-born citizen, after all, is still raised in a family whose ancestors within a few generations were lured to America by dreams of freedom and prosperity. America's increasingly manic lifestyle—a dysphoric extension of our passionate pursuit of material happiness fueled now by debt, rapid technological innovation, and around-the-clock commerce—has grown out of this migrant drive for betterment.

Adam Smith's economic philosophy has particular appeal to the migrant's well-developed sense of survival, and two centuries ago his dream came alive in the daily struggles of the colonists. In his *Wealth of Nations*, published just as American independence was declared, Smith championed the Americans' desire for economic autonomy. He openly admired the industry and the egalitarian vision of the settlers. "Though North America is not yet so rich as England," he wrote, "it is much more thriving, and advancing with much greater rapidity to the further acquisition of riches. Labor is there so well rewarded, that a numerous family of children, instead of being a burden is a source of opulence and prosperity." In the new land, economic success was achieved through the raw energy of individual ambition, by struggle and by hard work. In early America the idle rich and the destitute were almost nowhere to be found. The successful settlers were practical people who lived close to the land they cultivated, and those who undertook the challenges of the westward migration did so of their own free will. Thus it was in a genuine struggle with nature that the true character of American society was born.

In the instinctual premise of his economic philosophy, Adam Smith thus belongs to America as much as Thomas Jefferson or Benjamin Franklin. The Continental Congress of 1774, meeting two years before the publication of Smith's *Wealth of Nations*, had stated clearly that the colonists were entitled to "life, liberty and property," a phrase Jefferson changed to "life, liberty and the pursuit of happiness" in the Declaration of Independence. In 1776 nobody understood what "the pursuit of happiness" really meant, nor do we today, but the metaphor has always been clear: in the American temperament there lives a restless desire to achieve some ill-defined perfection, and toward that end, the pursuit of self-interest, as Adam Smith first championed, is a valued virtue.

A century ago, when European migration to America was at its height, in contrast to the crowded nations of Europe there was no bridle to future growth in America. Although still a raw nation, the bounding production, abundant virgin forests, vast resources, bustling harbors, and wealthy and resourceful citizenry all predicted that America would grow to dominance. The driven desire of the people—whether they were robber barons or street vendors—is what distinguished America from the rest of the world. It continues to be so. With millions of additional migrants being admitted each decade, bringing with them the same dynamic energy that characterized the first adventurers, it is a culture that accepts no boundaries.

Today America is a land of vitality and of abundance: the home of great universities, of unparalleled science, of biotechnology and medical miracles, and of the world's most successful software industry. And yet in its dominance, our nation still thrusts ahead with the same raw energy—the same mania of purpose—that to outsiders has long suggested a lack of social planning and a lust for material excess. America is different in its social balance. When compared to many of the European democracies, it remains a land of individual opportunity and self-interest, a place where the tireless engines of human desire can be tuned and raced in unfettered competition. But Adam Smith's dream of an evolved market economy, where the ingenuity and energy of self-interest finds balance with benevolence and mutual sympathy to the social benefit of all, is yet to be realized.

America's migrant society has built its own unique brand of aggressive capitalism, where the competitive accumulation of material wealth is an end in itself and the accrual of personal debt is but a means to that end. This modus operandi has emerged, in large part, because the nation's vitality springs from the émigré being free to write a new chapter in his or her life story without obligation to family or to culture of origin, and with a minimum of regulatory interference. Such freedom has been the key to America's material success. But in achieving that success, we have dramatically changed the social circumstances under which millions of Americans live and work until many, now pushed close to the limits of their physical and mental tolerance, are beginning to lose faith in the time-hallowed narrative of the American dream—that if you compete, work hard, and pay your taxes, then one day you will be rich and happy. Something is not right. We seem to have lost touch with the purpose of our quest. Increasingly, when the behavioral outcomes of our manic pursuit are measured, it is not happiness that we find but the disturbing trends of rising anxiety, obesity, and greed. In the face of this growing sickness it is time to pause and to reflect.

As Sigmund Freud observed in his essay *Civilization and Its Discontents*, published in 1930, civilization offers no gifts to liberty. The individual enjoyed far greater freedoms before the advent of organized community life. And yet the decisive step in civilization is the melding of individual and community. A civil society, in the ideal, is one where the liberty of the individual and the advantages of community life are balanced to mutual advantage. Such a balance is not easily agreed on, however, nor is it easily sustained, and in American culture that has been particularly true. But why is this so? Does the explanation for America's ambivalence toward the creation of innovative social structures that would help balance the seductive demands of the Fast New World lie in the nature of the migrant experience—where memories of past struggles are too vivid, or the fear of further loss is too great for trust to be placed in others? Or is this hesitancy toward social investment rooted in the restless, risk-taking temperament of those who elect to undertake the migrant's journey?

It is to such questions that I now turn.

Chapter Two

CURIOSITY AND THE PROMISED LAND: OF ORIGINS AND OPPORTUNISM

Give me your tired, your poor,
Your huddled masses yearning to breathe free,
The wretched refuse of your teeming shore,
Send these, the homeless, tempest-tossed, to me:
I lift my lamp beside the golden door.

Emma Lazarus
"The New Colossus," 1883

MY FLIGHT TO NEW YORK CITY from Los Angeles on that December day was uneventful. With a precision that we have come to take for granted in modern air travel, United Airlines Flight 956 crossed America's vast continent in just five hours and thirteen minutes, about the same time that it takes to prepare a Thanksgiving meal. A roiling winter storm had preceded us. It was cold, the pilot reported; snow covered the eastern seaboard from Virginia to Maine. Through the crisp air, as the plane banked in its approach to Kennedy airport, I could see Manhattan's familiar skyline standing etched and clear, as if some stage set, burnished in the evening light. I lifted myself against the restraining seat belt and there before me, within Liberty's glance, was a slip of land pressed hard against the New Jersey shore. It was, I knew, Ellis Island: the copper cupolas and the bulk of the Great Hall were unmistakable. Ellis Island: perhaps a mere slip of land but the place where the migrant forebears of some forty percent of the nation's citizens first set foot on American soil.

LIVING CREATURES move constantly across the face of the earth. For some, as for the moose and the caribou, it is a periodic migration driven by the opportunity of the seasons. For others, as with the Pacific salmon, it is a single excursion that may take the lifetime of an individual. In our mobility, we humans are no exception. In the short span of perhaps one hundred thousand years, from our cradle in Africa, we have wandered into each and every continent, surviving every climate.

The migrant has purpose. In contemporary human migration it is frequently to discard the yoke of social repression or to seek economic opportunity. Usually young males lead the journey, often traveling together in groups, as do other migrating primates. The Romans took good note of this and practiced forced migration, enlisting young men and garrisoning them in distant places. Many traveled in the hope of returning with riches. But invariably they were absorbed into the indigenous culture, marrying local women, and within a generation or two the homeland was a memory. Even in open societies, despite initial intentions the migrant rarely returns, and just as he is molded by the new culture, so does the migrant help shape that culture.

America is the quintessential migrant culture. While the United States is not the only congregation of migrant people in the world today, it is contemporary civilization's largest. Ninety-eight percent of Americans either were born elsewhere or were born into families that migrated to the United States within the last three centuries. Of those who have been party to America's unique experiment, many arrived in hunger and some in bondage, while others fled to their new land in fear, seeking a refuge beyond the reach of invading armies. Although diverse in origin, the tide has been consistent. Only during the Great Depression and the Second World War did the nation's annual infusion of migrant energy fall below two hundred thousand persons.

In the initial decades of the migration—beyond the natural barriers of sea and season—there were no criteria of admission to the American experiment, although there was a distinct preference for replicating the original European settler, preferably English speaking. Ireland's potato famine helped in that regard, feeding America's voracious appetite for increased population in the mid-nineteenth century. Those with disease, illiteracy, and socialist views were always discouraged, as were the people of Asia after 1882. The numbers of Italians, Irish, Poles, and Russian Jews who crowded into the ghettos of the northern cities at the turn of the twentieth century prompted the development of quotas based on national origin. Slowly those policies were relaxed to favor those politically persecuted or of demonstrable talent. However, in the last decades of the twentieth century—when Indo-Chinese boat people, Cuban exiles, and South American laborers sought the liberty and opportunity of America by means legal or illegal—the "poor" and "huddled masses" were again predominant among those who came. Thus America's ethnic mix has continued to evolve to the nation it is today, a unique distillate of the human species.

My own interest in migration and what drives those who choose to relocate their lives was kindled in the 1960s when, as a student, I made my first transatlantic voyage to America. After embarking from Liverpool on a dark December night, a shivering group of us gathered at the stern rail of the SS *Corinthia* to better mark our departure. Among my fellow passengers was an eminent Irish historian from Trinity College Dublin, a chronicler of the massive exodus that had drained Ireland's population during the nineteenth century. This man of generous gray mane and poetic turn of phrase had made the Atlantic crossing to New York many times. But, as he proudly informed the assembled company, his journey had always been by boat. The reason, he explained, as we stood watching the last vestige of Ireland's coastline disappear into the white-capped water that furled in our wake, was to pay homage to the courage of his migrant forebears. "Surviving the Atlantic in the 1840s was no picnic," he proclaimed. "There were no staterooms and stewards in those days. The vessels that carried those famine-starved Irish families were branded as 'coffin-ships'—fever-ridden and overcrowded. And for those who made it to the other side, life in New York was not a whole lot better." The professor saw migration as a process of Darwinian selection, where those who survived were toughened in mind and body. The migrants, in accepting the gamble and the risk, were a self-selected few. Even at the height of the famine in the West of Ireland, the majority prayed to find salvation at home. "Most human beings," the scholar concluded, "are mere homebodies at heart. That is why America is different."

I knew intuitively that he was right. As a boy I had worked each summer on a farm in rural England, to earn my pocket money. Many of those with whom I labored had never seen the sea. And yet it was but eighty miles away. Novelty and risky pursuit are not for the majority. The common instincts of our species are those of our mammalian ancestors: we tend to avoid strange places. Introduce a small mammal—a rat, for example—into a new cage or a laboratory maze and at first it will do nothing, or apparently nothing. The creature will sit in a dark corner and survey the scene. Only after reassuring itself that sudden changes are unlikely will it venture forth. The average monkey is much the same in its behavior when confronted with novelty, and in a more sophisticated way so are we. Given the choice, most humans prefer familiar territory.

Compared to when I was a boy, we are more mobile now, scurrying about in our machines. For those in the industrialized nations, daily travel has become a way of life. But this activity is nomadic, not migrant. In the original Greek a nomad—from *nomas*, "to roam about"—was one who sought fresh pasture, and cast in such a role, humans have been nomadic from the beginning. On the other hand, the verb *to migrate*—from the Latin *migrare*, "to move from one place to another"—implies deliberation and planned purpose. Our heritage as a species is one of nomadic pursuit—finding better pasture, hunting beasts of the field, or simply chasing dreams—to better serve our own survival and the comfort of those we love. And in many respects we have retained our hunting-and-gathering existence: much of our movement is to work and home again, to pick up the kids from school, to gather the weekly supply of groceries, or to visit friends and family. But deliberate migration is for the few. Despite our daily roaming, the vast majority of humans end up living close to where they were born—proximal to the place they call home. Even during the great disruptions of human history—when famine, war, and persecution have been rampant—*for every two individuals who sought their salvation in migrant flight, ninety-eight remained behind to accept what fate would bring.*

The migrant is the maverick who runs at the edge of the human herd. Migrants are a self-selected band of seekers—those of adventurous and curious mind—who in their restless approach to life lie at the extreme of the bell-shaped curve of behavioral distribution. And because of this eccentricity, given that America is a nation built almost entirely on the energy of migrant individuals, some important questions arise. As a beginning, how and to what purpose did such restless curiosity evolve and what do we know of its biology? How has the migrant mind-set helped shape our collective behavior as a commercial culture? And what contribution does this restless temperament now make to our manic pursuit? It was with these and similar questions in mind that early in my research for this book I spent an afternoon with Professor Lynn Fairbanks, a colleague of mine at the University of California in Los Angeles and an expert in primate social behavior. I was particularly interested in learning about the neurobiology and the individual differences that determine migration patterns in monkeys—and about Lynn's fieldwork in the Ethiopian Rift Valley, which many scientists believe to be the African cradle of our own primate species, *Homo sapiens.*

I was taken by surprise when, as we sat down, Lynn confessed with an impish grin that she was "a bit of a gypsy" herself. "I'm one of America's many internal migrants," she explained. "Restlessness is in my family. That's probably why I became a primatologist." Then, rummaging among books on a lower shelf, Lynn produced a leather-bound volume containing a history of her family. "Jonathan Fairebanke, my ancestor, was a prudent fellow by these accounts," Lynn said as she handed me the tome. "But if you want my honest opinion, he was an adventurer and little different in his behavior from any modern entrepreneur." "After all," she added, smiling again, "who but an opportunist or a hunted man would have crossed the Atlantic with a wife and six children in 1633." Lynn described a little about Jonathan as I leafed through the volume. He had been in his early thirties when he left England, and was the first relative on her father's side to come to America. "His wife, Grace Smith," Lynn explained, "and their six young children sailed with him in the *Griffin*, a vessel chartered by the Massachusetts Bay Company. His brother Richard—who became an innkeeper and later established the first post office in Boston—and Richard's wife came too. Imagine what it must have been like to sail the Atlantic in the sixteen hundreds. The *Mayflower* Pilgrims crossed in sixty-six days. Jonathan arrived just thirteen years later, and in a smaller vessel. In those days it took guts to leave a familiar place and start over in a new land."

Jonathan Fairebanke's behavior, Lynn's skepticism notwithstanding, is typical of the successful migrant. The curious mix of unusual daring and prudent self-preservation for which Jonathan's descendants remember him is commonplace among those who have beaten a path to America's shores. His reputation for prudence apparently was well earned. Indeed, packed into the hold of the *Griffin* were all the essentials required to establish a homestead in the New World. Basic furniture, linen, pottery, and pewter had been carefully stowed, plus the materials to build a house—the oak beams required for framing, windows, glass panes, and roofing—all of which were in short supply in the Bay Colony. Even the ship's ballast of pink English bricks had a purpose, becoming the chimney of the house Jonathan built in 1635 in "Contentment," Massachusetts, later renamed Dedham after a town in Essex, England. It still stands, preserved now by the Fairbanks Foundation as the oldest frame dwelling in America.

As Lynn clarified that afternoon in her office, migrant behavior—as measured by the distance creatures move between birth and the conception of the next generation—is of considerable biological importance because it leads to "gene dispersal" and reproductive advantage. "Out-migration, or *dispersion* as we primatologists like to call it, is dangerous but it opens up new opportunities," Lynn explained. "In most primate species some animals will ultimately leave the group of their birth and seek another habitat. Commonly it is the males, but for some—in chimpanzees, gorillas, and spider monkeys, for example—it is the females." Although there are fundamental differences tied to species behavior and individual intelligence, typically most out-migration occurs in adolescence, when risk taking increases. "It is important to understand, however, that in most monkey groups the adolescents leave because they want to," Lynn added, "not because they are driven out. In human terms it's a bit like a young man running away to sea, or preferring to search for a wife from another village rather than from his own.

"But there's also a second factor operating, which interacts with the risk-taking predisposition of those who migrate," Lynn continued, "and that is the competition for scarce resources. This is where social rank becomes important in determining which animals leave the troop. In bad times, when there is not enough food to go around, the high-ranking animals usually stay in place and the aggressive lower-ranking animals are those most likely to leave." Such dispersion is not something that occurs every year, or in every generation, but when it does occur, it has a major impact on future generations by weeding out the parent troop and potentially seeding new ones.

Lynn considered this out-migration in the primate world analogous to Jonathan leaving home to start his new life in America. The Fairebankes family was relatively affluent, with estates in the north of England, and Jonathan was a successful merchant who had been married for sixteen years by the time he made the decision to leave England. He was also well educated and resourceful, as his success in America was to demonstrate. But as Lynn explained, Jonathan was a child of his father's second wife, and under the system of patrilineage that prevailed in England during that time, it was traditional for the real property to pass to the eldest male heir. Regardless of how much Jonathan achieved in England, he would remain a second son and would never inherit his father's estates, which would pass to his elder stepbrother.

"For Jonathan to leave England and his family of origin was risky, but advantageous for his children," said Lynn. "If we put his situation in anthropological language, it is the dominant and established members of a primate group—those enjoying a habitat similar to that of their predecessors—who remain, whereas those who migrate must find their own way. In the monkeys there's considerable wastage—in some cases half of those who disperse disappear—but those who make their way into a new troop are often really smart and frequently emerge on top. Those subordinate animals that have inherited particularly assertive or intelligent genes are at an advantage because they will survive the challenges of dispersal. Scientists call this process *selection pressure* and it shapes all species, including our own.

"Another parallel to human experience," Lynn suggested during our conversation, "is the trade-off that the migrant monkey must make between facing intense competition within the ancestral territory and the hazards of leaving it. In human terms, if you want to stay in your own community and be number one, then you must be bigger and stronger, or richer and better educated than everybody else. But if you leave, you don't have to be any of those. You just have to be smarter and quicker in figuring out new ways of doing things. In today's language you need the survival skills of the entrepreneur. Sure, leaving a familiar environment is risky, but once outside, the rules are different and there's more opportunity. In the new setting, the competition is not predominantly with others over space and food, but about individual survival amid the challenges of a novel environment." It is here that temperament becomes important, as Lynn explained. Migrants have a different mind-set when it comes to risk. They acknowledge the danger in the risks they take, but in their curiosity about what's ahead, they also see opportunity—a personal challenge to their flexibility. "I think," Lynn said, "as a man of ambition Jonathan saw the New World as an opportunity, despite the risks, and I suspect that's true for most of the migrants who have found their way to America."

NUMEROUS STUDIES of migrant populations, from all over the world, support Lynn's conjecture. Optimism, self-interest, curiosity (often described as restlessness or novelty seeking), and a vigorous ambition are the best predictors of émigrés' adjustment to their new environment. Studies report that ambition and optimism are more commonly expressed in the men than in the women who migrate. In both sexes, however, it is emotional adjustment in their homeland—before they migrate—that predicts how well émigrés will adjust in the new country. In the success of British migrants to Australia, for example, good social skills and a sense of responsibility for one's own destiny emerged as positive variables, whereas emotional dependence on others was associated with a poor performance in the new culture.

The typical behavioral profile of the successful migrant that emerges from the international research is that of an independent-minded and socially competitive individual who is restless (and often impulsive in decision making) and driven to succeed. In those most successful the restlessness and impulsivity—which in humans, as in our primate cousins, has been found to be highly heritable—are commonly held in check by above-average intelligence and an internal sense of control. (Where such control is lacking, aggression and self-destructive risk taking may result, however, especially in men.) Because they are ambitious and seek social advancement, most migrants are eager and productive workers, laboring long and hard even at mundane tasks. Those most successful are also usually quick decision-makers and adept in communication, while those who are particularly skilled in resolving social conflict frequently emerge as group leaders under stressful circumstances. Thus the studies suggest that an intuitive understanding of social hierarchy and the intelligence to exploit that understanding, together with independence, a strong work ethic, and the ability to accept criticism with flexibility, are most commonly associated with social advancement and economic success in the new culture.

These are some of the competitive qualities of mind that have been carried to America by successive waves of immigrants for over three centuries. In the aggregate—as no doubt most readers will have already recognized—they are behaviors that overlap with the instinctual drives of self-love, curiosity, and ambition that Adam Smith considered to be the engines of a vibrant economy in a market-based society. A similar observation did not escape the eagle eye of Alexis de Tocqueville when he visited America in 1831, with Gustave de Beaumont. The ostensible purpose of the two young men, as commissioners of the French government, was to study the prison system in the United States. But what most fascinated Tocqueville—and what he described extensively in his famous treatise *Democracy in America*, the first volume of which appeared in 1835—was how the temperament of the migrant differed in ambition from that of the average European and how that variation was an advantage in the development of America's new democratic republic. "In Europe we habitually regard a restless spirit, a moderate desire for wealth, and an extreme love of independence as great social dangers," he wrote, "but precisely these things assure a long and peaceful future in the American republics."

Appropriate to his era, Tocqueville resorted to the metaphor of the "navigator"—a merchant seaman—to explain the differences he observed between the American and European mind-set. The European navigator, he noted, was prudent when venturing out to sea, doing so only when the weather was suitable. "If any unexpected accident happens, he returns to port. At night he furls some of his sails and when the whitening billows indicate the approach of land, he checks his course and takes an observation of the sun. The American, neglecting such precautions, braves these dangers. He sets sail while the storm is still rumbling. By night, as well as by day, he spreads full sails to the wind. He repairs storm damage as he goes, and when at last he draws near the end of his voyage, he flies toward the coast as if he could already see the port. The American is often shipwrecked, but no other sailor crosses the sea as fast as he. Doing what others do but in less time, he can do it at less expense. . . . I cannot express my thoughts better than by saying that the Americans put something heroic into their way of trading." The Americans, Tocqueville concluded, were born merchants.

SO WHAT do we know about the origins of these "heroic" talents and the love of risk that Tocqueville saw as bringing trading advantage to the young American nation? Under what conditions did such human versatility in self-preservation evolve and how is that versatility exaggerated in the migrant temperament?

The story really begins some 200 million years ago when our mammalian ancestors first appeared. That was during the Jurassic period, so popular in children's fantasy, when the dinosaurs were dominant and the world was a hot and steamy place. Then, during the Miocene—a mere 20 million years or so ago—a global cooling began, and it was under these challenging circumstances, as the food supply dwindled and competition for survival increased, that our direct forebears emerged. We know from the fossil record and genetic studies that humans, gorillas, and chimpanzees all descended from common ancestors—small apelike creatures, called *hominids*, that were distinguished by walking upright—who lived late in the Miocene period, some 5 to 7 million years ago. The first remains of a hominid skeleton—given the genus name *Australopithecus* or "southern ape"—were discovered in South Africa in 1925, but during the 1970s richer evidence emerged from excavations along the Rift Valley, the region in northeast Africa where Lynn Fairbanks, together with her colleague Clifford Jolly, have studied the migratory behavior of monkeys.

The Rift Valley is a unique and remarkable place. A massive geological fault line created as the African and Asian continents began to separate, it runs from the southern tip of Turkey through Israel and the Red Sea, into Ethiopia, and along the eastern shoulder of Africa. Four million years ago floodwaters draining from the Ethiopian highlands formed lakes, the ancient scars of which are to be found along the modern-day Awash and Omo Rivers of Ethiopia and Lake Turkana in northern Kenya. The products of erosion, immense quantities of silt and sand, and the subsequent formation of sedimentary rock along the shores of these lakes and rivers have made the region an archaeologist's paradise, and an archive of early human habitat. There are places in the Rift Valley, for example, where a day's climb from a crater's brim to the bedrock can embrace a geological journey of several million years. The evidence suggests that it was from this arid, subtropical cradle that our own species of *Homo sapiens* first evolved.

"It remains an environment of extraordinary scarcity," had been Lynn's comment when I asked her about the region. "After I spent time in the Rift Valley I found it easier to understand the genesis of risk taking. To evolve in such a sparse environment there was no choice—it was migration or death." The detailed maps and photographs that Lynn uses in her work tell the story. As the Awash River cuts down to its rocky channel, alternating geological bands of lake sediment, soil, and gray volcanic ash reveal the vast instability that pervades the history of the region. Even now the land is one of contrasts. Along the river canyon, giant fig and acacia trees flourish and offer their lush protective foliage, while beyond the rim is a hot flat world of scrub savanna. The forest monkeys of the region choose to live in the trees and among the vegetation that thrives along the river. The baboons in contrast, although they return to the canyon at night, spend considerable time out on the savanna digging for roots and tubers and sometimes eating flesh during the dry season, much as our hominid ancestors must have done.

Rick Potts, the director of the Human Origins Program at the Smithsonian Institution's National Museum of Natural History, believes that the rapid growth of the hominid brain that culminated in the evolution of *Homo sapiens* was a direct result of the intense pressure for survival caused by profound shifts of climate in this Rift Valley region, compounded by volcanic eruptions and earthquakes. Potts argues in his book *Humanity's Descent: The Consequences of Ecological Instability* that the evolutionary winners during these tumultuous times, which reached their zenith some seven or eight hundred thousand years ago, were not the specialists—such as the robust *Australopithecus* whose massive teeth were equipped to chew tough savanna roots and tree bark—but rather the lighter-boned, versatile, and more intelligent generalists of the hominid line. It is from these versatile generalists that our own species has descended.

Potts's ideas find resonance in the fossil record and in new discoveries from human genetics that supplement the archaeological evidence. An ongoing effort in genetic sleuthing, initiated by the late Allan Wilson of the University of California at Berkeley and by Luca Cavalli-Sforza of Stanford University, supports the thesis that *Homo sapiens* emerged as a uniquely intelligent species in the Rift Valley region approximately two hundred thousand years ago, strengthening the "out of Africa" theory of human evolution. The research also underscores the remarkable consistency of our genetic makeup as a species and helps clarify the migratory patterns of our forebears, suggesting that individual differences of skin pigmentation, facial features, and hair quality—through which we distinguish ourselves as Eskimo, Bushman, Caucasian, and so on—are genetic adaptations to climate and environment that have emerged since we left our African homeland to wander about the world.

The genetic analyses also emphasize that the intelligence that distinguishes us as *Homo sapiens* is of comparatively recent origin—emerging perhaps a mere two hundred thousand years ago, compared to the millions of years that the hominid line has been in evolution. Thus, in fact, the human brain—the organ that we revere as the seat of our unique capacity to reason—is a hybrid in its construction, where the new brain that is responsible for our extraordinary curiosity and ingenuity is inextricably intertwined with the same ancient systems of self-preservation and survival that serve many lower species.

This evolutionary layering is reflected in the anatomy of the human brain. Thus, if you were to hold a brain in your hands, most immediately you would see two wrinkled lobes of tissue that together are roughly the size of a cantaloupe melon. These are the two recently evolved hemispheres of the cerebral cortex (*cortex* in Latin means "husk") that are molded to fit within the skull. Together these hemispheres contain some 75 percent of the brain's neurons, the cells responsible for thinking. It is the cerebral cortex that confers on us our unique intelligence, but it is not responsible for survival or for sustaining the body's vital organs. Those essential functions are delegated to brain centers adapted from the ancient architecture of the reptilian brain. The cortex is merely the brain's new bonnet displayed much as the cap of a mushroom is displayed on its stalk. Only when turning the brain over are the ancient centers revealed, within a bulbous stem nestled between the two great hemispheres. Here lie the brain centers responsible for the machinery of breathing and the beating of the heart, plus the basic systems that serve touch and smell, our instinctual fear of noise, the desire for sex, social dominance, and territorial defense.

Now if you were to carefully inspect beneath the hemispheres' cap, you would discover another protuberance of tissue—not dissimilar in form to the nub of an old walking stick—that sits above the ancient reptilian centers at the brain's stalk. Here lie the centers of the limbic or old mammalian brain that are the crucible of emotion and social behavior. It was with the evolution of the limbic system (*limbic* means "border" in Latin, and the region is so named because it includes the oldest lobe of the new cerebral cortex) that the brain's mechanisms of self-preservation became substantially upgraded. Within the limbic structures are found the brain systems that maintain a steady body temperature, those that orchestrate the body's stress hormones, and also those that provide the physiological adaptation required to accommodate a seasonal planetary environment. But more importantly, the limbic brain also confers on us the advantages of emotional communication and the capacity for family life, which together have made possible the development of community and human society. The integration of these systems of self-preservation with the evolved sophistication of the new cortex is what gives the human brain its extraordinary creative power and the versatility to adapt to rapidly changing circumstances.

Such versatility, however, demands the precise control and swift transport of information. Thus, to coordinate the billions of neurons in the hybrid human brain, and to efficiently orchestrate the functions of its many hierarchically organized centers, elite sets of neuronal pathways have evolved. These information superhighways employ a special family of chemical messengers (also known as *neurotransmitters*), of which the principle members are *serotonin, norepinephrine,* and *dopamine*. Although the superhighways involve relatively few of the neurons in the brain (to be numbered only in the tens of thousands), their cell bodies are rooted in the brain's stem and their long axons spread upward like the branches of a tree to effectively connect the emergency systems of the reptilian brain with the limbic system and the new cortex. These messenger systems, working together, balance and modulate the brain centers that underpin our most complex behaviors.

It is in this modulation of brain activity that we find the biological roots of temperament and of those individual differences in behavior that help explain why some among us are adventurous and hardened mavericks while others prefer to stay quietly at home with the herd. Each brain superhighway carries signals with a specific behavioral impact (which I summarize here, but will describe in detail when I discuss the American temperament in my next chapter). Thus the serotonin system of neurons generally provides calming restraint, and the norepinephrine highways are activating in their action. The dopamine system, through modulation of the brain's reward pathways, plays a central role in curiosity and novelty seeking, behaviors that feature prominently in the typical migrant profile. Hence it is the relative activity of these information superhighways—the genetically programmed balance among these systems—that helps determine the differences in behavior that exist among individuals.

When it comes to self-preservation, nature is inherently conservative, and through evolutionary selection, over millions of years, the brain's survival systems have become extraordinarily efficient. The dopamine system of neurons is integral to that survival efficiency, helping us to decide on a minute-to-minute basis what in the environment should command our attention. Determining what is new is critical to staying out of harm's way, and curiosity and novelty seeking work hand in hand toward that end. Because most of what happens around us each day is predictable, processing every detail of a familiar habitat is wasteful of energy and possibly a dangerous distraction. Thus when our ancestors were living on the savanna, they paid little attention to the stable profile of the mountains on the horizon but were alert to any change or movement at the riverbank. Today neighborhood buildings provide a comparable consistency to the mountains in our everyday experience, but should we glimpse a stranger leaving from a house across the street, the unusual activity quickly commands our attention.

We are instinctually drawn to the unexpected. Novelty stimulates curiosity (which, you will recall, together with self-interest is central to Adam Smith's analysis of what drives human motivation) and invites investigation. The essential question then arises: What is the potential reward in exploring this unexpected experience, or is it something dangerous and to be avoided? Exploration involves risk, but it also increases the acquisition of knowledge, and the brain's dopamine superhighway system is essential to both. This is confirmed by extensive research in primates, which has shown that new learning takes place when unpredicted environmental changes occur and the firing rate of the dopamine neurons increases. When an experience becomes familiar and boring, even if previously it had been stimulating and pleasurable, then the dopamine nerve cells remain essentially quiescent—until another novel event occurs, at which point the firing rate again increases, drawing attention to the new situation. Thus the dopamine superhighways (frequently called the dopamine "reward" system, for obvious reasons) are what sustain our curiosity and bring novel events to the attention of the executive centers of the limbic brain and of the cerebral cortex for rapid assessment and action.

This dopamine-driven system of curiosity and reward, and the sophisticated ability to assess opportunity and risk, have played a seminal role in the success of our species. Many of the early hominids living in the Rift Valley region did not survive the abrupt environmental changes that confronted them. In those depriving times, the seeking out of rewarding opportunities and the ingenuity and intelligence to exploit them became behaviors essential to survival. As the Rift Valley dried up, diminished food choice meant either a life of crunching tree bark, as adopted by some early hominids, or an aggressive program of scavenging and predatory hunting of other animals to support a varied diet. Studies of teeth from the fossil record suggest that archaic *Homo* individuals—the more intelligent and adaptable members of the hominid line and our primitive ancestors—chose the latter option, eating a staple diet of tubers and bulbs, supplemented during periods of drought by meat, just as is the habit of the modern chimpanzee, our closest living primate relative. Some speculate that eating meat, and breaking the limited amino-acid intake of a vegetarian diet, facilitated brain growth and fostered our versatile intelligence. The increased protein in the diet helped establish a positive evolutionary loop, within which the rapid development of new cortical neurons became the wellspring of speech and reason. Thus it was *under frugal environmental circumstances* that curiosity and risk taking—that is, reward-seeking behavior—became selected as a vital asset, with the rewards for success being improved individual survival, stronger offspring, and further cortical growth.

When practiced alone, however, curiosity and risk taking leave little room for error. Learning the social skills of cooperation and of assisting others during depriving times through mutual understanding—empathic behaviors that Adam Smith in his writings summarized as *social sympathy*—helped moderate these dangers, further enhancing survival success. Thus our *Homo* ancestors chose to live in stable, hierarchically organized, and family-related groups, as remains our preference today. Through emotional gestures and a primitive verbal language they were capable of precise communication, and these behaviors were progressively enhanced by the growth of new cortical tissue. Particularly important was the augmentation of the brain's capacity for memory and the development of the frontal lobes, for this is where the massive amounts of information required for rapid assessment, planning, abstraction, language, and sustaining a complex social organization are processed and stored. Having the extra brainpower to exploit novelty as opportunity—to rapidly evaluate the prevailing circumstance, to communicate with others, and to quickly modify one's behavior in consequence—gave extraordinary advantage in exploration and in the hunt. That which early *Homo* ancestors foraged and killed, they shared within the group—and no doubt bartered and exchanged in a primitive precursor of Adam Smith's market economy. Our forebears no longer simply startled at the first sign of danger, but rather analyzed what had engaged their curiosity within a personalized framework of risk and reward, subsequently

communicating that analysis to others through the social glue of emotion and language. This intellectual amalgam was to emerge as the
unique signature of the mature human mind—the blending together of
reward-driven risk taking and curiosity with intelligence and social communication in the interest of self-preservation.

But what of the migrant? What role has curiosity and reward-seeking
behavior played there? It was some eighty to one hundred thousand
years ago that our species began leaving its Ethiopian cradle. Probably
the first such excursions were nomadic and seasonal and undertaken in
pursuit of an adequate diet, as is the habit of the handful of hunting-
and-gathering tribes that remain in existence today. Thus the first
migrants may have merely drifted out of Africa in search of a preferred
prey or by just following their instinctual appetites for adequate nutrition. Recent evidence suggests that the ancestors of some Russians, for
example, may have traveled north in the pursuit of mammoths, the lum-
bering ancestors of the elephant that flourished during the late Pleis-
tocene. In 1998, together with numerous stone-age tools, the remains of
more than fifteen such creatures killed approximately twenty-two thousand years ago were discovered in Zaraysk, a town south of Moscow.

In the time that our African exodus began, the world was a lot colder
than it is now. From geological evidence we know that until about thirteen thousand years ago when the world began warming up, glaciers covered North America and arctic conditions came and went with the
seasons. Landmasses were thus periodically connected. Through
nomadic dispersal of a mere twenty kilometers each generation, spread
over twenty thousand years, it is theoretically possible to walk the distance between Nairobi and Peking, or to reach the farthest shores of
Europe from North Africa. Pushing north from Ethiopia along the
shores of the Red Sea, it was a simple matter to turn right into Asia and
on to China, which the genetic archaeologists believe *Homo sapiens*
reached between fifty to seventy thousand years ago. Doubling back
around the Mediterranean and west into continental Europe took a little longer. From the extremity of Asia it was not difficult to roam into
North America, which conveniently was joined to the southern portion

of that continent. At the height of the glaciations (and even during the last Ice Age just eighteen thousand years ago) the Bering Sea would have been approximately three hundred feet below its present level, making it possible to cross by foot from Asia to America. Thus the genetic evidence suggests that Native Americans are closely related to present-day Siberians through common ancestors that migrated into the New World some fifteen to twenty thousand years ago.

FOR A KINSHIP group to walk from Ethiopia to the tip of South America, however, albeit over many generations, requires greater motivation than a nomadic search for one's next meal of mammoth meat or the perfect fruit tree. It suggests a curiosity and a daring in the leadership of the foraging band, and an appetite for risk, which is reflective of contemporary migrant behavior. Could it be that the instinctual curiosity and self-interest that facilitate survival in times of challenge, *at the extreme of the genetically determined spectrum of individual differences,* also determine migrant behavior? During my discussion with Lynn Fairbanks I asked whether there was evidence from her studies in primates to support such an idea.

Lynn nodded her head in affirmation. "Some monkeys are definitely more curious, more impulsive, and more drawn to unpredictable situations than others," she told me, "and they do seem to be the animals that most commonly disperse." Lynn cited growing evidence, some from her own research, which suggests that the drive to impulsivity—defined as the tendency to act quickly in novel circumstances, without restraint and without regard for the consequences (in monkeys one might call it the *Curious George syndrome*)—is powerfully heritable. A specific animal's reaction to an unfamiliar situation may be one of fearful avoidance, friendly curiosity, or impulsive aggression, depending where the animal falls along the continuum of temperament. A bold animal will quickly explore novel situations with little regard for risk while a shy animal is cautious, evasive, and fearful. Furthermore, Lynn told me, the specific behavioral response seems to be consistent for each animal over its lifetime, which suggests that it is an inherited characteristic. While in primates, as in ourselves, social experience is important in shaping this individual behavior—the infant born to a mother of dominant rank will have a different experience of winning and losing than will the infant of a subordinate female—in general, insatiable curiosity and a strong impulse to explore the unknown are instinctual and innate.

Lynn Fairbanks has investigated these variations in curiosity and impulsivity among the extended families of Old World vervet monkeys. Through a standardized procedure of introducing an "intruder" into a stable social group of monkeys, Lynn discovered that the impulse to investigate novel circumstances varies among individuals and with age. Adolescent monkeys—those between four and five years old—are more curious and impulsive in approaching a stranger than are older monkeys, but the individual differences prevail across the lifetime of the animal. Lynn observed that how quickly a monkey makes its approach to the intruder, how close it sits, and whether it scrutinizes, sniffs, touches, or threatens the visitor are behaviors that have remarkable consistency over time and in the presence of different intruders.

Lynn also found that the most impulsive and risk-taking males in her colony were those who had the lowest levels of the serotonin breakdown product 5-hydroxyindoleacetic acid (5-HIAA) in the cerebrospinal fluid, which is the fluid that bathes the brain and spinal cord. (You will recall that in the modulation of behavior, it is the serotonin system that opposes the curiosity-provoking dopamine superhighway and the alerting drive of norepinephrine.) These findings are in line with those from studies of aggression and impulsivity by other scientists working with a variety of monkey species who found that low brain serotonin activity—and thus a balance of brain chemistry in favor of the dopamine system—is associated with curiosity and risk-taking behaviors, especially in adolescence when dispersal is at its height.

There is also evidence that some individuals or subspecies, in whom the serotonin system only weakly opposes the dopamine drive, may be genetically "preprogrammed" for migratory behavior. Jay Kaplan, a professor in the Department of Comparative Medicine at the Bowman Gray

School of Medicine in North Carolina, while studying a managed colony of rhesus monkeys living on Cayo Santiago, a small Caribbean island off the coast of Puerto Rico, discovered that the males who remained in their birth troop beyond sexual maturity had a higher level of 5-HIAA in their cerebrospinal fluid. Subsequently, turning his interest to baboons living naturally in the Rift Valley, Kaplan compared males of the *Papio hamadryas* tribe, who rarely leave the troop of their birth, to the related *Papio anubis* baboon, for whom dispersal typically occurs around the age of puberty, and confirmed his earlier observation of an inverse relationship between serotonin levels and dispersal, which again suggests that dopamine drive plays an important role in migratory behavior.

"Explanations are never simple when it comes to behavior," Lynn Fairbanks cautioned during our discussion, "but the evidence is compelling in primates that curiosity and impulsivity breed true across generations, are closely linked with dominance of the dopamine system, and are also associated with migration. It's, however, always a trade-off," Lynn said. "Shy, low-ranking males are less likely to migrate and frequently die from disease. Males who are bold and aggressive in their curiosity, on the other hand, and who do disperse may grow up to have more offspring, control greater resources, and have access to large territories. But they are also more likely to be killed in a fight or to be eaten by a leopard." The ultimate success of any one individual is highly dependent on the unique challenges confronted during migration and resettlement, but in general, Lynn believes, the dispersion of the gene pool that resulted from migrant behavior promoted vigor and species improvement in the monkey colonies that she studied.

In human migration, not surprisingly, the behavioral trade-offs are subtler, but they are there and intimately entwined. Translating Lynn's primate observations into the language of international economics, for example, it is evident that the curiosity, risk taking, and survival skills that promote the successful relocation of the migrant also foster, across the globe, a positive redistribution of human capital—of energy, intelligence, skilled behavior, and experience—a phenomenon that has particularly benefited the United States in contemporary times. Rarely does migration involve "a simple transfer of skills and achievements, and even less often a transfer of wealth," writes Thomas Sowell, a senior fellow at the Hoover Institution of Stanford University, in his comprehensive book *Migrations and Cultures*. And yet "nothing is more common than to have poverty-stricken immigrants become prosperous in a new country and to make that country more prosperous as well." Studies of American émigrés have emphasized their extraordinary diversity in religious, economic, and social background and, at the same time, the remarkable consistency in attitude that they bring to the task of establishing themselves in the new land. While migrants often begin their new life earning less than persons of the same national and ethnic origin who are already established, over a short span of ten to fifteen years the first-generation migrant commonly exceeds the income levels of his or her countrymen. This upward mobility is evident in the statistical profile of immigrants to the United States, but it is also true in Canada and Britain among individuals of all ethnic groups. It is not material wealth that is transferred in the human migratory process but an attitude of mind that begets wealth, as Tocqueville observed during his visit to America in 1831.

But with this extraordinary facility for self-improvement are entwined potential pitfalls. In the migrant's entrepreneurial success, Adam Smith's instinctual engines of economic growth are tuned to their greatest efficiency, as is apparent in American culture. Curiosity, anticipating reward, assessing prospective gains, and making choices about which rewards to pursue are behaviors central to wealth creation, and, as I have noted, the evidence is rapidly accumulating that the dopamine reward system drives these behaviors. When a Wall Street trader is reviewing the continuous stream of electronic information that is a stock-market report, for example, it is the dopamine reward pathways within the trader's brain that provide the ability to focus and the frontal cortex that undertakes the executive analysis. Under optimum circumstances, based on the prudence of past experience, greater effort is then expended by the trader toward those stocks calculated to produce the greatest reward.

But there are complications: objective deliberation is vulnerable to distraction and distortion when our curiosity is tweaked by some novel product or new technology, as was evident—for virtually the whole nation—during the Internet boom and the excitement surrounding the "new economy" of e-commerce. Unexpected pleasurable reward, the anticipation of such reward, and a plethora of choice all have the same exhilarating effect. The explanation of these phenomena is that *the dopamine reward systems of the brain are easily hijacked*. Such temptations as gambling, day trading, and cocaine—at least initially—offer not only the fascination of instant reward but also the potential hazards of addiction.

The reward systems of every human brain—of every mammalian brain—are to a greater or lesser degree vulnerable to addictive hijacking. Thus America's greatest asset, the curiosity and risk-taking drive of her migrant people, is also potentially the nation's fatal flaw. It is a paradox of progress that during affluent times the drive for material success—rooted in the ancient instincts of survival—can make us sick. This is especially true when opportunity is freed from social and moral constraint, and when demand-driven novel environments such as the Fast New World dominate daily experience. I will begin to explore this conundrum in my next chapter.

It is also important to recognize that the restless, curiosity-driven émigré temperament that I describe here is not confined to those who are first-generation immigrants, but is pervasive in American life. Over 20 percent of Americans change their place of residence each year and have done so since the 1950s. From generation to generation there is a consistent movement of native-born Americans back and forth across the country. Rarely, and especially so in the urban centers of the East and West Coasts, does one find extended family living within commuting distance of each other. The migration and mobility of the American population within the nation's borders are greater than in any other industrialized nation.

The internal migration of members of Lynn Fairbanks's family within the borders of the United States is an example of such restlessness.

Although between 1636 and 1900 the house that Jonathan built was in the possession of the Fairbanks family, their westward migration continued. Jonathan Fairebanke's eldest son, George, moved to Sherborn, Massachusetts, which during his time was a frontier, while his third son, Jonas, helped found Lancaster, Pennsylvania, in 1657. Jonas's sons in turn became involved in the Indian wars and led a subsequent migrant wave that settled in western Massachusetts, Vermont, and upper New York State. While after that, as Lynn described it, "exhaustion set in, at least for a generation or two," the men in the Fairbanks family "retained a passion for migrant women." Lynn's father's mother had left Ireland at the age of fourteen, fleeing hard economic times, and her mother's parents had come directly from Yorkshire, England. In Lynn's own generation of the Fairbanks family she considered herself the "rolling stone." She quit college in Vermont after two years, worked in New York City, and then skied away a winter or two in Colorado before ending up in Boulder, "where I actually graduated." She began studying monkeys as a graduate student at Washington State before moving to the University of California.

"As a career that has indulged my sense of physical and intellectual adventure, primatology has been perfect for me," Lynn said. "I'm constantly reminded how fortunate I am, in being an American. Since Jonathan's time those with the migrant impulse to move on could expand across this huge continent. And, thanks to our early and successful fight for independence, unlike in Canada or Australia we have not been tethered by the traditions of a mother country. Flexibility and opportunity have been the great strengths of this nation. Those among us predisposed to restlessness were able to avoid the competition of the establishment, and in so doing frequently created something new and valuable. But for future generations it may be different. The cultural climate has changed. The physical frontiers are diminishing and commercial pressures are increasing. Whatever a young person wants out of life—be it a job, material possessions, a house, finding the best schools for the children, or whatever—there is fierce competition, and often it is money that sets the pace. Big commerce and big paychecks now dominate. In the past, faced with such circumstances the mavericks among us could pack up and seek their fortune elsewhere. It's part of our cultural mythology, part of following the American dream. At worst you could drop out and become a hippie, or move to California and study monkeys. But now in our consumer society, it's business or bust. With no wilderness to cross, autonomy is more difficult to establish and each new generation is compelled to compete as the market dictates. It's a different game and the risks and the rewards are more narrowly defined."

Chapter Three

THE FREEDOM
TO STRIVE:
OF RISK AND REWARD

The greatest risk is not taking one. They do not write the stories of those who play it safe. Yet most of us do. It is inherent in our nature to avoid risk. From the earliest age there is something that tells us to sidestep danger. Perhaps because of that, there is also something in us that admires the risk taker, the adventurer, the person with the courage to step up to the edge of the precipice and believe that he can make it to the other side.

Advertisement for the American International Group, Inc.
Economist, April 2000

WHEN ALEXIS DE TOCQUEVILLE and Gustave de Beaumont landed in Newport, Rhode Island, on May 9, 1831, Andrew Jackson was president and the United States had fewer than 13 million citizens. The pair spent nine months touring seventeen of the twenty-four states then in the Union, on foot and on horseback, and by steamboat and stagecoach, before returning to France on February 20, 1832. As a Frenchman, Tocqueville was passionately interested in how individual freedoms translate into economic vitality within democratic societies. He saw America as the grand experiment. "We are close enough to the time when the American societies were founded to know in detail the elements of which they are compounded," Tocqueville wrote in his introduction to *Democracy in America*, "and (yet) far enough off to judge what these seeds have produced."

Tocqueville and Beaumont never found their way to Los Angeles, and had they done so they would have discovered little more than a clutch of adobe houses and a Spanish mission. But Tocqueville did not doubt that the American territories would one day stretch to the Pacific Ocean. The people's restless pursuit of riches, he decided, would ensure America's expansion and economic success. "Most of the people in these nations [of the United States] are extremely eager in the pursuit of immediate material pleasures, and are always discontented with the position they occupy," Tocqueville wrote. "They think about nothing but ways of changing their lot and bettering it. . . . An American will build a house in which to pass his old age and sell it before the roof is on. He will plant a garden and rent it just as the trees are coming into bear. He will take up a profession and leave it, settle in one place and soon go off elsewhere with his changing desire. Yet at the end of the year crammed with work he has little spare leisure. His restless curiosity goes with him traveling up and down the vast territories of the United States."

Today the city of Los Angeles is living testimony to the migrant's restless desire that Tocqueville described almost two centuries ago. A vast grid of streets and superhighways—which when viewed from an airplane brings to mind some giant, misplaced, computer chip—Los Angeles is remarkable for its incessant growth and self-renewal. After World War II southern California was at the forefront of the rapid development that occurred in the aerospace, defense, and electronics industries, and this growth, together with an expansion in construction and entertainment enterprises, attracted a stream of immigrants and native-born internal migrants. While first-generation immigrants settle, today, throughout the United States, they are concentrated in the urban areas of just six states (California, New York, Florida, Texas, New Jersey, and Illinois). Los Angeles leads among those urban centers. LA, in short, is the migrant's city in a migrant land: a focus of international commerce, the acknowledged Mecca of a film industry with global reach, and a place of uncommon ethnic diversity. It is said, for example, that the children attending the LA school district represent 116 different languages.

In less than three generations the population of Los Angeles County and its immediate environs has swollen to some 14 million persons, and over that same time frame the terrain that first attracted many of those millions to the region has been dramatically reconfigured. The land devoted to agriculture dropped from 300,000 acres to less than 10,000 as 1,500 square miles of suburban construction spread itself across the Los Angeles basin and into the valley beyond. In the interim the citizens of wealthier means carved themselves housing sites out of the surrounding foothills and the mountains. By 1970 more than one-third of the county had been paved with asphalt to accommodate the automobiles that provide the far-flung citizenry with their only reliable means of transportation.

In its growth Los Angeles idealizes the imagery of the America dream. With deep roots in social fantasy, it is the world capital of futuristic metropolitan simulation. Through the theme parks it pioneered beginning in the 1930s and through media extravaganzas such as MCA/Universal's City Walk, LA parodies its own urban image even as it re-creates itself. By replicating the world of cinema and television—often populated by familiar cartoon characters—entertainment megacorporations offer tourists comfortable architectural bubbles that are segregated from the relentless throb of real city life. In part because of this reputation for fantastical imagery—especially with the tourism and entertainment industry now being southern California's largest employer—Los Angeles is commonly considered by many Americans as a caricature, worthy only of dismissal. This is a mistake, for the city evokes a future vision of America that deserves our thoughtful attention. It is not a vision of the scenario in *Blade Runner*—Ridley Scott's 1982 film and one of the darker Hollywood parodies in which actor Harrison Ford prowls the steel and microchip jungle of a rain-soaked twenty-first-century Los Angeles, stalking genetically engineered criminal replicants of humans—but one far more mundane. It is the simple notion—embodied in the city's theme parks and in its sprawling growth—that thanks to the ingenuity of its people, America is a nation with a limitless future.

While such a future vision might momentarily be called into question when one is driving bumper to bumper along a Los Angeles freeway, with one eye on the brake lights of the vehicle in front and the other on the rearview mirror monitoring the gestures of a driver who is speaking animatedly into a handheld cell phone, in fact this faith in American inventiveness is firmly held by the majority of citizens. It is the same self-belief that impressed Tocqueville during his visit, and that drove the wagons west in pursuit of settlement and fortune. Today we see a similar confidence placed in our scientific innovation, and in American technology as being the instrument of the world's future prosperity. The consistent underlying certainty is that regardless of the problems that we may encounter along the path of progress, we Americans will have the freedom, the resourcefulness, and the technical ingenuity with which to solve them.

Such faith in American cleverness is not entirely misplaced. In this migrant land our energy and restless curiosity continue to serve us well. American citizens have demonstrated again and again their leadership in technology and science. But in our success we must guard against complacency and a false sense of optimism. While judging on past record there is little doubt that America will continue to evolve as a fascinating, technology-based society, what the future impact of that evolution will be on how we live each day is becoming less certain. From the standpoint of individual health and happiness, one thing is already apparent. As I will highlight with three cautionary tales in the second part of this book, there is evidence that America's technology-driven Fast New World is already testing the limits of human physiology. In fact, the stimulus-saturated and helter-skelter existence that it fosters is at the root of the discomfort and of the health problems that many Americans are now experiencing.

In demand-driven urban habitats, such as Los Angeles, the chal-lenges we face today are unique in human experience. *Homo sapiens* rose to dominance, after all, in a physically dangerous and depriving environment, not amid the abundance of food, information, and mate-rial goods that Americans now enjoy. Life was simpler in the cradle of our evolution as a species: challenge produced clear, black-and-white results—either you were dead or you survived. Today it is no longer the life-threatening chance encounter that triggers physiological stress. Now stress is tied largely to social relationships and to the way in which our technology aids or hinders those relationships. The mechanisms of bod-ily defense that once gave short-term physical advantage are not well suited to the time-starved chronic competition of the Fast New World. The message is clear: if we are to adapt successfully to the novel habi-tats that we are creating for ourselves, we must be mindful of where we have come from and who we are as evolved creatures of this planet. While LA's theme parks depicting a fantastical, boundless future may hold us in awe, from the standpoint of human biology the future does have well-defined limits. And in America today we have begun to test those limits.

BUT WHY, you may ask, are Americans encountering these physiolog-ical barriers ahead of the rest of the world? To answer that question we must return for closer inspection of the American temperament and to further consideration of our cultural mythology as a migrant nation. For each of us, the way life is experienced is profoundly shaped by the way we approach it, and by the rewards and punishments that that approach engenders. It is in this interaction that temperament plays a critical role. Hence the shy person who engages his or her world with caution has a different experience from the bold individual who is assertive and pre-pared to take risks, just as Lynn Fairbanks demonstrated in primates with her intruder studies. Similarly, just as our collective behavior shapes cultural values, so does culture help shape the way in which we each behave. Thus in the United States the temperament of the classical émigré—a combination of restless curiosity and a competitive drive for social advancement—and the freedom of expression that American culture applauds are intertwined and mutually reinforcing in a continuously evolving cycle.

In thinking about this interaction and how it shapes life in America, I want to make an important distinction between temperament and character, the two key components of "personality." It is a distinction mirrored in everyday speech when we divide instinct from free will and inborn habits from what we learn. *Character*—habits and attitudes that emerge through self-awareness—is learned behavior that is molded largely by the family and the culture in which we are raised. In contrast, *temperament*—an inborn pattern of emotional style that emerges early in childhood and persists into adult life—is strongly heritable, accounting for approximately 40 percent of behavioral variance in twins.

Professor Robert Cloninger, a psychiatrist at the Washington School of Medicine in Saint Louis, Missouri, has developed an organized system of evaluating human temperament that is helpful in distinguishing it from character and defining its variations. Utilizing his Temperament and Character Inventory (TCI)—built from two decades of careful study—Cloninger has integrated information from the objective psychological testing of individuals with our growing knowledge of the brain's anatomy and chemical messenger systems. His research not only confirms that patterns of temperament are heritable, but also suggests that these different patterns indicate reflect variation in the genetic programming of neurochemical communication.

The common behavioral patterns of temperament appear to reflect the balance of activity among the dopamine, norepinephrine, and serotonin systems (the information superhighways linking the ancient reptilian brain stem to the new mammalian cortex, as I explained earlier in Chapter 2). Through his research Cloninger has identified behavioral clusters that describe four major temperament styles—along a shy–bold continuum—the poles of which he has named *harm avoidance* (shyness) and *novelty seeking* (boldness). Together with *reward dependence* and *persistence*—the intermediary factors along the continuum—Cloninger's analysis highlights the common patterns in which we interact with others and how we respond to social challenge.

Briefly, individuals with the temperamental style of harm avoidance are generally shy and inhibited. These people worry a lot and are fearful and anxious in the face of social competition. The evidence suggests that this temperament pattern is associated with a dominance of serotonin in the brain messenger systems. On the other hand, the temperament clusters of reward dependence, persistence, and novelty seeking—behaviors that overlap with curiosity—seem tied to activity of the brain's reward system and to the dopamine and norepinephrine superhighways. When in exercising our curiosity we stumble on some tasty food, engage in a new activity that we enjoy, get the best of some competition, or meet somebody we really like, it is the dopamine reward pathways of the brain that are activated, ensuring that we will seek to repeat the experience. Such pleasurable reinforcement initiates a "positive feedback loop"—a reward—and an individual's dependence on such outside reward is what helps determine his or her pattern of temperament.

In the heritable pattern Cloninger describes as reward dependence, individuals are sentimental, sensitive to social isolation, and highly dependent on positive feedback from others to sustain their own good feelings. Cloninger believes that such reward dependence is tuned by the norepinephrine system—the brain's superhighway that ensures that emotionally charged events are vividly encoded in our memory. By contrast, in those persons of persistent temperament, the need for social reinforcement is dramatically diminished. Thus persistent individuals are doggedly determined even in the absence of positive feedback. It is, in Cloninger's description of this temperament style, as if the brain's mechanisms of behavioral inhibition become "short-circuited" such that some perverse pleasure is gained even from the most difficult circumstances.

It is the novelty-seeking pattern of temperament, however, that is important in understanding migratory behavior. This temperament style appears to reflect genetic differences in the dopamine reward system of the brain. Those scoring high on this scale are bold and curious individuals who enjoy exploration and challenge, and who are typically risk takers relatively impervious to social feedback. Thus the classical temperament of a first-generation migrant who achieves success most closely parallels, in Cloninger's classification, a combination of novelty seeking and persistence—as, for example, in the case of Jonathan Fairebanke.

That patterns of temperament are strongly heritable has important implications for understanding the restless curiosity and risk taking that are so characteristic of American culture. If only 2 percent of the world's population is migrant, then it logically follows that Americans, in their willingness to take the risk of starting life anew, are a self-selected subgroup of that émigré population. And from this postulate, it also follows that within most American families there are members who carry some variation of a genetic constellation that in its purest form is expressed as the restless curiosity that is typical of migrant behavior. (U.S. immigration policies may have increased this genetic bias within the American population by giving preference over many decades to those immigrants who have previously demonstrated initiative and drive.) Therefore, what may explain Americans' restless engagement of the future that so intrigued Tocqueville over a century ago—and still persists in America today, especially in the mind-set of those who choose to live in cities like Los Angeles and New York—is an inherited association between the migrant temperament and risk taking. Perhaps it is this same temperament—determined by genetic variation among the brain's reward pathways—that drives our workaholic ways and shapes our optimism of the future? In short, perhaps America is not only a cultural experiment but also a genetic one?

WITH THESE ideas and questions in mind, one evening in the late summer of 2002 I sat down in Los Angeles with a group of young entrepreneurs to learn more about their lives. In particular I was interested in how risk taking and curiosity are expressed in contemporary America's commercial culture and whether such behavior is integral to the temperament of those who thrive at the manic edge of our society.

In organizing the evening I was aided and abetted by Anna, a woman whom I had first met when she was a postgraduate student in psychology at the University of Pennsylvania. Like Lynn Fairbanks, Anna is one of America's internal migrants. Lean and bespectacled with the crisp look that I associate with a Lands' End catalogue, she had grown up in the Protestant farm belt of the American Midwest. After working with me one summer as a research assistant, she had tried her hand at academia but was soon bored. "Perhaps it is because I was an MTV generation kid, but my attention span is too short to be a professor" had been her memorable wisecrack upon telling me she was quitting and moving to Washington, D.C. Gregarious, socially adept, and endowed with a prodigious appetite for work, Anna had risen rapidly in the fast-paced world of political management and had attributed this success to her grounding in psychology. In her doctoral thesis, she had explored the relationship between the emotional style of the therapist and the outcome in psychotherapy, and thus when I contacted her regarding my own investigations into temperament, she was eager to participate, inviting two of her friends from the business world to join us for the evening.

Our rendezvous was the Encounter Restaurant and Bar, housed in a giant disc perched on parabolic stilts some seventy feet above the frenetic hub of the Los Angeles International Airport. A first visit to the Encounter inevitably conjures up images of the Mos Eisley Cantina in the Star Wars epic. From the pulsing electronic jazz that heralds the closing of the elevator doors to the moonstone quarry walls, lava lamps, and crater-shaped bar—complete with light-emitting laser guns and cybernetic sound effects whenever a drink is drawn—the atmosphere is space age, and designed to be so. It had been Anna's idea to meet there. "Believe me, it's a lot more exciting than the basement of the Longworth Office Building," she had replied defensively when I asked about the choice. "And besides, it's convenient." (Anna runs the Washington office for a member of Congress and is constantly in and out of airports.) I reassured her. In fact I found the funky location distinctly in tune with my purpose.

Marcel, looking surreal under the restaurant's alternating illumination of magenta and electric blue, sat opposite me. Born in Paris, Marcel had been "discovered" while swimming for France in the Olympics, and had come to America as a teenager to study on an athletic scholarship. Injury had curbed his athletic prowess, but he soon enrolled as an undergraduate at Stanford, and later went on to the business school there. Then, after a spell working for a bank in Asia, and with some unexpected success in the international money markets, he turned to investments fulltime. After opening an office in Los Angeles, Marcel now offered what he described as a "boutique" service for selected international clients.

A lawyer was our other companion. Tom, whom I judged to be in his late forties and a few years older than Marcel, had been a leader in his class at Harvard and was now a successful business entrepreneur. He flew in from Arizona especially for dinner and arrived a little late. Vibrant with energy, Tom had a taste for the surreal. The unworldly qualities of the restaurant—courtesy of Walt Disney Imagineering—clearly delighted him. "There's nothing closer to the spaceport city of Mos Eisley on this planet than Los Angeles," was his comment as we shook hands. "If this is the Cantina, then I'm Captain Han Solo," he bantered, referring to the daredevil pilot in George Lucas's money-making space odyssey, "and you must be Ben Kenobi. No doubt our waiter will be R2-D2." Tom, I noted, certainly knew how to break the ice.

But as I next discovered, Tom's wit could also be disarming. "I hear you're interested in risk taking and what makes folks like me tick," he asserted as we sat down together. "Well, it's simple enough. It's the challenge of being at the cutting edge, of helping to create the future, of finding novel ways to be more efficient, that sort of thing. I'm really charged by what I do as a consultant. Some of my friends consider me an 'addict' when it comes to work, although that's really only one of my passions in life. In fact," he laughed, leaning across the table toward me, "my wife is convinced that I get the same sensation doing deals as having sex." I found Tom's openness and exuberance engaging and, with a smile of my own, asked if he cared to elaborate. From Anna's briefing I knew that each of our guests was highly accomplished, and she had told me earlier that "Tommy" in recent years had taken an interest in financing rehabilitation programs for stressed-out executives. The personal confession, however, had come as a surprise. Nor was I prepared for the sophisticated opinions that were to follow.

In Tom's opinion, to understand risk taking one first had to understand the roots of human pleasure—the "happiness thing." Particularly problematic was the definition of *addiction*, which Tom considered to be socially determined and dangerously confusing. Given the mounting evidence that there is a common chemical pathway of reward within the brain's circuitry, he argued, then the subjective excitements induced by cocaine, opiates, extreme sports, gambling, sex, shopping, doing business deals, or starting an Internet company probably have something in common. It was Tom's conviction that the "rush"—the cryptic label given to the subjective surge of pleasure that is associated with drug addiction—did not merely result from small molecules like cocaine or alcohol entering the brain, but rather "the hedonistic experience generated by the changing brain chemistry that such little molecules induce."

Thus Tom could think of "no logical reason" why in some people an acceptable social activity—such as playing basketball or trading on the stock market—"can't give the same rush of excitement as an illicit drug." In our social labeling we had confused the experience with what triggered it. "Fundamentally the rush comes from pushing the envelope," proposed Tom. "So if the push is tied to something society rewards, then we call it ambition. But when the majority finds that 'something' a little scary, then the guy's labeled a risk taker and a novelty seeker." In Tom's opinion, taking risk was just a way of finding one's ultimate place in the world. Searching for novel experience was part of our survival equipment, and the rush of excitement and fulfillment was the reward that kept us searching. "Real" addiction was something else and not to be confused with this basic quest for fulfillment. "Some of America's most celebrated idols," Tom declared, "including a president or two, have achieved their success by being risk takers and reward seekers." It was clear that as a self-styled maverick, Tom enjoyed thinking outside the box.

The word *risk* derives from the early Italian "risicare" that in rough

English translation means "to dare." Hence risk taking as a behavior lies beyond curiosity, implying choice and the freedom to choose. In pursuing a risky option, we have an awareness of less hazardous alternatives, but these have been rejected in favor of the gamble. An optimistic view of one's own ability and of the future is essential to risk behavior. Hence risk taking, as Adam Smith noted, is tied to the "conceit which men have of their own abilities . . . the absurd presumption in their own good fortune." Marcel caught the essence of such presumption when early in our conversation he provided the example of Mark Spitz, the legendary American swimming champion. During his swimming days Marcel had known Spitz well, and before the Mexico Olympics he had been surprised when Spitz publicly boasted that he would win five gold medals. "I think he won one," recalled Marcel. "At that high altitude he just hadn't got the right technique." Then four years later, in Munich, Spitz held another press conference. "This time he was going to win *seven* gold medals," said Marcel. "Many people laughed at such a bizarre announcement. I was there, competing against him, and I laughed too. But indeed he did go on to win seven gold medals, and that made him an American hero."

Marcel had learned something from his Olympic experience with Spitz and he reminded himself of it everyday—namely, that risk is an essential ingredient in the drive to succeed. It is through risk and pushing the social envelope—and here Marcel echoed Tom's opinion—that one defines one's place in a competitive world. I agreed. When human existence was linked more closely to nature, risk taking was a necessary hazard. Survival was tied to the everyday gamble of hunting, fishing, finding shelter, growing crops, and bearing children. Most people perceived their future as something outside human hands—a matter of luck and God's good graces—and most decisions were driven by instinct. Risk taking has long been integral to the human instinct of self-preservation.

How that instinct is expressed is determined today largely by the culture in which we find ourselves. This is underscored by the mushrooming growth of gambling in America since it was rationalized in the 1980s as an alternative to increased taxation. The state of Iowa, for example, where a Catholic priest was sent to jail during the 1970s on charges of running a bingo game, and which did not have a lottery until 1985, had ten casinos a decade later, plus horse racing, a dog track, and around-the-clock slot machines. While it is estimated that state governments actually lose money on such deals—forking out three dollars for rehabilitation programs and to the criminal justice system for every dollar of revenue taken in from the casinos—organized gambling is now an exceedingly popular public pastime, drawing more customers than baseball parks or movie theaters.

I asked my guests how they explained this shift in national sentiment. "The political acceptance of gambling was part of the thrust during the Reagan years to return America to laissez-faire economics," suggested Anna. Her friends agreed. "It was when we thought that Japan was about to overtake us that the brakes came off," said Tom. He recalled that when he began his career, in the 1970s, American business preferred married and conservative executives who liked to work for one company and slowly rise to the top. The stereotype he remembered was the local bank manager in the town where he had grown up: tall, thin, wearing a gray suit, a white shirt, and devoid of social skills. Such people were loyal and could be relied on to die at the desk. All that they expected from business was a clear hierarchy, satisfactory mentors, and the opportunity to climb the ladder. There was also a geographic locale to commerce. Cars were made in Detroit, by people living in Detroit, and were sold in America. "It was a military model," suggested Tom, "and in return for loyalty came caring and safety." Then somewhere in the late 1980s—as information management revolutionized everything from trucking to banking, the Soviet Union disappeared, and capitalism triumphed—the "celebrity" model of the business entrepreneur emerged. "With global market competition there came a desperate need for individualism and creativity," continued Tom. "Suddenly it was the free agent—someone unafraid of risk and willing to fly around the world, living out of a suitcase for six months, just to get ahead—who became the individual most in demand. These were heralded as the new frontiersmen, global cowboys in the image of Han Solo, but in my opinion America was returning to its instinctual roots as a frontier culture. The stability of the postwar years during the 1950s and '60s were an aberration. Now those prepared to die at their desks are gone."

"That change was beginning when I was at Stanford," volunteered Marcel. "Although it seemed to me—perhaps because I was fresh from France—that even before the shift occurred, the managers in the U.S. were greater risk takers than their European equivalents. The 1990s just accelerated that trend." I asked Marcel why he had stayed in America, being that many Frenchmen are so critical of the culture. He smiled. "Probably because I'm a contrarian," he replied. "I've always been suspicious of the herd and the unanimous viewpoint." Marcel appreciated the opportunity that youth and fresh ideas were given in America. "I like to discover things for myself," he said. "The thrill comes in learning how to beat the odds, in good times and in bad."

Anna was nodding. "In politics it's the same thing. There's intense competition to be part of a winning team. I learned that early on. It's a lot like Hollywood. Congress is its own little insular world," she continued, "and the rivalry is fierce. Burnout is common. We have every intrigue that is human—love affairs, back stabbing, you name it. Everybody has an inflated sense of self. 'Our industry just happens to be the guidance of the free world,' is the prevailing attitude on the Hill, 'and because that is terribly important therefore so am I.' It's like the Elvis Fan Club, all little world stuff, but with the difference that the risks you take may end up on the front page of the *Washington Post*."

"You might ask what drives us," Anna added, after a pause. "I think it's the thrill of being close to the leading edge of the most powerful democracy in the world, if only for one brief moment. It really *is* like living in Hollywood: a celebrity hierarchy, who's standing next to whom—that sort of stuff, the same social cachet. There's even a magazine devoted to it, a gossip sheet a bit like *Vanity Fair*, but with the unimaginative name of *Roll Call*. The irony is that the staffers who are the social glue that keeps the government together don't reflect the diversity of the people they work for. Rather they are selected for being out there at the edge, loving the excitement and the competition. Everybody is young, and hoping for a political career."

In Anna's opinion money is not the motivation. "Whereas people in industry count the number of dollars earned," she continued, "on the Hill we count the amount of time it takes us to earn them." She explained that although the Washington workday rarely starts much before nine or ten in the morning, it continues until nine or ten at night, with most people working on Sundays. The culture is driven by the next deadline. On the roll call of congressional members present each day is posted the number of days to the next election. The clock is always ticking, people are always running, and every deal is struck with one eye looking toward the elections in November. It adds up to a pressured existence, almost to frenzy. "You have to be young or foolish, or both, to do it for very long," Anna said, ruefully. "Sometimes it makes me wonder about myself, but then I realize that it is in the tradition of the American dream. For our crazy American lifestyle to work, everybody needs to feel that they are on their way to fame or fortune. Leisure doesn't fit with such a notion, so the hours worked have become a competitive index of how important we are in the social hierarchy. We don't live in luxury, we aren't celebrities, we can't measure the bills that we pass, but we *can* measure the number of hours we work. That's *our* score card," Anna concluded.

The Encounter Restaurant was filling up and there was a rising buzz of voices. Distracted, I found myself reflecting on our conversation and how similar my guests were in their approach to life despite their diverse backgrounds. Each had a unique style. And yet, as they spoke of their professional worlds, the enthusiasm for the competitive edge and the vigor of engagement reflected a common emotional tone. I was reminded again of Lynn Fairbanks and her cross-generational intruder studies of the impulsive primate temperament. Anna, Tom, and Marcel, despite differences in age and social origin, were—in their energy, optimism, and fascination with risk—of similar mind. These were "birds of a feather" that habitually flew in the face of life's challenge: individuals who in their aggressive "can-do" approach to life were shaping America's

Fast New World. This was the temperament, it seemed, that predisposed American culture to its manic pursuit.

From the stories being told that evening it was clear that Tom was a man of curiosity and a risk taker, but industrious and successfully so. Marcel, a quieter man, was clearly self-contained and extremely competitive. That Anna had the persistence and daring of the migrant, I already knew for she had wandered far from her Iowa roots. Anna is the eldest of five children. Her taste for the manic edge had emerged early and it had quickly set her apart. In the rural community where she lived, her forebears—a migrant tangle of German, English, and Irish ancestry—had tilled the soil for one hundred years, and in consequence everybody either knew each other or was related by birth. Anna had found such familiarity stifling. As she was describing her rural roots, I reminded her of a photograph from those early years that she had kept in her office while a graduate student. The camera had caught her, a young acrobatic Diana, balancing on one foot atop the vertical exhaust pipe of the family's John Deere tractor. Around her, standing in awe, were her younger siblings. Anna smiled at the memory. Enjoying novelty and challenge, she had felt "compelled," as she explained, to leave her rural roots. Anna had been of a restless temperament from the beginning.

Tom confessed that he too had always felt a restless streak. After finishing Harvard Law School, he first spent time in Japan. There were few American lawyers there at the time, and he soon became a celebrity in his role as a consultant on American business law. "I was having a blast, working my guts out, learning Japanese, and hooked on Asian women," he recalled with characteristic candor. Then, turning to corporate finance as a "turnaround artist," he quickly secured an international reputation. In its heyday the "turnaround" business was primarily supported by big banks, which "insisted on new managers to fix any ailing company they had helped finance during a takeover." Tom discovered that he was perfectly suited to the role of short-term executive and achieved great success. "For me each project was a game," he explained. "It was not so much the dollars I made which fascinated me, but rather that I was continuously learning. At the center of business success is the art of the deal. Making deals in the corporate world is a bit like gambling at high-stakes backgammon. The risk is high but if you have good skills—knowing the game, planning your moves, analyzing your opponent's strategy—the rewards are high too. You get deep into another person's life . . . the way they think, the way they feel, and the way they behave. For me the fascinating part is figuring out what they'll do next and staying ahead of the game."

I was prompted to ask Tom whether such sentiments were behind his earlier comment equating deal making with sex. Tom grinned. "Sort of," he replied. "I find I easily get hooked on things that I really enjoy, although I did learn a decade ago that it's possible to be *too* enthusiastic about something." After Marcel asked him to elaborate, Tom recalled how in the mid-1980s, when major banks in the United States were getting ready for "the recession which never happened," he had been asked to fix an international company that manufactured components for business machines and computers. "They offered me a huge package," Tom explained, "which I found impossible to refuse."

Tom had been living in Florida, happily married and with a teenage son, when he accepted the challenge. The company had offices in New York, Paris, Singapore, and Switzerland and manufacturing plants in Asia and Europe. In the United States the production center was based in Rochester, New York, so Tom quickly acquired a new house there with the intent of moving his family. His son, however, had different ideas, fearful that a change of high school would jeopardize his entry into college. "So," said Tom, "we did the best we could and I became a latter-day whirling dervish." He would leave Rochester in the evening on a Sunday and fly to New York and then on to Paris to arrive by 6:00 A.M. the next morning. After a day at the Paris office he would spend the night in his apartment there, and then drive to the factory in Rouen, spend a few days there, then on to Switzerland, back to Paris, sometimes to England, and perhaps on the weekend back to the Alps for some skiing. After Europe it was a plane to Korea, before spending time in Tokyo. He would then drop into the corporate office in Singapore before returning to Rochester—only to repeat the whole cycle a month later. "Whenever possible I'd pass through Palm Beach for a few days to see my son," explained Tom, "but otherwise this crazy game went on very successfully for two years."

Tom waved in the direction of the restaurant's observation window. Beyond the stark white stilts of our space module, the firefly flash of aircraft glowed against a sky of darkening blue velvet. "I got to know places like this real well," he continued. "Every month I was going around the world, and sometimes twice. Literally I slept for two nights of every week on an airplane. I knew I was living at the edge of my endurance but I didn't care. My family life was falling apart, but I had never felt so exhilarated."

Two events conspired to make Tom question the rationality of his exuberance. The first was at a law school reunion when several close friends commented that he looked so thin and unwell, they worried he might have cancer. Then, in Florida a few weeks later, as a favor to a colleague, Tom agreed to evaluate the financial viability of a rehabilitation center for stressed-out executives. "I had presumed that the Pines would be just another drying-out spot for alcoholics," explained Tom, "and indeed there was some of that. But in the process of assessing the market appeal of the place, I spoke to a few of those enrolled in the program. It was uncanny. I could have been talking to myself." Most of the people Tom interviewed were highly successful career professionals, and many were at the top of their game. "Some stories were painfully familiar. They had been riding the edge, peddling too fast, when something unexpected came along and bang . . . that was it. 'Stress junkies' the psychologist called them, which I guess in Cloninger's scheme would be persistent novelty seekers." Tom paused and leaned forward as if confiding a secret. "Anyway, it got my attention. I realized that but for the grace of God I might have been an inmate at the Pines myself."

AS I EXPLAINED to my guests during our evening together at the Encounter Restaurant, Tom's story is a graphic example of how life in the Fast New World can drive the brain's reward systems to their limits, and beyond. The dopamine superhighways do not discriminate among potential reward signals—the analytic centers of the limbic brain and the frontal cortex do that—but they do faithfully record those situations that require assessment. And thus when bombarded with novel stimuli—as Tom had experienced when living for a year at the manic edge of American culture—the dopamine system maintains the brain in high alert. It is this vigilance that is experienced as the exciting rush that Tom referred to earlier that evening, the subjective sense of pleasure that can drive people to accelerate their daily activity to the point of exhaustion, to gamble excessively, or to recklessly assume dangerous business risks.

This hijacking of the brain's attention by an overload of social stimulation engages the same chemical pathways of reward as do such drugs as caffeine, nicotine, cocaine, and the amphetamines. Drugs with abuse potential short-circuit and amplify the rewarding dopamine responses to normal social interactions by blocking the dopamine-recycling systems that balance dopamine with the other chemical messengers, such as serotonin, and protect the brain from excess stimulation. Cocaine or amphetamines, for example, when taken in small doses induce the rush of an immediate and pleasurable high. But with repeated use or excessive dose, the pleasure dissolves into a dysphoric and dangerous, drug-driven mania.

From the chemical action of these drugs in the brain and their addicting potential, we have learned much about the function and the genetics of the brain's reward systems. Researchers have discovered that the response to a specific drug differs among individuals. For example, with sufficient exposure to alcohol (a drug that indirectly stimulates the brain's reward circuits) we can each succumb to alcoholism, but for some people the rush of a drink is transforming and an experience they feel compelled to repeat. This suggests that in those who are prone to alcoholism (or to other forms of addiction) there exists a facilitating biology, which is genetically determined.

Pursuing such logic, Ernest Noble, the Pike Professor of Alcohol Studies at the University of California in Los Angeles, in the early 1990s reported finding in those suffering from severe alcoholism the presence of an unusual variant, or allele, of a dopamine receptor gene. *Allele* is the word geneticists use to describe the alternative forms that exist in any single gene, a gene being the distinct region of chromosomal DNA providing the coded sequence—the exact recipe—for the synthesis of a single protein. The proteins the genes create are the building blocks of the body, and the specific physical configuration of these proteins is what determines their precise function. The different body organs call on different combinations of genes to construct the proteins they need to operate effectively, and the brain, being the most complicated organ, utilizes about 40 percent of all available genes. The genetic recipe book, with its estimated thirty to forty thousand genes, is similar for each human. Yet for each individual the genetic plan is unique, because of chance variations in DNA sequencing (mutations) and the mixing of the genetic material received from each parent. These genetic variations are the alleles, and the slight differences in a protein's structure that they induce influence cellular function in subtle ways. Hence just as alleles provide each of us with distinctive facial characteristics, so do alleles contribute to the distinct behavioral signature we call temperament.

Professor Noble's discovery of an allele predisposing to alcoholism was controversial. While in later studies some scientists were able to repeat his findings—together with results showing a vulnerability to other drugs of abuse for those carrying the same allele—others failed to do so. (Upon reflection this is of little surprise because most of our complex behaviors are driven by genes working together rather than by any one of them alone.) However, Noble's work gave momentum to the idea that genetic differences make an important contribution to the behavioral spectrum of human temperament, including such novelty-seeking quirks as the enjoyment of extreme sports or Tom's addiction to life at the manic edge.

Subsequent research has given strength to the validity of these ideas, and the accumulating evidence emphasizes the central importance of the dopamine reward system. Particularly significant is the role of variations in the dopamine receptors that receive the information traveling along the dopamine superhighways from the brain stem to the limbic system and cortex. To date five members of the dopamine receptor family have been identified, logically termed D1 through D5. While all members work together in the transmission of information, the concentration of individual receptor types servicing the distinct pathways of activity and reward is different. Thus D2 receptors—where Noble discovered the allele (A1) associated with alcoholism—are particularly involved in motor activity, whereas the D4 receptors are localized largely along the reward pathways.

It is in the alleles of the dopamine D4 receptor system—the receptor system dominant in the reward circuits—that several researchers discovered a significant association between the presence of receptor allele D4-7 and high scores on the novelty-seeking profile of Robert Cloninger's TCI. It helps, in understanding the importance of these findings, to have a little technical information. The 7-allele of the D4 receptor is so named because a segment of the amino-acid chain that comprises the receptor complex repeats itself seven times rather than four (the D4-4 allele), which is the variant of the D4 receptor most commonly found in humans. Receptors in the brain are located at the synapses, the specifically engineered portals of communication across which neurons talk to each other. When a neurotransmitter—in this case dopamine—becomes bound with the protein of the receptor, much like a key fits in a lock, information is physically transported across the nerve membrane and into the cell, triggering an intercellular electrical impulse and continued transmission of information. Physiological studies have found that the presence of the D4-7 allele, when compared to that of the common receptor variant, D4-4, is associated with a "blunting" of this intercellular response, suggesting an insensitivity to the dopamine messenger.

Such physiological blunting may help explain why individuals like Tom, who are fascinated by novelty and risk, have a higher threshold for anxiety and fear when confronted with uncertainty or danger and reciprocally why they are easily bored. In genetically engineered mice, for example, from which the gene for the D4 receptor complex has been removed, or "knocked out," the animal shows little interest in exploring new territory. This association of exploratory behavior *across species* (genetic "conservation" in scientific language) with the D4 receptor complex suggests that the dopamine reward pathways have played an important role in mammalian adaptation to novel environments throughout evolution. The search for novelty—including exploration, curiosity, and the vigorous pursuit of knowledge—is instinctual behavior quintessential to survival and to human creativity (as Adam Smith had observed in *The Theory of Moral Sentiments* over two centuries ago). Thus it is not only individuals who enjoy skydiving, bungee jumping, or extreme sports who score high on Cloninger's novelty-seeking scale, but also political leaders, corporate executives, airline pilots, and a myriad of others who have helped mold America's migrant culture. What we now label as novelty-seeking behaviors have survival value, but such behaviors also play an important role in shaping curiosity and exploration.

AT THIS point Marcel, who during my rather technical discussion with Tom about the biology of temperament had been quietly tackling what Anna had characterized as an "Evil Empire" steak, pushed back his plate and stretched himself. "You know, for an average guy who plays the stock market for a living, this is heavy going," he said good naturedly, "but I think I'm beginning to get the picture. How's this for an analogy before I rush off to catch my plane. As somebody who enjoys driving fast cars, what I hear you saying is that in our temperament some of us are genetically tuned for faster acceleration and cornering than others. I can buy that. Ninety percent of the brain's activity is geared to providing the basic Volkswagen model and then there are other devices—this dopamine receptor and reward pathway stuff—that when optimally tuned become the Porsche-like bells and whistles that improve performance, but which just might land you in the ditch if you're not paying attention."

I found Marcel's comparison to be apt. All cars have fairly standard components, but it is modifying the mix of fuel that is injected into the engine, the precision with which the pistons fit their cylinders, the gearing of the engine to the driving wheels, and the stiffness of the springs to the road that together create the difference between a family sedan and a high-powered sports car. Individually each of the minor variations is of little significance—modifying one component by itself is not decisive and may even be dangerous—but when collectively tuned to mutual complement, they account for a dramatic change in a vehicle's performance. It is similarly so with temperament. An individual gene or its allele may code for only a minor difference in the dynamics of neural transmission—a slightly more efficient manufacturing enzyme, a receptor that binds its messenger less securely—but each variant contributes incrementally to shape an individual's behavioral approach to the world until there emerges a shy person, a novelty-seeking celebrity, or more commonly an individual whose emotional disposition rests firmly between such polar caricatures.

Novelty seekers make poor farmers—a fact to which Anna could attest from personal experience—but curiosity and risk taking are behaviors essential to exploration and migration. Restlessness, a willingness to take risk, a curiosity about what is over the next hill, and the persistence to keep moving in search of a better future are all positive attributes for the pioneer and the explorer. Without such qualities of mind those who first walked toward the Bering Straits some twenty thousand years ago would never have discovered the American continent.

So if the D4-7 allele is truly a marker of such behaviors, this should be reflected in a distribution pattern of the allele among the populations of the world that is similar to the ancient migratory paths of our species. And, indeed, recent research confirms that this is so. Dr. Chauseng Chen in the School of Social Ecology at the University of California, Irvine, has conducted an extensive study of the D4-7 allele. Chen analyzed the available genetic data in association with the major routes of ancient migration, estimating the distance traveled by each migrant subgroup from knowledge of the probable origin of their native language. From this research there emerges a coherent pattern where those peoples who stayed close to their original homeland have a higher percentage of the common D4-4 allele in the population and a lower prevalence of the exploratory and novelty-seeking D4-7 allele.

Individuals, for example, who remained within the African continent, or whose ancestors ten to twenty thousand years ago became the original farmers of the rich lands between the Mediterranean and the Persian Gulf—the so-called fertile crescent region—have a far higher percentage (between 60 and 80 percent) of the D4-4 allele, compared to those who continued the initial migrant expansion of our species across the Asian continent. (Parenthetically, within the African continent it is the Bantu who both migrated the farthest and have the majority of the longer alleles.) Thus, those who migrated from Taiwan and the Chinese mainland down the Malay Peninsula and into Micronesia have a greater percentage of D4-7 alleles in the population than the aboriginal people of Taiwan who stayed behind. Similarly, individuals whose ancestors crossed the land bridge of the Bering Straits and walked south into the Americas—particularly those who pushed down into the Southern Hemisphere, the Colombians and members of the Karitiana, Surul, and the Ticuna tribes—carry a *preponderance* of the D4-7 allele.

Interestingly the frequency of the D4-7 allele in the Japanese, a stable and conservative culture even in recent times, is extremely low, and in some individuals living in eastern Asia the allele does not exist. Thus given that American Indians and the peoples of northern and eastern Asia share a common ancestry, the strong probability emerges that it was the genetic mix that codes for curiosity and the exploratory urge—and for which constellation the D4-7 allele appears to be a marker—which differentiated the ancestral families of the American Indian from the settlers who remained behind in Asia.

At this point Marcel, who had been listening attentively, had a question. "So what you are saying is that we Americans because of our self-selection as migrants are probably genetically predisposed to be risk takers." I nodded in agreement. "OK, so here's the question. Does curiosity and risk taking," Marcel wondered aloud, "initiate the migration, or is it a tolerance for risk that serves the migrant once exploration is initiated?" In his own contemporary experience as an immigrant to America, he believed that both must be important. He suspected, he said, that a complex feedback loop was involved where migration was instigated by curiosity and a search for novelty, but later, individual initiative, risk taking, and high activity level—all behaviors that offer advantages to a group on the move—were reinforced by the demands of the migratory experience.

"To return to my earlier comparison," Marcel continued, "my Porsche gives its best performance in the mountains. On a slow rutted track it's no fun, but on a twisting mountain road, although my behavior might appear as madness to some, I enjoy pushing it to the limit. So my point is that any behavior has its preferred context—the situation in which we perform at our best. Risk taking does not occur in a vacuum, and reward is not the same for everyone. If like Anna I'm a little hyper and I enjoy new things and new people, but I'm living on a farm in rural Iowa, then the smart thing to do is to pick up and move to LA or to Washington. In a free country that's possible and it becomes the natural thing to do. And so the Americans like Anna—those who have inherited the restless genes—are always moving, always seeking the manic edge. Similarly if I'm a competitive swimmer living a boring life in a Paris suburb, then accepting an athletic scholarship to America is a good idea. Novelty-seeking people migrate to where there's action and novelty. In America risk taking is encouraged, so more risk takers come here and then there are more people in America who take risks. There's a cultural selection operating in the U.S. and it connects the novelty of fresh ideas with risk and reward. It's a positive loop and it's self-reinforcing."

Heads were nodding in general acceptance of Marcel's viewpoint. Certain cultural environments select for certain behaviors. It takes a different temperament to survive in Los Angeles and New York than in the rural Midwest. So, if in LA the culture selects on personal ambition and for exhibition—for firm bodies, fast cars, sexy clothes, and assertive selves—then that is the profile of individuals who live most happily and most successfully in LA. And with an intellectual twist, asserted Tom, New York has a similar culture. "But," he added, "regardless of where you live in America, if you're in business, then being a workaholic and taking risks are essential. To make it in America you must try, and try again."

"But that's exactly the cultural distinction between America and Europe, or Asia for that matter," chimed in Marcel. "In America there's no shame attached to failure. Making the team is important. Being first makes you a celebrity. But *trying* is essential. Public welfare and social support are not big in America, so migrants do not come here for that, whereas in some European countries that is sometimes the migrants' specific goal. And it makes for resentment in those individuals who have lived in the country for generations and pay the bills. You don't see that resentment as much in America because in recent memory we were all migrants. More people are willing to accept that you get what you work for. The drive is to do better, and to be better rewarded. The shame of failure is eclipsed by the greater cultural shame of not *trying* to do better. In America you can go bankrupt and six years later you're back in business. That *encourages* risk taking. So everybody is trying all the time. This is particularly true of new immigrants, because they come here with a dream. A migrant can't get to America without trying."

"And, of course, trying is just another word for risk taking," suggested Anna. "You can't try something new without accepting risk." Marcel agreed. In his experience in France, he said, one could not afford to fail. In most communities failure was unacceptable. Everybody knew about it if you failed. It wasn't discussed, but people avoided you. To fail was to disappoint a whole spectrum of people, be it your parents, your teacher, the grocer, the dentist, even yourself. Failure was shameful so the pressure not to fail was great. The best way to avoid failure was not to try—to avoid risk—and so that's what most people did. They stayed close to family and to where they were born and accepted the established social order. Hence the individual who left his or her home community was usually considered an oddball—the one who dared to go, a person who was willing to gamble. "I guess that's where genetics of temperament fit in," said Marcel. "Few people who come to America ever go home because risk taking in the right environment is addictive. The opportunities in America tweak those reward pathways and then you're hooked. The New World is truly a new world. Here the social pressures are exactly opposite to those with which I grew up in France. In America there's a fresh sense of freedom in everything and the sin is not to try. Taking risk is the expected social norm."

Marcel pushed back his chair and stood up, swinging a night bag across his back with one easy movement. "I've enjoyed it," he said, "but I must go. If I don't leave now, I'll be sprinting for my flight." "But that's the American way," quipped Tom with a grin, as he rose to shake hands. I glanced at my watch. It was late. We had been sitting together for over three hours.

SOME FIFTEEN minutes later, having said my good-byes, I stood alone amid the parabolic stilts and shifting luminescence of the restaurant's courtyard waiting for my car and thinking about the evening's conversation. Marcel, as a recent immigrant, not only possessed the restless inquiry typical of the American temperament but also reflected in his behavior the adventurous striving that it promoted. Alexis de Tocqueville, his fellow countryman, had formed similar opinions in 1831. "Choose any American at random," Tocqueville wrote in *Democracy in America*, "and he should be a man of burning desires, enterprising, adventurous, and above all an innovator." Tom and Anna, in the patterns of their own lives, provided further validation of Tocqueville's observations. Their enthusiasm, creative energy, and commitment to excellence embodied the best of the spirit of adventure that makes America such an exciting and intoxicating place. The American temperament of Alexis de Tocqueville's classical description has bred true. In validation of that truth it is the likes of Anna, Marcel, and Tom who now push the envelope of America's Fast New World. And it is the rest of us who scramble to keep up.

Suddenly my thoughts were interrupted, as a glistening jet thundered from behind a clutch of buildings beyond the asphalt and turned its impatient nose toward the sea. Above me giant light beams challenged and churned the thick night sky. An ocean breeze had arisen, pushing back the heat of the day. I was reminded that had I found myself in that spot perhaps just a century before, I would have been standing on a deserted shore. While no doubt I would have been similarly transfixed, my mindfulness would have been for a ring of majestic mountains and a canopy of stars rather than the chorus of aircraft and the probing fingers of searchlights that now commanded my attention.

In just a few generations the adventurous American spirit has erased from daily awareness the untamed landscape that first sparked the curiosity of our immigrant forebears. As a young migrant people, rushing forward in the eager hope of securing the future, we have replaced those ancient vistas with surroundings of our own creation. In our hunger and ingenuity we have invented a novel habitat for ourselves, one where the speed of our technological advance blurs Star Wars fantasy with reality and where a scarcity of time has replaced the natural barriers of climate, sea, and mountain. But with our invention has come a new set of challenges—as Tom discovered from his life on the edge—challenges that we are struggling to understand. In our relentless pursuit of prosperity we have changed the world in which we live from one of scarcity to one of excess. Driven now by the competitive demands of a commercial world that rarely sleeps and tempted by the seductive delights of our material affluence, we find ourselves floundering without constraint and testing the limits of human endurance. Amid a rising sense of discomfort we find ourselves over the top.

PART II

OVER THE TOP: PROSPERITY'S PARADOX

They [Americans] find prosperity almost everywhere, but not happiness. For them desire for well-being has become a restless, burning passion which increases with satisfaction. To start with emigration was a necessity for them: now it is a sort of gamble, and they enjoy the sensations as much as the profit.

Alexis de Tocqueville
Democracy in America, 1835

Chapter Four

AMERICA
BUBBLES OVER:
OF GLOBALIZATION
AND GREED

Speed is the form of ecstasy the technical revolution
has bestowed on man.

Milan Kundera
Slowness, 1995

IT WAS A PRESCRIPTION for economic success, just as Adam
Smith had predicted. Take a bountiful land, far distant from the peevish
disputes of other nations; fill it with free, headstrong people determined
to better themselves; foster risk taking, innovation, and personal profit
through open trading and private investment; and, bingo, you have fash-
ioned the finest engine of wealth creation that the world has ever
known.

Vast shopping malls stand throughout the Union, proclaiming America's material prosperity. These pleasure domes house treasures from
across the globe: everything from candy to cosmetics, potted plants to
pianos, toothpicks to televisions, each item meticulously shelved, bar-
coded, and enticingly displayed such that you are guaranteed to leave
with something you hadn't imagined. A typical supermarket in America

carries on its shelves more than twenty-five thousand items. Well over one thousand varieties of shampoo are available to us, and some two thousand skin-care products. In America we live amid an abundance of everything: of mechanical assistance, of information, of food, and of choice. Adam Smith's dream of "universal opulence" is now an American reality, but there's a nightmarish twist.

When it comes to living with extraordinary luxury, Americans are in the vanguard. In general, humans have little experience with affluence. After generations of frugality and adjustment to scanty conditions, we are poorly equipped—especially in our physiological adaptation—to handle an overload of anything, be that the information we are fed, the choices we are offered, or the food we eat. While few individuals have trouble identifying when they are hungry, defining that point during a meal at which one becomes satiated is a more difficult task. And so is that task even greater, we are learning, when it comes to material prosperity. When is enough, enough? And when does enough become excess?

These are questions that most of us have preferred to ignore. Rather than savoring the pleasures of the affluence we have achieved, we have abandoned the laws of thrift and embraced insatiable desire. America's pursuit of prosperity has become, in Alexis de Tocqueville's description, "a restless, burning, passion that increases with satisfaction." Seduced by the novelty and the opportunities afforded by our wealth, we have passed beyond need and fallen into an addictive striving for more: for more money, more speed, more house, more car, more food, more choice, and more power.

And here lies the nightmarish paradox of the American dream: in our striving for more, we are discovering a mismatch between the wealth of goods and the technology-rich environment that we have created, and the biological limits of who we are as evolved creatures of our planet. Suddenly we are aware of a Faustian exchange where our affluence and material comfort are trade-offs against a competitive, unstable workplace, diminished time for family and community life, fragmented sleep, obesity, anxiety, and chronic stress. This mismatch is not unique to

American life: it is emerging rapidly in many industrialized nations. But it is a discordance, as I have described, that is acutely evident in the United States because of America's rare cultural mix of sophisticated technology, mass affluence, and the restless pursuit that derives from the émigré temperament. An exuberance of spirit remains one of the great assets of the American people. But in a deregulated commercial environment, that exuberance has no natural bridle. Wealth, in the migrant vision, although coveted and eagerly sought, brings only transient pleasure, for prosperity lies forever ahead, beyond the horizon. For those trapped in such addictive striving, more is never enough.

In this second part of the book I explore some of the contradictions that lurk in the shadows of America's extraordinary prosperity, and offer cautionary tales to emphasize why in our search for happiness we must look beyond the simple pursuit of material affluence. First, in this chapter, I outline the history of the electronic technologies that have revolutionized data processing and global communication. It was the birth of the Internet, as the most visible example of this revolution, that helped drive America's period of greed and stock-market excess in the 1990s, and thus I follow my brief history with an analysis of that roller-coaster experience and what it teaches us about our cultural vulnerability to celebrity worship and the enticements of competition. Subsequently, in Chapter 5, I demonstrate how America's decline in physical exercise and our taste for high-calorie foods—in a mismatch between the human genetic inheritance and the contemporary diet—have confused the regulatory systems controlling body weight to precipitate a pandemic of obesity. Then in Chapter 6, through the personal story of Kim Phan, a successful young lawyer, I show how competitive, demand-based work environments when coupled with travel across time zones and chronic sleep deprivation can become breeding grounds for anxiety and depression, precipitating illness even in the most healthy among us.

There are common threads that run through these stories. First, each of the contradictions originates in part from the challenges Americans face in adjusting to the impact of novel technology and a surfeit of choice, both in the workplace and at home. But equally important in precipitating our discomfort is the speed of the innovation itself, and the extraordinary increase in commercial competition that has been stimulated by globalization. Cutthroat rivalry based on rapid technical advance is now the modus operandi of American business.

AS A BOY I was taught "necessity is the mother of invention." Technology, I was led to believe by my history teachers, evolved from human need: machines are an outgrowth of social progress. The argument made sense to me at the time, and in large part it still does. Thanks to technical advance, a greater number of individuals in America and the industrialized nations enjoy better health and a higher standard of living. But for most of human history the speed of innovation was slow and the social impact was gradual. Take, for example, the plowshare. The evolution of this simple tool occurred over several hundred years. Agricultural practice adjusted slowly to the changes, for the elapsed time—the cycle—between each innovative step was measured in human generations. Then, with the coming of the Industrial Revolution, the pace picked up. Technological innovation began to drive social trends and to synchronize national economies. In America canals and steam power initiated the first economic boom, while railroads, steel manufacturing, and the telegraph triggered the second. So it was with the automobile and the widespread use of electricity during the 1920s, before air travel and microelectronics emerged in the second half of the twentieth century. Progressively the cycle of technical innovation has shortened: from generations, to years, and now—with the coming of telecommunication satellites and chip technology—to a matter of months. This acceleration has turbocharged the commercial world, making continuous technical advance essential to a merchant's economic success and critical to sustaining growth in the consumer markets. In consequence, we are now constantly bombarded with advertisements for innovative products that are vital to our personal pleasure and to our social position. The aphorism of my youth now stands on its head. Invention has become the mother of necessity—and also the proud parent of relentless social competition.

Tools and machines are no longer merely an extension of human need and of what we do in the workplace. In America's technology-driven society, machines increasingly shape who we are and how we relate to the world and to each other. Collectively, modest mechanical things have acquired power in our lives and none more so than the tools that now extend human communication. As evidence of the addicting qualities of modern information technology, the next time you are traveling by air, witness the number of cell phones that emerge as soon as the plane touches the runway, and even before the seatbelt sign has been turned off. The cellular telephone, within a few short years, has become the indispensable tool of the contemporary nomad.

Cell phones and the Internet are the icons of an electronic revolution that has transformed human communication and dramatically quickened the pace of life in America. Forever fascinated by speed, we have used this innovative technology to create for ourselves a competitive twenty-four-hour society where we need never be out of touch. A business opportunity will never again be lost because we were at dinner, in the bathroom, or just away from our desk. In the virtual universe that we have created, defining political events in the world and the latest statistics on activity in the global marketplace can be brought to our attention within moments of their happening. The world has become connected, and it is a connectedness that is orders of magnitude beyond anything humans have ever experienced. The Fast New World soars above the constraints of geopolitical boundaries and makes possible the conduct of daily life in "real time." It's a euphemism, of course, for *real* time can only be that which happens within the privacy of the human mind, that coming together of perception, deliberation, and deed that we call *thought*. But, thrusting such philosophical caveats aside, it is life in real time—where information cascades on us at electronic speed—that defines the Fast New World.

The electronic connectedness that we are now experiencing is truly novel. For centuries the speed of human communication was determined by physical distance. Runners, horses, and crude signaling—with beacons of fire, smoke, and even mirrors—sped the transfer of information in emergencies, as later did the development of the telescope and semaphore language, but fast and accurate communication over long distances had to await the magic of electricity. That moment came when Samuel Morse established America's first telegraph between Washington and Baltimore, in 1844. In those days the American West was coveted but still largely uncharted wilderness. Mail services were uncertain, and the railroads were primitive. But a revolution in transportation, made possible by steam power, was already increasing the speed and lowering the cost at which people and materials could be moved. Established time zones across the world, money transfers, ordering of flowers by wire, and news dissemination were all novelties in the telegraph era, and soon Morse's device was America's dominant mode of rapid communication. So much so, that when Alexander Bell introduced his invention, the telephone, in 1877, American business was skeptical of its future utility. After all, the telephone provided no paper record of a transaction.

With Marconi's discovery that electromagnetic radiation could be used to transmit wireless signals, radio and television were added in the first half of the twentieth century, although television developed slowly until communication satellites and cable systems revolutionized the medium. By the end of the 1980s, however, it was possible to broadcast television signals via satellite directly to a small receiving dish located anywhere on the globe. Thus, with two-thirds of the households in the world having a television set, it became theoretically possible for a majority of the 6 billion members of the human race to passively watch the same live event, unfolding in real time. In a little more than one hundred years electronic communication had reduced the world to a "global village."

It was Alexander Bell's invention of the telephone, however, that first catalyzed the connectedness of *interactive* international communication. First, fiber-optic cables and computer-operated switching systems revolutionized carrying capacity, such that millions of conversations and messages now can be transmitted simultaneously. Then, with the microchip and global positioning satellites, came worldwide mobility and the option of contacting a person rather than a place. Radio and "hardwired" telephone transmission is now complementary—cellular and cordless telephones are actually radio transceivers—and with the latest generation of satellites, international calls between mobile phones have emerged as standard practice. The telephone has become the handmaiden of the Fast New World, and the barriers of geography have been weakened. Time zones and language are now the obstacles to global communication, rather than distance, mountains, and oceans.

But if the telephone is handmaiden, then the computer has been midwife to our information wizardry. Developed originally as a weapon of war—as a machine to calculate the trajectory of artillery guns in World War II—the computer's evolution is a tale of blistering progress. Since the early days of the Enlightenment, inventors had dreamed of a mechanical abacus that might keep track of accounts. One of the first was built in 1642 by a nineteen-year-old Frenchman named Blaise Pascal, who sought to assist his father in the onerous task of tax collection. Pascal's device and all those that followed were analogue calculators, where the achieved summation of numbers is represented by a variation in position of the cogs and wheels of the machine. Digital computing, by contrast, represents information as discrete units—as when we use our fingers to count, or when we employ numbers to calculate something on paper. Thus the first challenge in constructing an electrical calculator had been to figure out how electricity, something that generates energy, could be translated into elemental units of information.

As is frequently the case when human curiosity is unleashed, the reasoned path was not direct. Indeed, it was the needs of the telephone that helped foster the initial insight. To manage the relay of signals through early telephone systems, a network of mechanical switches was required. At first these were operated manually, and then in the interests of economy Bell Telephone's engineers developed electromechanical devices that opened and closed automatically depending on whether an electrical circuit was active. In the 1930s George Stibitz, a Bell Labs' mathematician, began using these electrical switches to represent information, distinguishing between 1 and 0 by whether the switch was open or closed to electric current. Coding a series of relays to represent Arabic numbers by the sequence of those that were open or closed, Stibitz assembled—on his kitchen table as the story goes—a circuit of lamps that could count.

The computers we use today have come a long way from George Stibitz's "breadboard" circuitry. The first machines used as their electrical decision makers vacuum tubes that had been designed for radios. Transistors, made from crystalline mineral materials, comprised the second generation. But it was not until the invention of the silicon chip, in the 1960s, that the integrated circuit became possible and the cost of building computers dropped dramatically. With this unification of memory, logic, and control circuits, the miniaturization of the technology moved ahead rapidly, and the speed at which information was processed increased exponentially, making possible the personal computer and user-friendly software. Computer networking, employing existing telephone lines to create virtual communities, quickly followed, with the most visible examples being the World Wide Web and the Internet systems that provide access to it. Life in interactive "real time" had arrived.

The Internet was born as a concept in the 1980s, through a government-university liaison. Initially the idea was to link the world's established information centers in an interactive web as a tool to encourage scientific collaboration and social exchange. Stuffy academics provided its parenting, and thus there was little fuss in its early years as such individuals have little interest in business. It was only when Mammon stepped in—initially in the person of Jim Clark, the wealthy founder of Silicon Graphics who launched the web-browser Netscape with an erstwhile graduate student named Marc Andreessen—that the commercial potential of linking consumers with retailers sparked the interest of investors and entrepreneurs. Once that interest was ignited, "e-commerce" and the Internet were to become the fastest-growing method of mass communication in history—and, at the height of the mania that gripped America in the late 1990s, also the most lucrative.

———

FOR THE American merchant in the 1990s, the seductive power behind web-based commerce was its promise of a supercharged upgrade of the consumer society that had begun seventy years earlier. That was when geographically separated manufacturers, retailers, and consumers were systematically connected together for the first time, thanks to improving road conditions, the U.S. Postal Service, and the Sears catalogue. The Sears catalogue had been among the first to offer an in-depth description of what to expect if you bought a certain product. With Internet technology the temptations of the paper catalogue were now upgraded to the speed and convenience of an interactive screen. Through the wizardry of electronics, a virtual shopping mall was now potentially available in every home, and with that came the possibility that every desire could be instantaneously serviced. Here was the market paradise of which Adam Smith had only dreamed, where each individual was freed from the constraints of place and time to "truck, barter, and exchange" at will. No previous technological innovation had so underscored, or promised to so blatantly exploit, the motivating power of the market in the life of the individual citizen.

It was this potential of e-commerce to supercharge the consumer market—further promoted by the enthusiasm with which Americans habitually greet commercial opportunity and technical advance—that catalyzed America's Internet mania in the decade of the 1990s. The around-the-clock business activity made possible by the Fast New World brought intense competition to commerce. An electronic flow of money and information, streaming in real time around the globe, made international investment and multinational corporations the norm. With web-based technologies, diversified manufacturing and retail companies can create integrated systems of information that dramatically increase the speed of business transactions while personalizing their relationship with suppliers and customers. Thus e-commerce companies can pitch "tailored" offers directly to customers, based on their previous purchases. Similarly, integrated information systems allow multiple vendors access to inventories and sales statistics: who is buying what, where, and from whom. Internationally distributed production may thus be tailored to demand and to shifting tastes, ensuring that the retailer never runs out of stock. The interactive technologies of the Fast New World opened a new commercial frontier. Never before had a set of technologies so well served the expansive international vision of America's business leadership.

The timing of this perceived commercial opportunity was also important. The birth of the Internet coincided with a period of unusual exuberance in America, and with a renewed faith in the nation's destiny as an exemplar society. With communism vanquished, and nature's barriers of darkness and distance removed by international telecommunication, capital markets and technology were poised to save the world. America's long-promised "New Order of the Ages" was in sight. It was the end of history. The Internet in bringing people together would prevent wars, reduce pollution, and combat inequality. Global collaboration among nations would solve world hunger, and the sequencing of the human genome would eradicate cancer and other diseases. Ray Kurtsweil, the inventor and futurist, and like-minded techno-utopians predicted that the world was changing so fast that computers and the human brain would soon intermingle, ushering in an "age of spiritual machines." We would transcend the mortal condition of humankind to achieve a higher plane of pleasure and social integration. It was, as one observer remarked, as if the 1960s flower children had returned, but with a commercial twist.

Indeed, in retrospect, there are those who dismiss the experience of the Internet and the economic bubble that it spawned as isolated folly, as an example of a time when youthful indiscretion drove a whole nation to improvident excess. Such opinions are shortsighted, for at least two reasons. First, the temptations, time pressures, and competition of America's Fast New World are here to stay. Thus the bubble experience offers an opportunity to better understand the behavioral impact of such demand-driven environments, and how we may better accommodate them in the future. Second, the Internet story is a cautionary tale. As I have detailed in earlier chapters, there is much in the American temperament that should make us wary as a society of succumbing to periods of maniacal excess. Our obsessive search for novelty, a love of celebrity, and our fascination with the climactic moment—in the casino, in the commercial, in reality television, and in the action movie—speak to an exuberance of character that under permissive conditions can transmute into mania. In the self-confident expansive atmosphere that prevailed in America in the 1990s—in commerce, in sports, and in our conduct as the world's dominant power—those conditions were at hand. E-commerce was merely the trigger—the electronic cocaine—that hijacked the nation's reward circuits and gave focus to our mania.

Thus from our collective behavior during the Internet stock-market bubble, we have much to learn about our potentially manic ways. And yet, in distinction to Adam Smith, many economists remain disinclined to consider such market cycles of boom and bust as driven by human emotion. Perhaps the fear is that to do so will diminish their science. However, as a psychiatrist—having always considered economics closer to behavioral psychology than to physics—I have no such constraint. In my analysis of the bubble decade of the 1990s I find a useful comparison between the frenzy and subsequent letdown that we experienced as a nation and the swings of emotion that occur in manic depression. In those who suffer this common disorder, periods of high energy, creativity, and overconfidence alternate with angry self-criticism, pessimism, and social withdrawal. The parallels are striking and for ease of description I cluster them here into four stages.

The beginnings of mania are innocent enough. The *first stage* is marked by happiness and optimism. People feel good and there is a sense of excitement and expectation in the air, comparable to the enthusiasm that surrounded the birth of e-commerce and the emerging bull market in Internet stocks (the word *mania* is only rarely used by economists in describing market cycles, the anthropomorphic reference to bulls and bears being preferred). The *second stage* of a developing mania—described by psychiatrists as *hypo*mania, meaning *under* mania—is expansive, marked by an infectious exuberance and competitive self-promotion. As was the case with many of the Internet entrepreneurs and the venture capitalists that supported them, individuals commonly come to believe that they have a clear and unique vision of the future—that they have been chosen for a special mission in life—and others fall under the spell of that messianic dream. This aggrandizement feeds on itself, and a taste for risky adventure and profligate spending begins to push aside mundane concerns (such as business plans and profitability) until the *third stage* blossoms and the mania proceeds rapidly to full flower. In mania itself, as self-serving speculation escalates, personal judgment and objective reasoning are progressively compromised. Greed, irritability, and devious behavior emerge, distorting the earlier mood of euphoria. Social confusion develops as the individual, once so revered, becomes seen as increasingly ridiculous, illogical, and intolerable—and even dangerous to the well-being of others. In the *fourth stage*, with the manic flight exhausted, the wave of frenzy breaks and the bubble collapses, inevitably to be followed—as in the economic cycle—by a period of anger, accusation, recrimination, and depressive self-doubt.

AS AN AID to understanding America's Internet mania, this comparison goes beyond metaphor. The behavior of an individual suffering from mania is associated with an overload of dopamine in the brain. It is an overshoot of the normal reward circuitry—frenzy beyond happiness—where the brain's chemical and emotional equilibrium is driven off balance by excessive social and physical demand acting on a permissive biology. Looking back on the factors that drove America over the top in the 1990s reveals that something comparable happened to the everyday life of our nation. It was during those bubble years that the lure of profit and of personal reward—together with the competitive 24/7 work schedules, the sleep deprivation, and the anxiety of living on the edge—played on the permissive biology of the migrant temperament to drive American society beyond happiness and toward the dysphoric state of mania.

In the early 1990s, in addition to America's self-congratulatory mood—the happy innocence of stage one in the manic cycle—other social forces were priming our manic flight. First, the frontier image of the Internet as the gateway to an expanding global market prompted dreams of a new gold rush, tapping deeply into the curiosity and the love of risk that lies at the commercial root of our migrant culture. Second, the interactive and integrative technologies that launched the Internet bubble were more immediate and more powerful in their influence on individual behavior than had been earlier technologies such as electricity, the social impact of which became evident only with novel applications of its use. And third, the Internet drew heavily on the ingenuity of the nation's young people, a group marked by energy and a willingness to gamble outside the box. The financial barriers to software development were comparatively low and the technical skills required to enter the game were skewed in favor of this band of computer-savvy youth, the first generation of humans truly at home in the world of hard drives, gigabytes, and the language of microelectronics.

During the 1990s American youth was also resolute in its pursuit of commercial success. Reminiscent of the adolescent primate who risks all when dispersing from the home territory, many young entrepreneurs entered the Internet economy with the conscious intent of avoiding the established business hierarchy. The traditional disdain of youth for the established order was evident, but in the decades following the Vietnam conflict the focus of youthful desire had shifted dramatically. Now the dream, shaped by an entrenched materialism, was of celebrity and money rather than social activism. The annual survey of entering college freshmen, sponsored each year since 1966 by the American Council on Education, reflected this trend. In the 1998 survey of nearly 350,000 students, 75 percent considered financial success to be their primary objective, while 41 percent sought a "meaningful philosophy" in life. These figures were a precise reversal of the original survey, the curves having crossed in the early eighties, and they chronicled a declining interest among students in issues of social concern and in the environment. Hence, in 1998, half the graduating classes from the Harvard,

Stanford, and Wharton business schools opted to try their luck in the money-spinning Internet industry. In doing so they were joined by young migrant adventurers from India and China—as many as one-fourth of the dot-com start-ups were launched with the aid of migrant brain-power—who had been lured to America by the special visas offered to skilled computer programmers.

The likes of Jeff Bezos and Stephen Case were to become the poster children of this new generation of entrepreneurs. Bezos was only thirty-five years old when on December 27, 1999, at the pinnacle of the Internet frenzy, *Time* magazine proclaimed the ebullient founder of Amazon.com to be its "Person of the Year." Offering a new spin on the sale of books, later on music and video, and then on just about everything, the laughing billionaire—he's "manic without the depression" wrote the journalist who profiled him—fervently believed that Amazon.com would "change shopping for ever." Stephen Case, the chairman of America Online (AOL)—the company that first made Internet communication available to a mass public—had similar visions of his place in the world. With a background in advertising, Case had risen to billionaire riches through his unshakable conviction that typing on a computer keyboard would one day be as important in the field of communication as talking on the telephone. Thus, on a chilly winter's day in January 2000 when he announced AOL's deal to buy Time Warner, the world's largest media company—using AOL stock, the value of which had risen an extraordinary 59,000 percent since its initial public offering eight years earlier—the excitement of the moment was palpable. From the festive tone of the *Economist's* cover article about the merger it was clear that even that conservative voice had succumbed to bubble fever. Referring to the $165 billion deal as the "The Big Leap," the magazine proclaimed that "nothing can be the same again" in the competitive world of entertainment and information services. Case apparently agreed. At the press conference he put it succinctly. "This is not about money," he insisted. "I want to change the world."

The infectious enthusiasm, the self-aggrandizement, and the special mission of Bezos and Case are reminiscent of the second stage of mania.

In their behavior these young men were typical of individuals who helped create the expansive mood that made the Internet bubble a reality. Bezos and Case and the many hundreds of entrepreneurs who rode the wave of e-commerce in the 1990s were the "pushers"—those who pushed the envelope of credibility—in America's addictive striving for more. But it was the rest of us—we, the "buyers" of the technology stocks that symbolized the seductive pleasures that the pushers envisioned—who made the mania possible through eagerly following their lead. After all, none of the mathematics made sense. With blind enthusiasm the investment community, public, and politicians suspended objective judgment to accept the messianic vision of something called a "new economy."

During these giddy, self-indulgent years of glorious hypomania—when America awoke each day to the sweet smell of prosperity and the promise of ever-growing riches—American business had much in common with Hollywood. The Jeff Bezoses of the world sold magazines. His signature desk—an unfinished wooden door with four-by-four lumber legs held in place by angle iron—together with his blue button-down shirt and loafers were the celebrated symbols of the new workaholic, 24/7, dot-com lifestyle. That Amazon had lost $350 million on sales of nearly $1 billion in 1999, the year that Bezos appeared on the cover of *Time*, was apparently of little moment. With the promise of Americans spending $5 billion online for gifts during that holiday season, Amazon's share price had rocketed to $94. Jeff Bezos was an American celebrity.

As this celebrity fever gripped the land, the old notions of balance sheets, and of revenue and expense, were suspended. America was now living in an illusory world, one where the nation's future would magically unfold in a cornucopia of ever-growing riches. The marketing industry—the masters of illusion—was having a field day. For the new-economy companies, especially for those with little evidence of tangible products (the majority), public recognition was essential to a rising share price and many start-ups were spending 70 percent of their budget on advertising. The new economy was all about grabbing market share and casting oneself as a future titan. New television channels devoted to business and finance sprang up, with chat shows indistinguishable from those that surround entertainment and the cult of the Hollywood film star. The investors—the "buyers" in this illusion—followed the careers of the shooting stars of the Internet world, and in compliance the analysts and advisors of Wall Street ran articles not on companies but on individuals. The executives—the pushers of the illusory envelope—also rose to the occasion, demanding more and more salary, stock options, and other forms of compensation in line with their new celebrity status. Soon the chief executive officers of many e-commerce and telecommunication companies and even those of the old-line industries were being paid more than the hallowed stars of the sports world and of the Hollywood screen.

Amid growing public clamor, as the mania blossomed to its third stage and to full flower, an army of young entrepreneurs jostled for fame and riches. Internet start-ups were spawning in the hundreds. By the arrival of Independence Day 1999, the mania was rampant. "More than ever achieving the American Dream is a game of chance—and picking the right stock," commented *Newsweek* magazine in its cover article "The Whine of '99: Everyone's Getting Rich But Me!" Greed and envy had become a national disease. The article profiled "ordinary people" who had become instant millionaires through the stock options of booming start-ups, or by day trading themselves to riches. These latter, the "casino capitalists," were predominantly individuals in their twenties who spent eight hours each day trading Internet shares at a home computer. Amazon, AOL, and other dot-com companies had become the darling of these day traders, whose exploits in return had raised the market capital of the young companies faster than they were hemorrhaging money.

At the height of the Internet mania, the prices of initial stock offerings were growing in multiples that make the South Sea Bubble seem like a vicar's tea party. One much-cited example was that of Priceline.com, a Connecticut-based firm trading cheap airline tickets and hotel rooms online. At a time when the market was truly bubbling, Priceline had offered 10 million shares, 7 percent of its total complement, to an eager public. Within seconds the stock moved from the offering price of $16 to over $80. Although in the previous year, 1998, the company had lost $114 million on revenues of $35 million, on paper the $80 stock price made Priceline's valuation of $11 billion comparable to that of American Airlines. Such "irrational exuberance" on the part of the speculative trader was also driving the stock prices of companies like Amazon, where the equivalent of 100 percent of traded stock (about one-third of the total) was changing hands twice each week. That largely the founders, and the people who worked for them, held the stock of many dot-com companies explained why suddenly America was full of freshly minted millionaires. For most day traders, conventional market evaluations—derived from an analysis of debt, earnings, and projected profits—were of no consequence. This was a game of risk where the connection between the value of the shares and the underlying business was irrelevant. Hence for those who ran start-up companies, the temptation was to go public and quickly sell out. "I have new ideas on a weekly basis," explained one young magnate who was interviewed by *Newsweek.* "I'm a serial entrepreneur, who nails it, sells it, and then moves on to the next idea."

Suddenly the inventor had become the product. It was, as one commentator said, "Andy Warhol with stock options," a pervasive aura of mad genius unbridled. Stories of excess were legion. In keeping with the manic mood, "extreme" had emerged as the nation's new buzzword. In the commercialization of everything, even America's fascination with risk had found its own market. Our search for "the edge" through freestyle skiing, mountaineering, ice climbing, paragliding, and any other "extreme" activity—defined simply as "when you screw up, you die"— had spawned a whole new industry, from the Extreme Coffee Company and extreme sausages to the Extreme Teen Bible. Impresarios of all ages and ethnicity described themselves as "grabbing" at life, "rewriting" the rules, "bursting" old boundaries, and "hurling" themselves at opportunity. And why not? they asked. Why climb the corporate ladder when public enthusiasm and a seemingly bottomless supply of money had provided an elevator?

By the millennium's turn, the manic cycle of celebrity and self-interest had climbed to its irrational peak and the downturn was in sight. As the megalomania broke in the spring of 2000, and blind competition began to give way to questioning and to more sober thought, the public confidence in Internet stocks began to falter. Through the summer months, amid growing anxiety, the nation entered the fourth stage of the manic cycle and headed sharply downward, toward a depressing postparty readjustment. The market capitalization of Amazon—the proud prototype of a dot-com company—fell from $30 billion to $12 billion. Profits for Jeff Bezos had remained illusive. By the summer of 2001—less than five years after Amazon was first publicly traded—the company had sold an impressive $5.9 billion in books, toys, and electronic gadgets. And yet through it all had flowed red ink, for over the same time period Amazon had piled up $2.7 billion of debt. Bezos, with his usual charm, faced his critics and remained optimistic. The mystery of how profits would magically emerge from growth was about to be revealed. Unfortunately a year later his investors were still waiting and the talk turned, as the *Economist* wryly observed, "from praising Amazon to burying it."

As the economy slowed through the year 2000 and into 2001, it dawned on an apprehensive public that it was not only Internet stocks that had been absurdly overvalued during America's manic flight. In the bursting of the bubble the dot-comers—rapidly renamed the dot-goners by an ironic press—were but the first to fail. Over the ensuing months, the price of shares in the media, technology, and telecommunications industries of the Fast New World—the information-age stocks—all fell precipitously. Within a year of its signing, market analysts were questioning the AOL–Time Warner deal. Stephen Case's exuberant dream— that in the creation of "Time-Online" the traditional media of magazines, music, radio, and cable television could be united with the Internet to dominate entertainment, news, and e-commerce advertising—smacked increasingly of grandiose folly.

By springtime 2001, many of the dot-com companies that had enjoyed triumphant entries into the public market were either in bankruptcy or with shares trading at below $1. Some 12 percent of the Internet-based companies going public between 1994 and 1998 had failed—an extraordinary figure by historical standards—with many companies having existed for only a few months. Investors, at least on paper, were some $3 trillion poorer, and tens of thousands of former high-tech employees were on the streets looking for work. America's megalomania had collapsed into a wicked hangover.

With the gloomy days that followed, as is invariable in the aftermath of mania, came a period of angry self-reflection and a search for scapegoats. The Wall Street analysts and investment banks, which in the estimation of the *New York Times* had garnered some $600 million in bringing worthless stocks to market in the final months of the bubble, were an early target. Previously, before the competitive excitement of the Fast New World, the ground rules had been simple. Investment banks brought to public offering companies that had a proven product and a stable management team that understood the importance of turning a profit for the investor. But during the Internet stock bubble, the rules of the game had been rewritten. The investment houses' main objective had been to grab young companies before their competition did so. At the height of the mania any statement of a company's credibility by a celebrity analyst had brought a deluge of investors and new money, although frequently at high interest rates. In 1998 alone, Wall Street had issued $141 billion of "junk" bonds, and three years later, when company revenues began buckling under the weight of a crumbling economy, many companies were unable to meet their interest payments. As these companies defaulted on their debt, it became clear that dubious business practice had not been the exclusive province of small upstart ventures, but that it also existed in much larger companies and in the major accounting firms that advised them, for whom lucrative consulting had often conflicted with the role of financial watchdog.

As public outrage mounted, clear evidence of unbridled self-interest and of greed began to emerge. During the mania, nobody—apparently not even the accountants hired for the purpose—had been paying attention to annual financial reports. The Texas-based Enron Corporation was to achieve particular notoriety. Described by its chief executive as "the world's leading energy company"—later revised in a manic moment to "the world's leading company"—it had always been unclear how Enron made its money. Those who asked were treated with the contempt and arrogance that is typical of manic excess. Enron, they were told, simply created new markets for energy and made everybody richer in the process. It was only after the editors of *Fortune* magazine began questioning Enron's accounting practices that the company fell under greater scrutiny. As the questions mounted, Enron revealed, in a public "restatement" of its finances, that between 1997 and 2000 some $1.2 billion had been left off its balance sheets. In an effort to obscure the real debt of the company and to boost share price, a smokescreen of financially questionable "trading partnerships" had been contrived by the executive leadership, apparently with the knowledge and assistance of the company's auditors. Along with this information there also emerged the sinister story that as Enron had stumbled toward bankruptcy, it had paid 144 senior executives $310 million. Furthermore, these same executives had exercised stock options and received restricted stock of some $435 million. Over the same time period, as Enron's stock value had collapsed, the twenty-four thousand employees participating in the company's retirement plan had lost about a billion dollars in equity.

It soon became apparent that the executives of the Enron Corporation were not the only new-economy giants with clay feet and a maniacal greed for riches. Another spectacular example reported in the press was that of Gary Winnick, the CEO of Global Crossing, a telecommunications company founded to link the major continents of the world by broadband cable. Winnick's vision of the future was simple enough, indeed brilliant: while fiber-optic cable was available across a number of continents, it had never been laid under the ocean. Undersea cable would enable the transmission of thousands of simultaneous communications, and with the expansion of the Internet into a global system, the demand for Global Crossing's services would be infinite. Winnick's enthusiasm and his extraordinary marketing skills generated the necessary financing to start the project, and the stock-market mania provided the rest such that at its height the company stock was valued at approx-imately $50 billion. When the dot-com bubble deflated, however, and the Internet companies that had been expected to spur telecommunica-tions demand began to implode, Global Crossing's stock value sank from $61 to $16. Revenues, always a trickle, were unable to sustain the loans that had been assumed. For a few months creative accounting filled the gap with "round-trip" money swaps between Global Crossing and some of its partners, together with, as in the Enron case, the development of complex financial instruments and strange balance sheets, apparently to hide the realities of the diminished company.

Winnick, a celebrity among Wall Street analysts, in the few short years of Global Crossing's existence—before the company's bankruptcy in 2001 when stock was trading at under $1—drew $750 million in per-sonal reimbursement. In addition, he sold off personal stock at huge profits and gathered exorbitant fees from consulting and other real estate deals between Global Crossing and his own private investment companies. Other directors received some $582 million, the five CEOs during the life of the company collected $104 million, and early investors $3.8 billion, while Wall Street analysts and the investment bankers who had put the telecommunications giant together also made substantial profits.

Through the spring of 2002 the list of celebrity scandals continued to grow, bringing to mind the 1987 film *Wall Street* and the guiding philos-ophy of its lead character, Gordon Gekko: that "greed is good; greed is right; greed works" (at least for a time). Thus the chief executive of Tyco, a conglomerate of companies, stood accused of evading taxes on fine art that had been bought with money loaned to him from the company's cof-fers. The former boss of WorldCom had persuaded his telecommunica-tions company to lend him hundreds of millions of dollars, which he then wagered in the stock market in an attempt to sustain his company's share price. The board of Adelphia, a publicly owned cable company, assumed the risk for $2.3 billion worth of bank loans for the founding family, which owned 20 percent of the company's shares.

Such stories are nothing new in the annals of human behavior. Greed and unethical practice are as old as history. Adam Smith knew that and repeatedly warned against them in his writings. Nonetheless the American public was shocked by such avarice in a group of individuals who were already extraordinarily rich. From the White House, Mr. Bush expressed his outrage that a "few bad apples" could threaten "our entire free enterprise system." As the president's critics were swift to point out, however, Mr. Bush's personal fortune had been made by some timely sales as a board member of an energy company in Texas, just before bad news had plummeted the share price. Similarly, the same critics observed, the vice president, Dick Cheney, had indulged in some interesting accounting activities when he was the chief executive of Halliburton, allegedly at the suggestion of Arthur Andersen, the accounting firm that had been discredited during the Enron scandal.

Bad apples in the barrel they may have been, but the stories of executive greed also reflected the culture of covetous self-interest that had become pervasive in America during the bubble years. In the last decade of the twentieth century, many American business leaders became extremely rich. In 1985 the highest-paid CEO in the land was Lee Iacocca of Chrysler, who took home $20 million. In 2001, it was Larry Ellison of Oracle, who made $706 million from the exercise of stock options that the company had given him in earlier years. This dramatic change reflected a new guiding philosophy in the compensation of American business executives—that through the use of stock options and other equity-linked incentives, the interests of the management should be aligned with those of the shareholders. This proposal, founded on Adam Smith's philosophy of self-interest being the engine of economic growth, had been eagerly adopted in the desire-driven culture of America's Fast New World.

Unfortunately, as anyone with a practical knowledge of human instinctual behavior would have predicted, the compensation plan was conceptually flawed. Rather than rewarding executives for working to enhance a company's long-term growth, thus benefiting investors, the plan gave incentive for executives to focus primarily on strategies to increase the short-term market return—and thus their own income—on the company stock that they had optioned. Ingenuity had created a mis-match—an environment so tempting to avarice that inevitably self-interest had overwhelmed any social concern for others.

Thus during the bubble years, dot-com entrepreneurs and telecommunications executives—emboldened by a blindly enthusiastic investment community and rising stock prices—in the hubris of their manic flight invested billions of dollars in building e-commerce and a broadband capacity that could not be sustained when the global demand slowed. As Edward Chancellor observed in an essay entitled "Perverse Incentive," which appeared in *Prospect* magazine during the summer of 2002, "The alliance between shareholders and managers had faulted on the greed of the latter. Before shareholders realized they had been robbed, corporate insiders were cashing in on their options. It is no coincidence that insider sales reached a record $11 billion in February 2000, just as the . . . bubble was about to burst." In a climate where global trading had weakened the usual business constraints, top executives were skimming incomes in excess of market value from those whom they employed and from the shareholders. The emotional climate in America, as Federal Reserve Chairman Alan Greenspan described it, had gone from "irrational exuberance" to "infectious greed"—or in my comparison with the cycle of manic depression, from the energy and euphoria of hypomania to the avarice and excess of florid mania. "For the most part this stuff was hiding in plain sight," remarked one market analyst referring to the greed and accounting problems that emerged as bubble stocks collapsed. "Why did people do this? Why did people look the other way? It's a question for psychiatrists, not economists."

IN ADAM SMITH'S vision of a market society, greed is held in check by social pressure and, if all else fails, by regulatory policies such as those that have been slowly dismantled in America since the fall of the Berlin Wall and the triumph of laissez-faire capitalism. Smith was suspicious not only of government interference in market practice but also of the distorting self-interest of the powerful merchant. It is unlikely, however, that in seeking to release human initiative from the leg irons of eighteenth-century mercantilism, he could have imagined the temptations that are represented by contemporary America's highly competitive and commercial culture. Nor could Smith have countenanced an electronic world of instant communication in which market forces would slip beyond local control to be extensively manipulated by clever and powerful people as a means of serving their own self-reward. Knowledge of such a world would have dashed Smith's fervent hope that market self-correction and a desire for social acceptance are sufficient to contain avarice.

And yet the Fast New World has catalyzed such a cultural shift in America. The ancient reward-seeking behaviors of our species, particularly represented in the restless temperament of the migrant, have been magnified to reveal a fundamental paradox of human freedom: that the healthy instincts for self-preservation—self-interest, curiosity, and ambition—when consistently and excessively rewarded by affluent circumstance and a plethora of choice will run away to greed. Technology's removal of nature's barriers to travel and communication, the promotion of the celebrity model of success and of market-style incentives at every level of society, and the endorsement of massive debt as a method of financing have together fostered an addictive culture of covetous desire—a commercial juggernaut over which social sensibilities exert little constraint. In consequence, the social balance that is so important to a civil society, and that was championed by Adam Smith as fundamental to his economic philosophy, has been lost to unbridled self-interest.

Considered within the framework of neurobiology, however, and in acknowledgment of the fundamental role of reward in motivating human behavior, such a shift in America's social balance was predictable during the bubble years of the 1990s. And thus it should come as little surprise that some executives, lionized as celebrities and in a position to use investors' money to their own advantage, retreated to a mania of greed and self-preservation when an economic downturn threatened their prosperity. Indeed, perhaps what *should* be of surprise is our moral outrage at such behavior, when as a culture we applaud competition, celebrity, and self-aggrandizement, the fertile soil in which greed and mania take root. And it must also be accepted that such behaviors, when so deeply rooted, are hardy perennials. Thus, if in America we choose to exercise the economic advantages of the unrestrained competition that our Fast New World can deliver, and to embrace a market society of megacorporations where Adam Smith's instinctual engines of economic growth essentially are allowed to run free of social constraint, then the occasional outbreak of greed and covetous desire is the price that must be paid for the choice we have made. In the manic society, as in mania, when the human will is made subservient to instinctual desire, more is *never* enough.

Chapter Five

A GROWING BURDEN: OF APPETITE AND ABUNDANCE

The twentieth century may yet be remembered
as one of monstrous mass feeding.

M. F. K. Fisher
The Art of Eating, 1989

THE MORE MOBILE WE ARE, the less active we become. It's
another paradox of America's Fast New World, and also the one most visible. A dramatic decline in daily exercise, together with an unbridled
enthusiasm for tasty high-calorie food, has fostered a pandemic of obesity in America. As our prosperity has grown, so has the national waistline.

In England, where I grew up in the 1950s, 80 percent of children
went to school without supervision, walking or riding a bicycle. I suspect
many Americans growing up during that era had a similar experience.
Half a century later, however, here in the United States, virtually 100
percent of children are chauffeured to school by their parents or arrive
by bus. I am fortunate: I still walk each day to work—it takes me just
twelve minutes—but in Los Angeles, where cars outnumber each pedestrian by the tens of thousands, I am considered an oddity.

In the decades since John F. Kennedy was elected president in 1960, the U.S. population has increased by almost 100 million souls—by over 40 percent. And yet over 75 percent of the population lives in urban areas, and the majority of us still reside within fifty miles of the Atlantic or the Pacific Ocean. In all, 97 percent of Americans are clustered on just about 3 percent of the 5.5 million square miles that make up this bountiful land. We live in congested, densely packed, but sprawling cities. It is here, in these urban areas, where most of America's 400 million motor vehicles are to be found. And we use them: 85 percent of the miles we travel are by automobile. Some 86 percent of us commute to work each day, usually in our own vehicle and alone, logging up almost two hundred thousand miles during a working lifetime, a distance that is equal to approximately seven or eight trips around the world. And— here's the bad news—the average time of our commute increased by 36 percent between 1983 and 1995, with a lot of that extra time spent just sitting in sluggish traffic, on interstate highways built for speed.

It is no secret that America's dependence on the automobile has created its own problems. The ability to drive long distances has encouraged a monotonous city sprawl, such that only when the fast-food chains begin repeating themselves is it clear that one is entering another community. In Los Angeles, which grew with the motorcar in mind, the density of the city is too low and the distances are too great to be effectively serviced by public transportation. A growing disparity of income has encouraged this trend, and a mobility class structure has developed, with buses for the poor, limousines for the wealthy, and cars for the rest of us—although we each must struggle along the same congested streets.

We have not forsaken our habitually nomadic ways—as this frenzy of motorized activity makes clear—but for all our bustling about, walking and bicycling are in steep decline in America. And with them has gone the routine of daily, built-in exercise. Incongruously, in an effort to repair such deficits, those who can afford the membership fees, and the time, now drive occasionally to a gym. But children no longer walk to school. City life is potentially dangerous, and in most neighborhoods the distances are too great. And besides, with both parents working, who would be at home when the children returned?

In fostering this decline of the nation's physical fitness, the automobile has been aided and abetted by the many ingenious gadgets that have been invented to free our busy lives from strain: the garage door opener, ideal for inclement weather but now used year round; the cordless phone that saves that tiresome walk across the living room; the indispensable television remote control; the moving walkway at the airport; and, of course, the drive-through window at the fast-food restaurant, making it so convenient to eat quickly when "on the go."

It is those tasty goodies at the drive-in, the unlimited supply of energy-rich, cheap fast food (pizza costs about a dollar per thousand calories), and the highly palatable family meals in the grocery store, together with the nation's dramatically reduced physical activity, that have led to America's obesity epidemic. Roughly half of the average family's food budget is now spent on food eaten out, and 45 percent of the dinners eaten at home have no home cooking associated with them. Our rapidly expanding national waistline has been further encouraged by the cultural conviction, when it comes to food, that larger portions are the definitive evidence of value. Thus, originally (in those old glass bottles), one serving of Coke was six and a half fluid ounces. Now the average plastic bottle contains five times that amount. Similarly McDonald's original hamburger contained 260 calories: today the standard order is the double cheeseburger, with 444 calories, while the Big Mac Extra Value Meal contains 1,250 at a cost of $3.59.

WHILE WE may presume that what we like to eat, and plenty of it, must be good for us, it isn't. Humans have evolved excellent mechanisms to defend the body against starvation and weight loss, but the body has few regulatory systems to guard against excessive appetite and weight gain. An abundance of food, such as we enjoy in America today, is a novel experience. Just as exercise is no longer about the necessity of moving from place to place or of running for one's life—or for one's dinner—eating is no longer about hunger.

The statistics are alarming. Using the classification scheme established by the World Health Organization, in 2001 approximately 60 percent of Americans were considered overweight and 27 percent of those were obese, with a body mass index (BMI) over 30. (It is important to realize that these statistics do not reflect a national state of Rubenesque chubbiness. A woman who is five-feet five-inches tall and of median build usually weighs between 127 and 141 pounds, and 20 percent increase in weight above that range places her in the overweight category. The BMI is calculated by dividing an individual's weight in kilograms by his or her height in meters squared, and thus to be considered obese, the same woman must weigh more than 180 pounds.) Middle-age women, those in their fifties, were especially represented in these statistics, with over 35 percent of them meeting the BMI criteria for obesity. A similar dramatic weight gain is evident in America's children, with one in four of the nation's youth being overweight.

The explanation for this "broadening" of America is to be found not in some seismic shift of the human gene pool but rather in its stability. Our weight gain is not a function of defective physiology; it is a predictable response, given our thrifty origins, to the environment that we have created for ourselves. Kelly Brownell, a psychologist and obesity researcher at Yale University, has argued that America's lack of exercise and our easy access to the mélange of appetizing high-fat, high-carbohydrate foods have created a toxic environment. While genes and self-control play a role in weight gain and the health problems that result, it is in large part this toxic environment, Brownell insists, that has been responsible for the nation's extraordinary weight gain in the last decades of the twentieth century. Furthermore, he suggests, this "toxic food environment" should be of comparable concern to Americans as was our earlier concern about tobacco. "We have taken Joe Camel off the billboard," says Brownell, "because that was marketing bad products to our children, but Ronald McDonald is still considered cute."

From studies of individuals who have moved from the developing world to the United States over the last twenty-five years, the evidence is on Brownell's side. Mayans from Guatemala, for example, who have migrated to Florida and California—when compared with Mayans remaining behind—demonstrate weight gain in just one generation, with the children of these immigrant communities weighing on average twelve kilograms (twenty-six pounds) more than their relatives in Guatemala. Mexican-Americans who now live in California exhibit similar statistics. The Centers for Disease Control and Prevention and the National Center for Health Statistics report that among Mexican-Americans between the ages of twenty and seventy-four, the prevalence of those overweight is 69.3 percent (for both men and women), with 24.8 percent of the men and 36.1 percent of the women being obese, representing one of the highest rates of obesity worldwide. Thus, these studies strongly suggest, as Brownell claims, that there is a causal relationship between the contemporary American diet—it is estimated that one-fourth of American adults eat fast food each day—and the nation's growing obesity.

Well-designed research has shown that regular physical exercise has a protective effect against obesity and can mitigate the morbid health consequences of a high-fat, high-carbohydrate diet by increasing energy expenditure. America's high-tech environment, however, tends to actively discourage physical activity—as evidence, walk into any department store, or airport, and count the number of people climbing the stairs versus those riding the escalators—such that 25 percent of adults admit to being completely sedentary, and another 40 percent rarely exercise. These habits begin early in life. The Internet, television, and electronic games all increase the time spent in sedentary pursuits, especially for children. Even in junior high, only about 30 percent of girls are actively involved in sports, and half of those cease their participation before leaving school. This trend has accelerated—and has become self-perpetuating—as many schools have cut sports programs, citing falling interest and rising costs. And, justified similarly by financial necessity, as the time spent on mandatory physical education has been cut back, the fast-food vendors have been invited into the schools as official caterers to provide soft drinks and luncheon services.

Here advertising has played an important role. McDonald's prides itself on selling not hamburgers but "food, family, and fun." In the same vein Burger King promotes their "Kids Club" program where children play games and they, not the parents, get to exclusively decide their choice of meal. Both efforts exploit a fundamental principle of marketing—to develop brand loyalty early on and to keep the children returning to their favorite fast-food provider with their own families a generation later. "We all have special memories about McDonald's," says Patrick Knoll who is the creative director of the Chicago advertising agency that develops McDonald's commercials for children, and his campaign seeks to strengthen those memories. One thirty-second spot, now famous, shows a young father playing with his gurgling infant. "There will be a first step, a first word and, of course, a first french fry," intones the soothing voice of a young woman in the background. The only problem with such images, as consumer advocates have emphasized, is that one-third of American children between the ages of four and twelve are now overweight.

To some Americans, after a couple of decades working out at the gym and being obsessively concerned with cholesterol and low-fat diets, the nation's growing obesity has come as something of a surprise. And, indeed, many such individuals eat rather well and have avoided the fattening trend: they are predominantly citizens of higher socioeconomic standing for whom money is not a consideration when it comes to feeding the family. But with extended commuting times now the norm, and with fewer hours in the day to cook at home, all families regardless of economic status have shifted toward precooked, fast, and time-convenient meals. And therein lies the problem: it is not just the quantity of what America eats, but also the nature of what is eaten, that has fostered growth in the nation's waistline.

AMERICANS HAVE not always been fat. During the 1960s and the 1970s the number of individual Americans considered obese stayed fairly constant at around 13 to 14 percent. The exponential weight gain that has culminated in more than one-fourth of Americans being obese and nearly two-thirds being overweight began in the 1980s, and gathered momentum during the 1990s. And looking back over those years, it is evident that good intentions helped pave the way.

During the 1970s, concern over the killer diseases of atherosclerosis and heart attack and a growing body of research into the origins of these disorders led to a massive public health campaign to reduce cholesterol and animal fat in the American diet. The postulate, based on what was considered good epidemiological evidence, was that red meat and cholesterol-containing products, together with cigarette smoking, were bad for your health and major contributors to cardiovascular disease. And, most importantly, they were *modifiable* risk factors. In response to this information, the nation's consumption of tobacco rapidly dwindled, and in 1977 a Senate committee led by George McGovern published its dietary goals for the United States, advising that Americans significantly curb their fat and cholesterol intake to reduce the chances of heart disease and stroke.

On the menus of the nation's upscale restaurants, chicken and fish were soon pushing aside the time-honored entrees of sirloin and roast beef. In the supermarket, mothers paused at the shelves to scrutinize the new labels proclaiming "Nutrition Facts," obsessively checking the family's favorite food items for the presence of cholesterol and total fat. In self-interest the food industry responded, reducing the amount of saturated fat and replacing the lost calories with carbohydrates and high-fructose corn syrup. (Several efforts to create fat substitutes were poorly received, as most of them had unpleasant side effects such as diarrhea and intestinal discomfort.) Refined carbohydrates—pasta, rice, and bread—were now the foundation of the highly recommended Food Guide Pyramid and the healthy anchor of America's new low-fat diet. And because carbohydrates, calorie for calorie, are the cheapest and most profitable form of processed food to manufacture and to store, the food industry—in the best American tradition—applied itself earnestly to providing the customer with both abundance and choice.

Almost thirty years later it is increasingly recognized that our hopeful, 1970s understanding of the role of fat and dietary cholesterol as risk factors in the genesis of heart disease is grossly oversimplified. From 1970 to 1985 the overall death rate from heart disease, for middle-aged individuals, declined by approximately 3 percent, but these gains have not been sustained in the most recent studies. Despite less smoking, an overall reduction in the percentage of saturated fat in the diet, and a decline in blood cholesterol levels, the incidence of heart disease has not continued to fall as anticipated.

In fact, there are two types of cholesterol circulating in the bloodstream: high-density lipoprotein (HDL)—the so-called good cholesterol—which is elevated, for example, by the consumption of olive oil and other unsaturated fats, and low-density lipoprotein (LDL), the "bad" cholesterol, an elevation of which does correlate with an increased incidence of heart disease. However, in the genesis of cardiovascular disease for each individual, the interactions of cholesterol, blood lipids, and other risk factors including the predisposing genetic-family history are idiosyncratic. Thus there is no linear relationship between the *consumption* of fats and the development of arteriosclerosis, although there is most definitely an association between *being* fat and suffering heart disease, and also between obesity and diabetes. Hence what many individuals who develop diabetes and heart disease have in common is being overweight. Fast food is dangerous as a regular diet principally because of the weight gain it induces.

America's growing portliness is explained by the simple equation between energy intake and energy expenditure. When we eat starchy foods, especially refined carbohydrates, in excess of our energy requirements, they are rapidly turned into fat. Key to this conversion is the role of insulin, which in addition to the regulation of blood sugar also has the function of shunting spare calories aside for storage and future use once the immediate metabolic needs of the body are satisfied. This shunt is an ancient and prudent physiological adaptation, a reflection of mechanisms that had been selected out over many generations when uncertainty was the fundamental rhythm of life and—as is written in the Bible—lean years invariably followed those of plenty. Thus the physiological frugality that fosters the body's hoarding of the processed carbohydrates that are dominant in the contemporary American diet, we owe to our forebears.

BEFORE AGRICULTURE became a way of life, approximately five hundred generations ago (looking back some ten thousand years), we scavenged as best we could, and had done so for one hundred thousand generations before that. It was our capacity to conserve and to survive on meager rations that gave us a distinct advantage in those early years. Relying on our superior skills of communication, we lived in small bands of related individuals, perhaps twenty or so. To survive famine and physical hardship, we ate fruits, nuts, flowers, the roots and tubers that we found on the plain, and even tree bark. The archaeological evidence, and the diet of those rapidly diminishing peoples who still forage for their subsistence (the Kung, the Australian aborigines, and the Tasaday are examples), suggest that as we became masters of the hunt, this sparse vegetarian diet was supplemented heavily with meat. Not the tender sweet meat of the American supermarket that contains 25 to 30 percent fat, but the lean meat of game, with a fat content of no more than five percent, that itself had run the savanna life—the deer, the bison, the horse, and the mammoth. The archaeological records also suggest that during those Paleolithic times we were taller, well over six feet in height on the average, and lean from sustained physical exercise.

So it was only when agriculture appeared, just ten thousand years ago, that the sedentary life began. With the cultivation of small grains and fruits, and later with the domestication of cattle, the human diet slowly changed toward the cereal starches, sugars, and dairy fats with which we are now familiar. After the Industrial Revolution, as agriculture became centralized and we began purchasing food rather than growing it ourselves, physical activity declined further and the dominant health prob-

lems of today—obesity, hypertension, heart disease, and adult-onset diabetes—began to emerge. These diseases are modern ills, probably
unknown to our ancestors. And that should come as no surprise. Of the
four basic food groups in the contemporary Western diet—meat and
fish, vegetables and fruit, breads and cereals, milk and dairy products—
the last two did not exist in the diet of our forebears. Theirs was a frugal physiology adapted to the vagaries of the hunt, and that physiology
persists within each of us.

Over succeeding generations physiological accommodations to the
addition of starches and fat to the diet have occurred. One example is
the phenomenon of "lactase persistence," where the intestinal enzyme
lactase, which digests the disaccharide sugar *lactose* present in breast
milk, persists in its activity beyond childhood in many individuals living
in northern Europe, and among members of certain nomadic tribes of
Africa and Asia where milk drinking is part of the culture. Once domestication of cattle occurred, fresh milk and its fermented products
became a valued part of the diet for those moving through arid climates
or struggling with the privations of winter, and there was clear adaptive
advantage for individuals who could continue to digest lactose into their
adult years. Leena Peltonen, a professor of human genetics at the David
Geffen School of Medicine at the University of California, Los Angeles,
together with her colleagues, recently clarified the genetics of this interesting adaptation. And as one might suspect from an understanding of
human history, it is the lactose *intolerant* among us—those who buy the
"Lactaid" milk products at the grocery store—who carry the ancient
gene, while those of us who blithely drink fresh milk are the upstarts and
genetic variants.

This adjustment to the persistence of lactose in the adult diet has
occurred over many generations, and then only in populations where the
consumption of dairy products has become an important part of the culture. But it is an illustration of similar physiological adjustments—of
which, as yet, we have little understanding—that the European population must have made to accommodate those dietary changes driven by
the coming of agriculture and Western industrialization, until a stable

(and reasonably healthy) "cultural-genetic" balance was achieved. Thus in many contemporary European societies, especially Finland, the Netherlands, and Sweden, obesity is increasing only slightly in men and not at all in women. This enduring balance of diet and metabolism, however, has been achieved over several centuries. By comparison, the challenges of fast food and the contemporary American diet, in which increased fat consumption is now supercharged with high-density carbohydrates, have been with us for less than two generations, offering little time for metabolic adaptation. In Britain, a nation that follows American trends more closely than do its European neighbors and where snacks and fast food are increasingly popular, we find a similar trend in weight gain as we have seen in the United States: between 1980 and 1994, obesity rates in Britain jumped from 6 to 15 percent in men and from 8 to over 16 percent in women.

THE BIOLOGICAL mechanisms that determine body weight are dependent on the interaction of probably several-dozen genes that influence appetite, satiety, and the metabolism and conservation of the calories we eat. Thus, in addition to reduced exercise, the mismatch between the genetic heritage of America's ethnically diverse population and the novel environment of the fast-food diet that now drives our growing obesity is promoted by several factors. Of particular importance in determining the severity of the mismatch, however, is the *speed of exposure* to the supercharged carbohydrate and high-fat diet (whereby calories are consumed in excess of energy needs), especially in ethnic groups with a history of successful conservation during previous times of scarcity. *As a result, Americans who are genetically equipped to survive most proficiently during depriving times are the ones who now suffer the most.* It is the Mexican-American population (who carry a mixture of partially adapted European and poorly adapted-to-plenty Native American genes) and the Native Americans themselves—being descendents of migrants who first settled the American continent—who are most vulnerable to the contemporary American diet. Genetically tuned for effi-

cient adaptation to a frugal habitat, they have fallen victim to a potentially lethal challenge—that of living amid novel abundance against
which they have no natural physiological protection. Under such circumstances the best defense is that of knowledge and of the human will
employed in a thoughtful campaign to increase physical exercise and to
reduce caloric intake. But in America today that is a Herculean task for
such behaviors run antithetical to the consumer-driven, exercise-starved
culture that we have built for ourselves.

It is here that the story of the Pima offers us an important cautionary
tale. In their migration, the native peoples of the Americas—descendents of the Siberian hunters who crossed the land bridge between
Siberia and Alaska approximately twenty thousand years ago only to
become marooned when the great glaciers melted back into the
oceans—became experts in survival. Over a period of ten thousand
years, prior to the coming of the Europeans, these migrant hunters
spread throughout the continent, developing their own ethnic communities and showing remarkable adaptation to the prevailing environmental circumstance, be that one of arctic ice, mountain, desert, forest, or
jungle. Those we now know as Eskimos adapted to life at the edges of
the Arctic Ocean. The Great Lakes tribes fished and invented the light-
weight birch-bark canoe, whereas others, drifting farther south, followed
the caribou to the Great Plains. There during the spring and summer
they hunted the large game—the bison, the caribou, the mammoth, and
the moose—drying the meat, fashioning clothes and stone tools, and
then retreating to protected mountain valleys during the harsh winter
months, especially in the north. Others eventually settled in the areas of
the Southwest, where the coastal tribes of California lived off abalone,
shrimp, mussels, oysters, crabs, and sea snails, gathering the acorns
from the abundant oak trees and pounding them into flour to create a
carbohydrate staple.

But it was the tribes living in the hot and arid basin that now includes
Nevada, Utah, Arizona, and the eastern part of California who faced the
greatest challenge. Forced to eke out an existence hunting for rabbits
and snakes, and eating insects, roots, berries, seeds, nuts, and virtually

anything green they could find, starvation was always close at hand. The Pima people, whose tribal name originates from a misunderstanding by Spanish missionaries of the Pima word for "no" (the Pima language is of the Aztec-Tanoan linguistic family and they call themselves the O'od-ham, or "river people"), were among those who learned to adapt to such a marginal habitat. Moving up from central Mexico some two thousand years ago to settle the land where the Gila and Salt Rivers meet in southern Arizona, the Pima built elaborate canal systems to trap the rivers' flood. Fashioning dome-shaped houses from mud and brush, they supplemented a meager hunting diet—the Pima were unusually skilled with the bow and arrow—with pumpkins, corn, and beans grown on the irrigated land. Spinning native cotton for clothing, curing buckskin for winter warmth, and learning to weave a basket so fine that it will carry water, the Pima built an ecologically balanced culture that thrived for well over a thousand years.

Today, the Gila River is dry and the fields of squash and beans have gone, as the water of the region has been drained off to serve the rapid growth of Phoenix, just half an hour's drive north of the Pima Reservation. The Pima are still an agricultural people nurturing orchards of orange trees, pistachios, and olives, but as a way of life, hunting and subsistence farming disappeared long ago. And in the wake of that disappearance has emerged a scourge of obesity and diabetes.

The traditional Pima existence had been sustained until the late nineteenth century, when the European-American farmers settling upstream first began to divert the waters of the Gila River, disrupting the community's ancient patterns of irrigation and throwing it into poverty. Over subsequent decades, malnutrition and even starvation became commonplace until, with their population dwindling, the Pima were forced to accept as dietary staples the white flour, lard, and sugar provided to them by the U.S. Government. It was the beginning of a dramatic shift in nutrition and lifestyle for the Pima. In the 1890s they had been physically active and their typical diet, rich in starch and fiber, contained about 15 percent fat. Now, in addition to adopting a sedentary lifestyle, the Pima began consuming much the same food as other Americans, a diet in which some 40 percent of calories is derived from fat. World War II, when many Pima served in the U.S. Army, only accelerated these dietary trends, and in 1963, following a National Institutes of Health survey of the health status of several Native American tribes, the extraordinary level of obesity and diabetes suffered by the Pima came to national attention. Today, save for the isolated Nauru Islanders in the West Pacific, the Pima nation is plagued by a higher rate of obesity than any other ethnic group in the world, with about half of those who are over the age of thirty-five suffering the dangerous complication of insulin-resistant diabetes.

Diabetes is an illness where the normal regulation of the body's sugar metabolism is impaired, resulting in high circulating levels of blood glucose—the body's fuel—that over time can cause severe damage to the cardiovascular system, kidneys, and other body organs. Normally the ß-cells of the pancreas precisely control the level of blood glucose by varying their production of insulin. In the rarer form of diabetes (type I), which usually begins in childhood, this production is impaired and breaks down. A series of studies undertaken by the Pima people, the National Institutes of Health, and the Indian Health Service, however, found that insulin concentrations were normal or elevated in individuals who suffered the combination of obesity and diabetic blood sugar levels, indicating that it is not the failure of the pancreatic ß-cells but a *resistance* of body tissues to the action of insulin that causes the blood sugar elevation (type II diabetes).

After a high-carbohydrate meal when the blood glucose level rises, as part of its regulatory responsibilities insulin decreases the mobilization of energy from the body's fat storage system and converts the blood sugar not needed for immediate energy into glycogen. This glycogen is then stored in the large muscles of the body for future use. In an individual who is "insulin resistant," the metabolic enzymes that drive this process of glucose conversion behave differently in response to the insulin signal and the blood sugar level is raised. It has been proposed that in times of privation and low carbohydrate intake, such a metabolic shift had the survival advantage of reducing the energy supply to the muscles in favor of the brain, and of the mammary glands for the production of milk. If this "thrifty gene" theory is correct, then within Native American migrant groups—many of which faced chronic nutritional privation—natural selection would have favored individuals whose metabolism was genetically programmed through insulin resistance to maintain high blood sugar levels during periods of starvation. And in some tribal peoples such as the Pima, geographic isolation, together with its associated inbreeding, would have magnified this selection process.

So let us presume that in a balanced but marginal nutritional economy—as had been established by the Pima prior to the settlement of European-Americans—insulin resistance would have had a significant advantage. Then, as their traditional lifestyle of hunting and subsistence farming was lost and the balance of their long-established economy was overturned, discordance would have emerged between the thrifty genotype that the Pima carried and the new circumstances that they faced of reduced daily exercise and a high-calorie diet. The resulting positive energy balance would then foster obesity and diabetic levels of circulating blood glucose. That such a mismatch is the explanation for the obesity of the Arizonan Pima is reinforced by recent study of the Mexican Pima of the Sierra Madre, which is where the southern remnants of the extended Pima tribe that once stretched down from Arizona to central Mexico now live. The Mexican Pima have maintained their agrarian culture, and in contrast to their cousins in Arizona, most of them are thin and only about 8 percent of the community suffers from diabetes. They also work hard, laboring physically for about twenty-three hours a week, whereas the time the average Arizonan Pima spends exercising each week is less than two hours. But most importantly, the Mexican Pima still live on a diet of beans, corn, and potatoes, with perhaps a chicken once a month, consuming in total some twenty-two-hundred calories a day.

The complex carbohydrates consumed in beans and corn are distinctly different from the refined carbohydrates and sugars present in a McDonald's fast-food burger, and they are also metabolized differently. The complex carbohydrate molecule, commonly contained in grains and dietary fiber, is not broken down as quickly to sugars and thus stimulates only a moderate rise in circulating insulin. On the other hand, cereals that have been milled, as are found in the sesame seed bun, are more digestible and together with refined sugars, as found in candy bars and soft drinks, will rapidly induce high blood sugar levels and insulin resistance. In the Arizonan Pima, under such circumstances, a self-perpetuating vicious cycle has developed, and thereby hangs another cautionary tale.

It is now clear that Pima children born to mothers with diabetes are at greater risk to develop it themselves. From the results of a longitudinal epidemiological study of the Pima that began in 1965, it became apparent that children born to women who suffered type II diabetes during pregnancy had a significantly higher risk of becoming obese at an earlier age, and of developing diabetes, than did the offspring of non-diabetic women. The suspicion arose that the mother's diabetes was adding to the baby's risk of developing the illness, independent of diet and genetics. This suspicion was confirmed when a further study of sibling pairs—children who shared the same mother and therefore were presumed to be of comparable genetic susceptibility, but who were born either before or after the maternal diagnosis of diabetes—found that the children born *after* the diagnosis suffer more obesity and are at greater risk for type II diabetes than their older brothers and sisters. Thus a disabling illness, initiated by the disruption of an ancient balance, has now become self-perpetuating within the reproductive cycle.

The Pima, in their capacity to cope with the adverse circumstance of a depriving environment, are at one extreme of the adaptive physiological scale. And it is that same capacity, to conserve every extra calorie that they eat, which now causes them great harm. For those Americans of European ancestry, the complications of a consistent diet generous in fat and refined carbohydrate have taken longer to emerge. This is because agriculture and dairy production began in Europe and the Middle East long before other regions of the world, and hence most European-Americans have had time to adapt to a diet of abundance. But that was before we introduced fast food and frenzy as the standard American lifestyle. Now we are all at risk. Of the estimated 16 million Americans suffering from diabetes, approximately 14.4 million (90 percent) have the obesity-related, insulin-resistant variety. And with the number of citizens who are obese increasing rapidly, the prevalence of diabetes will certainly also rise for Americans regardless of ethnic origin. While at the moment European-Americans have a lower incidence of insulin-resistant diabetes than do the Pima and other Native American peoples, under the challenge of our new supercharged high-calorie diet—especially when combined with a sedentary existence—that gap will narrow significantly in coming generations. And of even greater importance is that a lack of exercise and a high intake of dietary fat—above all, saturated fat—promote insulin resistance in animal experiments, and simple sugars will do the same, *especially in the young.* This research suggests that the excessive intake of sugar-laden soft drinks by young Americans is particularly dangerous for the nation's future health.

America is not unique in the growing obesity of its people. Obesity is becoming a problem worldwide, wherever diets are changing from that of low-energy to high-energy foods and work-related exercise is falling. In China, for example, although the prevalence of obesity is infinitesimally small, with the growing Americanization of diet and of lifestyle, the rate at which citizens are becoming overweight is now about 1 percent per year.

But it is America, with our technology-rich culture, that has been in the vanguard of the industrialized nations when it comes to weight gain. And all the evidence suggests that our leadership will continue. In just one generation it is estimated that the number of Americans who walk more than thirty minutes each day has fallen by half, and the daily energy expenditure on exercise has fallen by about 250 calories. With almost two-thirds of the nation now overweight, America has crossed a significant social threshold. In practical terms the problem is easily framed: contrary to what we might wish to believe, it is not that aircraft seats have become smaller, but that Americans have become larger.

SO WHAT compels Americans to eat to excess? Tom Wadden, an obesity researcher at the University of Pennsylvania, has suggested that in

America eating has been transformed from a basic necessity of life to a commercially driven, reward-centered recreational activity—as exemplified in McDonald's familiar jingle "you deserve a break today." Amid the frenzy of a demand-driven, twenty-four-hour society, food has become divorced from hunger and from nutritional need, with the result that the natural relationship between our bodies and what we eat has fallen out of balance.

The sophisticated science and biotechnology employed in manufacturing the artificial flavors that now make America's fast food so tasty have contributed significantly to this loss of balance. The instinctual drives that served so well in frugal times are now hijacked by such flavors to great commercial advantage. The original McDonald's french fries, for example, gained their reputation not because they were made from scratch everyday, but because of their taste: the thinly sliced Russet Burbank potatoes were fried in 93 percent beef tallow. It was the hint of meat that gave the fries their unique flavor and, parenthetically, provided more saturated beef fat per ounce than did a McDonald's hamburger. Prepared in this tasty fashion, McDonald's fries have helped change the way we eat potatoes. In 1960 Americans consumed, per capita, about eighty-one pounds of fresh potatoes and four pounds of frozen french fries. By the year 2000 the comparable figures were fifty pounds of fresh potatoes and thirty pounds of frozen fries. In 1990, after criticism regarding the amount of cholesterol in its food, McDonald's switched to vegetable oil in making its french fries, but thanks to the flavor industry, the meaty taste remains. And we keep coming back, drawn to that flavor by an ancient appetite. As a result, today McDonald's is the largest single purchaser of potatoes in the United States, processing and freezing approximately 2 million pounds of fries each day.

We humans, like other mammals, largely *smell* what we taste. Often what we believe to be the taste of a favorite food is its aroma. The sensitive olfactory system in the lining of the nose can detect thousands of different chemical substances, in minute quantities, and the brain integrates such signals with information on taste coming from the taste buds in the tongue and the palate. There are some half-dozen basic categories of taste that we innately distinguish: sweet, sour, salty, astringent, bitter, and a fresh meaty-mushroom taste that the Japanese call *umami*. In the distant past, the ability to tell these tastes apart was an essential survival skill. Sugars, carbohydrates, and some proteins are sweet, for example, and we are drawn to sweet substances as a ready source of energy. Sweetness is thus a taste that is almost universal in its appeal. Similarly, salt is essential to survival, and the desire for salty food is intimately linked with the body's electrolyte balance. A sour, acidic, or bitter substance, on the other hand, is initially repugnant—as is meat that has putrefied or become contaminated in some way—and is rejected as potentially dangerous, especially in childhood. Most young children prefer sweet foods to bitter and spicy ones but can learn to enjoy the latter, depending largely on with whom they eat them. Hence McDonald's commercial strategy of catering to families and young children makes good physiological sense. Developing a taste for the foods we ultimately prefer is largely a process of socialization, and flavors discovered and rewarded in childhood can drive a lifelong craving.

Artificial flavoring is now the backbone of the American food industry. Processed food accounts for some 90 percent of the food purchased in America today, and in that processing most of the natural flavor is lost. But, thanks to taste being mainly about smell, by harnessing the wizardry of modern chemistry to sort and recombine literally thousands of volatile compounds, the flavor industry can now copy almost any natural flavor and suit it to any particular palate. In fact, the industry provides the flavor not only for McDonald's fries, but also for just about every other snack and fast-food product on the market. With annual revenues climbing into the billions, and after a half-century of practice, the American flavor industry knows what we like. And what that means, after a generation or two of family conditioning, is that we are hooked on their magic. Thanks to tasty and consistent flavoring, the American public is getting exactly what it wants from the fast-food industry, and we *enjoy* what we eat.

THE AMERICAN supermarket is the ultimate valley of plenty. No longer are we subsistence farmers living meagerly on sparse acres, or hungry hunters searching desperately for a kill. The sweet-tasting fruits of late summer, and the salty fresh meats are all there, displayed in delicious abundance on grocery shelves. Can there be any wonder why we gorge, when for generations we have instinctively sought, cherished, and hoarded such delights? But amid this bounty we have lost perspective. In the greater order of biology, instinctual appetites have a greater purpose. The immediate drive to satisfy them is just the hanging thread of a complex physiological web.

For our forebears, wandering the equatorial grasslands, to find sweet fruit was a rare delight. When such good fortune presented itself, they stuffed greedily: insulin did its work, and the grove was marked in their mind for return the following year. Salt, in low levels in most foods other than meat, was even scarcer, and the kidney conserved accordingly. And perhaps of significance in helping explain our latter-day passion for french fries is our forebears' eagerness for fat. Indeed, the desire of the modern-day hunter to target prey in the late summer and fall—just before winter begins and when the quarry is most fat—derives from intelligence with an ancient root.

Jay Kaplan, from his work with macaque Old World monkeys, has suggested that this ancient intelligence is tied to fat being a dense and valued source of energy, and that in consequence alterations in dietary fat and cholesterol have a profound effect on social behavior. During ongoing investigations designed primarily to tease apart the complex interaction of the social environment and a high fat intake in the development of heart disease, Kaplan observed that a cholesterol-lowering diet, given over a period of twenty-two months, increased aggression and impulsivity in experimental animals. The agonistic behaviors were most apparent in the lower-ranking animals that were forced to cope with an unstable social situation. Furthermore, the aggression diminished when a diet high in fat and cholesterol was reinstated, suggesting to Kaplan that the low fat intake was specifically magnifying the competitive behavior.

The human brain consumes approximately 20 to 25 percent of all the calories that the body uses when at rest, and requires stable supplies of energy for optimal function. Thus it makes sense within an evolutionary framework that in large-brained primates, including us, a falling blood cholesterol level would induce risk-taking behavior, such as hunting and competitive foraging, as an appropriate adaptation to the threat of dietary privation. Reciprocally, sustained periods of energy abundance will foster complacency and physical inactivity. Thus after a heavy, high-fat meal most of us prefer to sleep—or to watch televised sports from the comfort of the couch—rather than to engage in violent exercise.

As Professor Kaplan is the first to emphasize, this adaptive interpretation of the association between cholesterol metabolism and behavior is unsupported, as yet, by experimental data from humans. However, to dismiss out of hand a potential association on this basis would be premature. We share in common with the living primates some 98 percent of our genetic code, and a comparative scientific approach similar to what Kaplan has suggested has great potential value in unraveling our vulnerability to the challenges of the Fast New World. Nature is conservative, and thus the genes of ancient nutritional survival—the so-called thrifty genes that once were advantageous but in our new environment bestow susceptibility—are probably conserved within the common genome of present-day primates and humans.

The diet and the physical activity of a present-day primate living in its natural habitat probably differ little from those of early man. Under natural conditions an obese monkey is hard to find. But when animals are confined and fed an "affluent" American diet, the disorders of civilization—obesity, atherosclerosis, and high blood pressure—rapidly emerge. And as Kaplan demonstrated, in a chronically unstable social situation that mimics our own competitive environment, the repeated challenge and physiological stress of maintaining social rank contribute to arterial disease and obesity. And this is where a comparative genetic approach can be valuable. Thus the gene variants that successfully protect some Europeans from developing diabetes on a high-fat, high-carbohydrate diet, for example, are unlikely to be found in the hominoid line, for the human variant represents a recently selected mutation. In this instance it is the *loss* of the ancient thriftiness that confers protection from our "civilized" environment. Reciprocally, in individuals who *do* develop diabetes under the stress of a high-carbohydrate diet—as do monkeys exposed to the same conditions—the thrifty genes that now offend are likely to be conserved and still present in the hominoid gene line.

This comparative approach has proved successful in unraveling the mysteries of angiotensinogen and human hypertension. Angiotensinogen is an abundant protein, circulating in the blood, which plays a central role in the complex regulatory systems that maintain blood pressure. When a variant of the angiotensinogen gene was discovered in those suffering from high blood pressure, it was presumed that a specific mutant responsible for some forms of hypertension had been identified. Only later when it became clear that the variant was more widely distributed in the Japanese, Nigerians, and African-Americans (plus a variety of primates, including our closest relative, the chimpanzee) than in the European population, where it had been originally identified, was it realized that the "mutant" predisposing to hypertension was the ancient genetic form. Retrospectively, as with the story of lactose intolerance, it all makes sense. In Paleolithic times one of the greatest challenges to life was blood loss from injury, and the ability to rapidly increase blood pressure was vitally important. Today the situation that pertains is exactly the opposite. In America's Fast New World, the critical challenge is to regulate excessive *increases* in blood pressure induced by social stress, a sedentary lifestyle, and a high-salt, energy-dense diet.

THUS A THEME emerges. The human animal is ideally equipped for sustained physical activity and survival under frugal circumstances. Our body metabolism is finely tuned to precisely control blood pressure, blood sugar, cholesterol, and numerous other physiological parameters within *lower* limits of tolerance, but few bodily systems are devoted to the *upper* limits of tolerance and to the control of excess. Humans are confused by excess in all its forms, including food. Diligently we eat what is placed before us, and if the plate gets bigger, we eat more. High levels of sugar in the blood were a rarity during the evolution of our species. There were few fruit trees and their bounty was seasonal. Thus calorie conservation was our practice then, and it remains so today, with the evidence of our efficiency clearly displayed in unbridled weight gain. Likewise, given the scarcity of salt, we have had little experience in controlling the sustained increases in blood pressure induced by a salt-rich diet, especially when combined with a demand-based work environment. Despite our pretensions to being above the animal herd, in our evolutionary fit, whether we like it or not, we are creatures still tuned to our ancestral environment.

America's Fast New World is the antithesis of that original habitat. Today, in distinction to our forebears, life has become technology and calorie rich, but time and exercise poor. It would be difficult to invent an environment of greater contrast. And yet this challenging new world has evolved with little public concern for its physiological and social consequences. Why is that? we must ask. Have we, amid our reward-driven abundance, fallen into a dangerous complacency?

I believe we have. That material prosperity may have a pernicious potential is the ultimate paradox of the American dream. By most Americans such an association is not to be countenanced. Indices of the nation's rising anxiety are dismissed as evidence of individual weakness, and weight gain as something bothersome—something genetically determined and beyond individual responsibility for which medical science will soon discover a magic bullet. The leptin story is a case in point. When leptin—the hormone product of an "obesity" gene that was first isolated in mice—was discovered in 1994, it was hailed as the great hope for the obese, and pharmaceutical companies were soon bidding tens of millions of dollars for the privilege of exploiting the finding. Leptin is produced largely in the fat cells known as *adipocytes*, but also in the stomach and the hypothalamus of the brain (among other areas). The levels of leptin in the blood are correlated with total body weight, but the hormone has not yet proved to be of practical value in the treatment of obesity. While as an individual's weight increases more leptin is secreted, the body becomes less sensitive to its action, and when an effort is made to lose weight, the production of the hormone falls. Unfortunately, it is clear that as an appetite-suppressing panacea, leptin just doesn't work.

Disappointed but unperturbed Americans continue to clamor for a simple way to curb appetite. The fast-food industry spends about $10 billion a year on advertising, but ironically the weight gain that is the evidence of its success has spawned a diet industry with annual revenues triple that amount, approximately $34 billion. Since the Food and Drug Administration deregulated dietary supplements in 1994, some twenty-five-thousand new products have reached the market. Particularly popular have been nonprescription pills and other over-the-counter weight-loss agents that require little in the way of sweat and sacrifice. The number of outrageously fraudulent products is on the rise: slimming seaweed soaps that remove fat in the shower; pills guaranteed to drop pounds without diet or exercise. The gimmickry knows no bounds.

In the best American tradition the obesity pandemic, rather than triggering a national campaign of education and exercise to aid those who suffer the most to help themselves, has spawned a whole new industry that seeks to profit on our nation's growing disability. Rationalization abounds. Big has become beautiful. Children who are overweight are no longer fat, but "fluffy." Teenagers who wear large clothes are now embraced by clothing manufacturers offering everything from denim to bike shorts. Health clubs for children are on the rise, with aerobics classes and miniature stair-climbing machines: a group providing exercise programs for private elementary schools now has nineteen franchises in thirteen states. Diet books proliferate. Two of the most popular, *The Zone* by Barry Sears and *Dr. Atkins' New Diet Revolution* by Robert Atkins, promote the idea that we should get back to eating a diet that our genes are designed to manage—higher amounts of protein and lower levels of processed carbohydrates—as the key to weight loss. And in Franklin, Tennessee, the best-selling diet author Gwen Shamblin runs the Weigh Down Workshop, a multimillion-dollar business developed around the idea that one is morally obligated to slim down for Christ.

Such ingenuity is quintessentially American and entirely in keeping with our restless migrant quest for the novel solution, but we have lost sight of the forest for the trees. As a nation we have grown fat because of the diet we have adopted and the choices we have made, and without thought and different choices we are likely to grow fatter. These are simple facts. Now it is time to grasp the considerable knowledge that we have about ourselves and about our evolutionary ties to an ancient biology, and use that knowledge to exercise our human will in the interests of health and our common welfare. With a redirection of our ingenuity, we can do it—we can reduce the mismatch between biology and environment that is making us sick—although the evidence is that it will not be easy. America has recently adopted drug-free zones, smoke-free environments, and exercise-free schools. The last idea was a mistake, but it's part of a dangerous trend. Type in the keywords *diet and obesity* on the Amazon web site for books, for example, and 189 titles will be presented for your consideration. Try *exercise and obesity*, however, and the choice is reduced to twenty-five. With all our concern about food and diets, the importance of exercise in maintaining the intricate orchestration of the body's physiology has dropped from general public awareness.

When, by necessity, children walked to school and physical activity was essential to the work we did each day, our imperative need for exercise largely took care of itself. The technology of our Fast New World has blunted those mundane opportunities, and we have been slow to realize the health consequences of the change. There is overwhelming evidence in the medical literature that sedentary individuals do not have a normal physiology, and that physical inactivity promotes ill health. And yet, all too often, physicians prescribe exercise only after such disabilities as obesity and diabetes have emerged.

The ultimate goal is to prevent disease before it occurs. And that is where we must be willful. If activity has disappeared from the routine of American life, then we would do well to institutionalize it. Learning the discipline of regular physical exercise should be mandatory in school, together with the discipline of mathematics. And I'm not referring here to competitive sports. Even a brisk walk for thirty minutes each day can have a salutary effect on maintaining the intricate orchestration of the ancient genes that control food intake and energy expenditure. Thus it was a step to be applauded when in the spring of 2002 the Bush administration launched a modest advertising campaign aimed at promoting exercise in children. Similarly, the Los Angeles school board has sought to ban the sale of sugar-laden sodas in schools in their district. Such steps are a beginning, but America has a long way to go if in the face of our abundance we are to change public opinion about diet and exercise.

So I was reminded in November 2002 when I attended the annual meeting of the Society for Neuroscience, held that year in Orlando, Florida, the home of Disney World. One afternoon, after sitting for several hours in the conference hall, I decided to go jogging, only to discover that pedestrian walkways are rare in Disney Village and hard to find. Obviously Orlando, as was Los Angeles, had been planned with the car in mind. Nonetheless I persisted. The weather was sticky and warm, and after a mile or so I found myself at a busy intersection and a red traffic light. The only other pedestrians in sight were an elderly couple who had parked their car nearby and were looking for the visitor's center, where they hoped to buy tickets. I was of little help and suggested that they ask at the McDonald's across the street. "Thanks, we will," said the woman as the light changed, and together we started across the line of traffic. "And you be careful," she added with genuine concern in her voice. "You can kill yourself running in weather like this."

Chapter Six

THE TIME TRADE:
OF CLOCKS AND
COMPETITION

While the law [of competition] may sometimes be hard
for the individual it is best for the race, because it
ensures the survival of the fittest in every department.

Andrew Carnegie
North American Review, 1889

IN THE ULTIMATE PARADOX of America's Fast New World we
are running short of time. Time is now our most precious commodity. In
the headlong pursuit of prosperity we have traded time for money. We
no longer speak of "passing" time, and certainly not of "killing" it, but of
"spending" it as we would spend money. And so, as with money, we
guard our time, we hoard it, and we hunger for more.

It is a recent craving, this hunger for time. For thousands of years the
rhythmic pacing of life by day, night, and season—the divisions imposed
on us by the sun and our spinning planet—was our only measure of
time. Ritual helped mark the passage of each day while annual festivals
provided anchors for memory and expectation. It was not until the
invention of the mechanical clock and the flowering of the Industrial

Revolution that time became important in everyday life. The clock, by accurately dividing time into units, made possible the coordinated activity of large numbers of people. Soon, rather than being paid for a task, workers were being hired by the hour, and de facto the clock had become a measure not only of time but also of money. Time was a commodity to be bought and sold.

While the railroad and the telegraph injected a sense of urgency into commercial life, our preoccupation with time today is largely a product of the Fast New World and the electronic automation that now magnifies market competition. To fuel the nation's supercharged economic engines, many American industries have adopted a 24/7 workweek. Real-time rivalry has similarly increased the competitive demands on individuals, and twelve-hour workdays are now common practice. At the millennium, approximately 20 percent of the U.S. workforce was employed in shifts, or worked at night, and the numbers are steadily increasing. Millions of other citizens find themselves tethered to their jobs around the clock by the same nomadic tools—cell phones, pagers, and wireless e-mail—that were heralded first as instruments of liberation. Technology and the market are in cahoots, and a swarming sense of urgency grips the nation as we squeeze the maximum commercial value from each precious moment in life's span.

It is a paradox of America's prosperity that despite a massive increase in disposable income, especially in the professions and in business, many families consider themselves too busy to enjoy their affluence. Material wealth has been decoupled from contentment and personal fulfillment. The time investment devoted to securing wealth has crowded out family life and threatens the intimacy on which humans thrive. Divorce, drug use, and single-parent households compound the problem, and the number of professional women remaining childless has increased. Even for the intact family, changing work patterns and an increasingly competitive culture have diminished the closeness among family members and increased the daily demands on children. A challenging plethora of organized after-school activities is now a feature of childhood from the earliest years, with even first graders carrying schedules.

A further irony is that families earning the most money are frequently those with the least inclination to slow down. Goal-oriented, hard-working parents demand high-energy offspring, and in such families individual achievement is prized above the cultivation of intimacy. Competitive sports and extracurricular activities—learning to ski, to dance, or to play a musical instrument—are often the object of financial extravagance, with money replacing parental involvement. "Quality time" is scheduled to replace the "togetherness" that the family's high-velocity existence has made obsolete, and the restorative "vacancy" of a school vacation disappears as camp and other activities are structured to achieve maximum return with a minimal investment of parental time.

For many Americans the "free moments" that once glued a busy life together have almost disappeared. We cut corners where we can—with fast food, fast service, fast banking, fast cars, and fast communication—but as the demands of the workplace have increased and family time has eroded, Americans have been forced to invade those hours previously reserved for sleep. As a result, the nation is now significantly sleep deprived. A survey conducted in the winter of 1997 by the National Sleep Foundation found that during the work week the average American borrows up to two hours each night from his or her sleep bank. For individuals living at the leading edge of our manic society, a chronic sleep debt, driven by sixty- to eighty-hour workweeks, is nothing unusual and sometimes boasted of with pride. And for the majority, the traditional eight hours of sleep—commonplace in the agrarian economy of a century ago—has been replaced by fatigue, an alarm clock, and a desperate hope that the weekend will bring relief.

THE SPECIFIC amount of sleep required within a twenty-four-hour period varies among individuals, with a range of five or six to ten hours and an average need for about eight. We can teach ourselves to sleep less for limited periods, but there is little that can be done about changing our total sleep need. Those who believe otherwise implicitly seek to erase from human behavior the evolutionary imprint of our planet. The earth's rotation around the sun dictates that living creatures are exposed to an alternating world of light and dark every twenty-four hours. It being difficult to perform optimally under such varying circumstances, most animals in their evolution have adapted to one environment or to the other. Nocturnal creatures, such as raccoons and owls, withdraw to a secure refuge during daylight hours while others, including chickens, squirrels, and us, sleep during darkness. Thus, just as day alternates with night, animals oscillate between behavioral engagement with the world and retreat from it. This oscillation is an active coordination of body and behavior by a brain clock mechanism that is millions of years old. As is our need for intimacy and for family and friends, our need for sleep is an ancient biological imperative.

From the standpoint of efficient competition in the global economy, it would be advantageous if we could ignore these ancient body clocks. The Fast New World has essentially three time zones—pioneered by the financial markets dividing themselves among Tokyo, New York, and London—and international commerce is now an enterprise that never sleeps. Late in the evening in Los Angeles, when I confirm my United Airlines flight from New York to London, the individual on the other end of the telephone line frequently will have a British accent. That's because the airline's operators are asleep in New York but just beginning their shift in Britain. Multinational companies are working in similar global relays to speed the latest software upgrade, design a better light bulb, or close a financial deal. In maximizing the efficiencies of the virtual corporate web, the clocks of commerce seek to ignore the rhythms of the sun. Faithful to its ancient imperative for survival, however, the human brain cannot.

The brain's "biological clocks"—named the suprachiasmatic nuclei because anatomically they lie above a crossing of the optic nerves—are actually a cluster of about ten thousand nerve cells located in the hypothalamus of the old mammalian brain. These pacemakers drive our circadian (from the Latin *circa dies*, meaning "around one day") patterns of rest and activity, and coordinate a flux of hormones designed to maximize our efficiency during daylight hours. This rhythm of efficiency varies among individuals, although most are more alert after awakening in the morning than in the late afternoon. With the rising sun each day, as the eyes take in the morning light, a signal is transmitted via the optic nerves to set the timing of the master clocks. In humans these chronometers are genetically programmed to run with a cycle slightly longer than twenty-four hours—close to the earth's rotation around the sun but not rigidly so, and thus the sun must reset them each morning. This "imprecision" is important, for it provides the flexibility to remain in harmony with the changing light of the seasons and offers, in our age of rapid transport, the potential of coping with self-imposed time-zone changes.

It is through these brain chronometers that the physiological rhythms of the body, including our intellectual alertness, are adjusted for optimal daytime performance. Without such adjustment we are mentally diminished. The system is extraordinarily sensitive: sleep deprivation over one night—a reduction in sleep time of as little as two or three hours—can result in sleepiness and fatigue lasting for several days. This is because the sleep drive increases progressively during wakefulness, and decreases only as physiological recovery occurs during sleep. Thus sleep deprivation interacts with the time course of the circadian clock, and together they determine alertness and the drive for sleep within each day. A third factor in the equation is that the total daily sleep requirement has a variance among individuals from two to four hours, and the phase of the circadian performance cycle from two to three hours. This helps explain why individuals who by phase are "evening types" are more tolerant of working late at night, and thus do better at shift work. Similarly, naturally short sleepers can better tolerate sleep debt than naturally long sleepers, with less impairment of performance during periods of sustained wakefulness. Thus, under the demands of a twenty-four-hour society, those who have little need for sleep or who have low vulnerability to sleep loss have a considerable business advantage. An individual of manic temperament who sleeps only four or five hours, and who is alert and working with the Tokyo stock exchange at 4 A.M. New York time, has the competitive edge over any colleague who requires eight to ten hours of sleep each night.

To sharpen that competitive edge—and in an unconscious effort to override the brain's clocks and escape the chains of our planetary environment—hard-working Americans have embraced the buzzed vigilance and hard-beating heart of caffeine addiction. With the average American worker now running a sleep debt of between two to five hundred hours each year, the demand for coffee has exploded. Coffee is particularly effective in reducing sleep inertia, the feeling of grogginess and intellectual impairment that many individuals experience immediately after awakening. Inertia is most troublesome in those who are already sleep deprived and suddenly awakened—as with an alarm clock—from a short sleep or nap. Coffee gives a shot of caffeine to the brain, peaking in the bloodstream about half an hour after consumption, and does not lose its efficiency with repeated use. America's increased demand for coffee started in Seattle, the home of Boeing, Amazon, and Microsoft and a city where during the manic pinnacle of the 1990s one could work any sixteen hours of the day that one chose. The trend spread rapidly and caffeine soon became America's stimulant of choice (and, second to oil, the world's most actively traded commodity). Where many cultures enjoy a leisurely breakfast before work and perhaps even a lunchtime nap, to meet the demands of their Fast New World Americans have adopted the morning latte and the afternoon frappachino, with booster shots of expresso in between.

THIS TIME-PRESSURED, caffeine-driven existence is one that Kim Phan knew well. Indeed, in many ways, Kim's story is that of the American dream writ large. In the decades that elapsed since Kim fled with her family from Vietnam, she achieved astounding economic success. From her early years as a music teacher, living on tuna fish salad and selling encyclopedias door to door, she ascended the professional ladder to become a respected international lawyer. Kim's accomplishments were a tribute not only to her energy and native intelligence but also to America's market culture where talent and hard work are swiftly rewarded with financial success. But Kim's story also illustrates the hazards of life at the manic edge—how loss of sleep, the relentless competition of a "wired" workplace, and the deferral of intimacy in the pursuit of a career may precipitate crippling anxiety and self-doubt in even the most resilient of individuals.

Kim worked for one of the most aggressive law firms in the city of Los Angeles, where she specialized in corporate mergers and acquisitions. By her own account she was good at her job. Being of ambitious and agile mind, Kim relished the excitement and novelty of what she did and of achieving that which others thought unachievable. "I love working with my wits," Kim told me, "when there's nothing in my experience to pull from and when every problem is an immediate challenge, a test that can't be prepared for." Deadlines, complex decisions, fierce professional rivalry, uncompromising colleagues, and tight international travel schedules were her bread and butter. She thrived on such a diet and achieved what many of her friends had thought impossible. Despite being a woman and an immigrant, Kim had climbed the corporate ladder until it was generally acknowledged that when an innovative solution was required for a complex problem, she was the young go-to lawyer with few peers.

Kim lived with her pager turned on twenty-four hours a day, and she was paged seven days a week. Even while sailing—on the rare Sunday when she could get away—somebody from her office would invariably contact her and intrude. She took it all in stride. "It's better to be paged while sailing than not sail at all" was Kim's philosophy. Electronic communication had definitely eroded her privacy but she accepted it as a technical advance that enabled her to use her precious time to the best advantage. Frequently, when she was away from Los Angeles, even her secretary did not know her exact whereabouts in the world. Thus her nomadic tools—her pager, laptop, and cell phone—went everywhere with her. Overnight delivery, fax machines, and e-mail had also become necessary services for Kim, as for so many in America's corporate world.

Despite Kim's love of the Fast New World, however, and her personal dependence on technology, she had her misgivings about life in "real time." With the emphasis on the speed of transaction as the key to profit, she feared that the urgency of negotiation, in combination with the exhausting travel demands of a global market, threatened the objectivity and quality of corporate decisions. Kim believed that prior to the fax machine and e-mail becoming standard methods of circulating documents, there had been greater opportunity for thoughtful deliberation. Negotiations proceeded at a slower pace: the briefs and draft agreements had to be sent by mail, and changing a document was cumbersome, fostering compromise and reducing the compulsion to negotiate every detail. "There would come a moment," Kim explained, "when you would look at a point and say, okay, I can live with that." Word processing totally changed such behavior. Now perfectionists had no bounds, and arguments over detail replaced an intelligent discussion of principle.

In the real-time world the pressure to move quickly was intense. The global game was played against the clock, with a fast turnaround synonymous with success and profit. "So now everyone's running on steroids," Kim said. "Young as I am, even when I began in this game it would take eight days to get the mail back and forth across the Atlantic. Now it takes eight seconds; just the amount of time needed to punch the numbers into the fax machine." A document may have taken thirty days to draft but in the real-time world a response was expected in thirty minutes. In Kim's opinion, while electronic systems increased the speed of international business transactions, that advance was synonymous with neither efficiency nor quality, simply because machines could not substitute for the personal contact required to glue a final agreement together. "So my job has changed," Kim explained, "and the backbreaking part is now the travel required as markets have gone global. It's an essential part of my business—I've found no substitute for being physically present during the final phases of a negotiation—but the stress can be exhausting."

Kim spoke from bitter personal experience. In her late thirties, with the whole world her oyster, she had become suddenly anxious and fearful of the future. Kim was in Paris when the first episode of panic occurred. She was negotiating the sale of a small California-based company that made electronic circuit boards to a European conglomerate. For over a month she had been living on coffee and little sleep, working fifteen to twenty hours each day to complete the transaction before the end of the financial year. It was not an unusual job, but it had become protracted and intense after her discovery of a technical problem with the company's existing certificate of incorporation. The document, which had been drafted by her law firm some years earlier, included a provision that preferred stock be given to the stockholders in lieu of dividends, with the promise of later conversion into common stock. Kim had discovered early in the restructuring that the original calculation was in error and the quantity of common stock authorized in the charter was insufficient to cover the compounding growth of the preferred stock plan. Kim's boss and senior partner, "JP" Moran, whom Kim described as "never the easiest of men, especially when criticized or under pressure," had been embarrassed and infuriated by the discovery of the error. His team had drafted the original charter, and he feared it might jeopardize the sale of the company. In his irrational anger, he had insisted that Kim engineer a solution, and should she fail, he would hold her publicly accountable. "So there I was," Kim said, "in Paris, in real time, but totally alone."

Kim was fluent in French, having learned the language as a child in Vietnam, and she had worked frequently in France. But it was wintertime and, in stark contrast to Los Angeles, Paris was dark, cold, and wet. To carry forward the delicate negotiations between the European and American principals, Kim was flying back and forth between California and Paris at almost weekly intervals. "Everything seemed to be working against me," she said. "The nine-hour time difference was bad enough but it was also the holiday season and there were flight delays and cancellations, plus JP was being impossibly arrogant." Kim had developed sinusitis, and to relieve the headache and congestion, she began taking cold medicines. "My sleep was totally fragmented and the more fatigued I became, the more coffee I drank, until I was feeling hyped up and miserable at the same time." Kim had always prided herself on being calm under stress, but the fatigue and tension so disturbed her thinking that she started to make small mistakes, especially when angry with JP or during difficult negotiating sessions. Then, walking back to her hotel one bitterly cold night, she began experiencing stomach pain and nausea, and the doctor that she consulted, thinking that Kim might have appendicitis, admitted her to a hospital.

Kim had never been hospitalized before and her anxiety rose exponentially, especially at the thought of possible surgery. Battling such fear, she eventually fell asleep only to be awakened by a nurse who wanted to set up an intravenous drip. "As she put the needle into my arm I must have fainted," said Kim, "because my next memory is of a masked individual poking me and discussing how difficult it was to find my blood pressure. I was sweating and trembling, feeling dizzy and unreal, with an intense feeling of suffocation—of not being able to get a deep breath—and I could sense my heart pounding. I was terrified. My first thought was that I was dying. Then suddenly the whole thing subsided. For the rest of the night I just lay there exhausted, while churning through my mind were thoughts of our escape from Vietnam."

The vivid return of these ancient memories confused Kim. She had been a young girl when Saigon fell, and in the years of her American success she had rarely thought about Vietnam. But suddenly the images were again bright and intrusive: the wailing of sirens as tracer shells lit up the night sky; the screams and the smell of burning oil; the blind, visceral panic and the terrifying jeep ride to the water's edge and to the waiting pontoon. She intuitively understood the survival value of the terror she and her family had experienced during that ordeal, but it made no sense to her that anxiety and fear should suddenly invade the security of her life as an affluent American attorney.

Kim's hospital stay was brief. After various tests, the French doctors declared her to be suffering from "nervous exhaustion," not appendicitis, and she was discharged with instructions to rest. "That was the good news," Kim told me, "but subsequently I began worrying about dying in my sleep." She considered such fears irrational, but they persisted. Lying quietly in bed she would feel that she was suffocating—that she couldn't get enough air—and, occasionally, having fallen asleep, she would awaken suddenly with her heart pounding.

Kim finished the Paris project on time, but her vibrant self did not return. She began experiencing similar episodes of panic on occasions that surprised her—as on a weekend skiing trip when she paused on the mountain to tighten her boots. In another instance, during an argument with JP, she was forced to excuse herself and to lie down on the floor of her office until the feelings passed. Over subsequent weeks the night terrors subsided, but Kim found herself uncharacteristically anxious and antisocial, with a rising self-doubt. In her logical mind, to be paralyzed by repetitive attacks of panic and anxiety smacked of a weakness of character and a loss of personal control. Amid luxury and professional success, Kim felt personally diminished. "Lying awake in the early morning hours I began thinking that I was a fake," she confessed to me. "I'm admired by others as the smart immigrant who made it. I'm a respected and skillful attorney. But I'm also forty years old, divorced, childless, and running on a treadmill that others control. It's not that I'm a fake lawyer, but sometimes I do feel like a fake person: that I've lost a sense of meaning in my life."

WHEN I DESCRIBED Kim Phan's experience to my colleague, Alexander Bystritsky, a professor of psychiatry at the University of California, Los Angeles, and an expert in panic disorder, he found the theme of her story a familiar one. The acute development of panic, as Kim experienced in the Paris hospital, is a misinterpretation of an ancient survival alarm, Bystritsky explained, when normal vigilance becomes heightened or confused under stressful circumstances. When confronted with potential danger or intense competition, the human brain reverts to alarm systems that are tried and true (to our "immediate instincts," as Adam Smith expressed it). The powerful human intellect is placed aside and we retreat to those ancient mechanisms of alarm that served our forebears, for whom physical survival was a daily challenge.

Anxiety is thus the human emotion most intimately linked to primordial fear. The feelings are familiar to each of us: an anxious sense of foreboding as the heart picks up its beat, an urge to pace, a knot in the stomach's pit, and a darting attention that destroys concentration. These are the signals of mind and body fused in watchful arousal. As fear increases, as Kim had experienced in her escape from Vietnam, primitive emotion races ahead of conscious thought, and a flood of stress hormones engage the body in emergency mode. Now the reptilian brain takes command. The heart pumps faster to supply the large leg muscles on which escape will depend, and the breath is drawn faster and deeper to deliver those muscles with oxygen. The pupil of the eye dilates, facilitating vision and escape. The stomach and bowel are summarily emptied and appetite is abandoned, for preserving life in a crisis depends on rapid mobilization of the energy stored in liver and muscle, not on digestion's deliberate work. Then, with the body in emergency mode, the sweating begins to better discharge the heat of the approaching struggle.

This primitive alarm reaction—what behavioral scientists call the *acute stress response*—can be life saving, as in Kim Phan's flight from Vietnam. But in America today the threat of death is no longer the prevalent danger. The locus of challenge has shifted from one of bodily harm to the fierce competition of a time-pressured commercial society. Survival for those who compete in the Fast New World is a challenge beyond the time-limited terror of running for one's life, for the race is never over. There is always a new deadline to be met, an opportunity to exploit, a key person to persuade, and another deal to be struck. Exposed to such relentless competition, as the physiological alarm bell sounds repeatedly, a system designed for emergency response slides slowly into a state of chronic arousal, until cascades of stress hormones flog the body organs much as a desperate rider flogs his tired and stumbling mount.

Bystritsky believes it is the proliferation of these socially competitive, demand-based work environments—with their associated stressors of sleep deprivation and real-time engagement—that is responsible for an increased prevalence of anxiety, panic, and social phobia in America. In two national epidemiological surveys, conducted approximately ten years apart, the prevalence of anxiety disorders in the United States has almost doubled, from under 19 percent to 33 percent of the population. Similarly there is an increased reporting of social phobia, which Bystritsky interprets as a coping strategy whereby those individuals prone to anxiety deliberately avoid the fast-paced world. Although greater public awareness may help explain these results, the prevalence of obsessive-compulsive behavior—the checking disorder—did not increase over the same time period, suggesting that a cultural shift has occurred in America that fosters anxiety disorder.

"In the U.S. we have created many ideal environments for breeding anxiety and social phobia," Alexander Bystritsky remarked during our discussion, "and I suspect the fiercely competitive law firm in which Kim worked is a perfect example of such an environment." He was correct. A big law firm, as Kim had described it to me, is a competitive and unstable hierarchy, with the cheap labor at the bottom renewed each summer by a detachment of new recruits. The partners, "the guys on the top of the pyramid," such as her boss, JP Moran, bring in the clients while the associates do the legwork, competing relentlessly with each other in the hope of being recognized. Kim felt that the women lawyers in her firm were more insecure and worked harder than the men. "Not that the men don't work hard," she added. "Everybody does, but I think the women compete among themselves for the prestigious projects in order to be recognized. The competition never goes away, and so any social attachments are superficial. The associates speak to each other, but in general they don't share professional information or help each other out. There's always the fear that if one person does well, they will get the better job next time." In consequence, I learned, everybody worked twelve-hour days because the unspoken truth was that only a small percentage of the associates would survive to gain partnership. "Initially I was terrified of making mistakes," said Kim. "I discovered early on that what you learn in law school doesn't teach you much about *practicing* law. I knew little about court procedures, commercial litigation, negotiating between rival parties—that sort of thing—and absolutely nothing about staying alive within a group of hungry, ambitious colleagues. I didn't know what I was doing. Any secretary knew more. But then I figured out that everybody felt the same way, but most covered it up with bravado. After that, I relaxed and started to enjoy the game. It was still stressful and hard work, but I knew what I was doing and felt good about being capable."

Kim had also been fortunate. When she first joined the law firm, JP Moran had taken her under his wing. "The fact that I was a woman and young and attractive all appealed to him," Kim explained. "He recruited only the smartest people to work for him: JP's group had the most capable lawyers, the most challenged, and the ones that work the hardest." Moran reveled in intense competition, admiring the industrial overlords of America's Gilded Age as paragons of initiative. "Survival of the fittest" was his favorite cliché. Nor did he deny that his whimsical attachment to the appellation "JP" reflected a strong identification with J. Pierpont Morgan, the investment banker with whom Andrew Carnegie and others, at the dawn of the twentieth century, had formed the United States Steel Corporation. It was, Kim had reflected, an appropriate affinity for JP in both business style and character. Both men were predators—bold, brooding, and fiercely competitive—who in their success had only disdain for those who fell behind.

Each junior associate in JP's group billed between 300 and 350 hours each month, which meant that year after year Moran brought in a disproportionate share of the firm's revenue—sometimes more than the rest of the firm put together. "If you listened to JP, you soon became pumped up," Kim commented. "We were the elite brigade in an elite law firm." To her surprise Kim discovered that she loved the work. To be involved in a high-powered, high-pressured acquisition project was an exciting experience. There was a sense of exuberance, of speed, of importance, and a successful project brought bonuses. JP had control over the lion's share of the firm's resources and he looked after the winners in his brigade. "There were many nights," said Kim, "when I would go home totally exhausted, but feeling incredibly happy."

IN COLLEGE Kim had been a music major, studying piano at a conservatory in Ohio and later teaching music in the public school system of Cleveland, where the family had ended up after their resettlement in the United States. Among the some three hundred thousand refugees who had fled from South Vietnam after the fall of Saigon, the Phan family had been fortunate. Their pontoon had made it to a Vietnamese boat lying off the coast, and later they had been rescued by a U.S. destroyer, eventually being interned at Camp Pendleton in Orange County, California, before being sponsored by a lawyer and his family in Ohio. It was he—a "wonderful man," as Kim remembered him—who later encouraged her to take up law.

Kim was married in college to another musician, who was "kind, gentle and easy to talk to." Initially they had many common interests, and one of Kim's fondest memories was playing the piano together over the weekends. Following graduation, after teaching music for a while, her husband had opened a record store, which proved to be a financial disaster. For two years it consumed money, and with Kim's job as a public school music teacher being their primary income, the couple were soon close to the breadline. As well as being poorly paid, however, Kim also discovered that teaching bored her. "I liked the relationship with the kids, but I spent most of my time being a baby-sitter," Kim recalled. "The fire rapidly went out for me as a teacher, which is why I decided to change my life and became a law student.

"Unfortunately that didn't work for the marriage," Kim continued. "When I became a summer associate, I began to fall into the work habits that I have now. I'd start in the morning at 8 A.M. and finish at 8 P.M. at night. Soon my husband was saying that that was not a lifestyle for him, and when I graduated and was offered the position here in California, it was obvious to both of us that we should split. We had no children, after all. He is so different from me. After the music shop failed, he took a middle-management job in a sporting goods store. I'm almost ashamed to say so, but I found it stifling to be with somebody who was happy to work for a mediocre salary in such a dead-end job."

After the boredom of teaching, Kim found the competitive world of law a "fascinating and exhilarating labyrinth," filled with opportunity and challenging problems. But it was also money that had drawn her to a high-status law practice. For Kim, money represented security. "When the music store was failing, I would work through my lunch hour to earn an extra $5.65," Kim explained. "I sold encyclopedias door-to-door at night, and gave piano lessons in people's houses on the weekends. I had watched my parents live from hand to mouth in the same way and just didn't want to do that for the rest of my life." After resettlement, during Kim's adolescence, the Phan family had been poor. Her father, who in civilian life in Vietnam had been an engineer, could not get such employment in the United States and in desperation started a small market garden to feed the family. "Never once did I hear him complain, regardless of the hardship," Kim said. She admired her father's stoicism but decided there must be another way: law had provided that for her when music failed. "As a lawyer my security is that I can take care of myself," Kim explained. "It has been a conscious trade-off: I have too little time for myself and my family, but I no longer worry about paying my mortgage, or the cost of dinner."

IT WAS this trade-off that Kim found herself questioning after the onset of her anxiety, and subsequently during her period of social withdrawal. When I asked Alexander Bystritsky how he understood Kim's seemingly sudden shift in emotion and self-appraisal, he was quick to remind me that anxiety, per se, is not a pathological state but a warning. "We intuitively understand the sentinel role of anxiety in an acute emergency," Bystritsky said, "but find that same concept more difficult to grasp under circumstances of competition and chronic stress. Kim's anxiety signaled a mismatch—a growing conflict—between her established career and what she valued in life."

In a healthy individual, Bystritsky explained, happiness is constantly being redefined. In youth, especially in American culture, the promise of happiness seems easy enough. You just work hard, fall in love, run fast, grow rich, and you will amount to something. Only later does the question, amount to what? begin to arise. Happiness in most cultures is tied to intimacy, which is sustained through a circle of friends and family bound together in trust and mutual support. Intimacy provides comparable bedrock in American life, but a greater cultural emphasis is placed on the importance of material prosperity in securing such attachments. "Unfortunately it's an illusion," said Bystritsky. "After a certain level of income, all the evidence suggests that happiness comes from the interaction with other people, not from material possession. American society is both alluring and destroying in that regard. It seduces with the message that given money and hard work everything is possible, but then, through the same cultural message, drains the time and energy required to achieve intimacy and personal happiness. So it was for Kim: up, up, up until she reached a threshold when—precipitated by JP's irrational anger and withdrawal of support—first fear and anxiety broke through and then later, in withdrawal, she began to question what her life was all about. Had she given up the intimacy of marriage and children, and the cultural expectations of her family, merely to create an *illusion* of happiness based on financial security? As a fundamentally healthy individual, Kim found herself confronted by an ancient superior force—an ancient alarm system—that called her frenetic activity into question."

Hence Kim's anxiety did not feed simply on some resurrected ghost of her Vietnam experience—although the terror of that ordeal had probably sensitized her and later facilitated an understanding of the panic episodes—but rather on a damaging accumulation of chronic stress. Beneath Kim's existential anguish churned a physiology pushed to its adaptive limits. The feeling of suffocation that had so frightened Kim in the Paris hospital, and the breath holding commonly seen in panic, Bystritsky believes to be the survival equivalent of when a fearful animal freezes in the presence of a prowling predator. During the freezing reaction, the blood vessels constrict through sympathetic activation, but the heart rate does not increase until the animal is discovered or seeks to escape. However, when physical flight is closed as an appropriate option, as in the demanding social confrontations of today's workplace—or when one is confined to a hospital bed—the changing physiology and anxiety can explode into the symptoms of panic.

The disruption of Kim's sleep-wake cycle by the frequent trips back and forth between Paris and California—together with the severe sleep deprivation imposed by her work schedule and coffee consumption—also magnified her anxiety and mental fatigue. The relationship between the number of hours awake and intellectual fatigue is not a simple one. For each of us, performance is more efficient at certain times of the day than at others, depending on the phase of the brain's pacemaker, the number of hours we have slept the night before, and our total habitual sleep need. Kim was by habit a short sleeper—and one who slept lightly—and the repeated circadian disruption imposed by her transatlantic travel had a catastrophic effect on her mental acuity, compounding the strain she felt in meeting the imposed deadlines for the project. Furthermore, as Kim learned to her cost, consciously attempting to remain awake and alert through the use of coffee and other stimulants, such as cold medicine, does not control the phase of the brain clocks. An increase in daytime sleepiness can be detected after just one hour of circadian disruption—an ordinary occurrence for those just traveling within America's borders—and this rapidly escalates with the increased phase disruption of repeated transatlantic crossings, which was Kim's experience.

As sleep deprivation increases, despite all compensatory efforts, performance deficits rise in tandem. Emotional irritability grows, while reaction time, the accuracy of short-term memory, and logical reasoning are diminished. And should the privation continue over several nights, a phenomenon known as "forced napping" begins, where an individual falls asleep during periods of reduced stimulation, such as when driving a car alone at night along a quiet road. These changes in performance predictably occur in everyone who is sleep deprived—regardless of intelligence, occupation, education, motivation, or commitment to the task in hand—and if the deprivation is sustained, chronic fatigue and stress-driven anxiety become almost inevitable. Indeed, in a study conducted by the National Institute of Mental Health, symptoms in 58 percent of those who suffered from panic disorder worsened after they were partially deprived of sleep over a single night. Thus, as Kim had learned in Paris, sleep deprivation and anxiety can reinforce each other in a progressive cycle.

But even with these acute stressors, Kim's story might have been different—with the ancient alarm bells quiescent—had her Paris struggle not been superimposed on the chronic challenge of a capricious and intensively competitive professional environment, plus nagging family concerns. At the beginning of the Paris project, two or three weeks before Thanksgiving, Kim's father had suffered a transient impairment of his speech that the doctors, in retrospect, considered evidence of a minor stroke. Characteristically her father had dismissed the episode, insisting that Kim attend to her business rather than traveling home to Ohio for the Thanksgiving holiday. "So I didn't visit," said Kim. "I justified it by telling myself that my mother and my sister and her husband were there and that they would cope, but I felt guilty later. His illness took us all by surprise. Although my father's now in his seventies, he still runs the market garden and is an anchor for the whole family."

Her father's episode of illness also triggered in her mind thoughts about the importance in her life of her family attachments. Her father's selfless behavior, and her love for him, stood in stark contrast to the anger and irritation that she felt upon JP's "disloyal retreat" when the errors in the corporate charter were discovered. Thus, deep down, Kim had already begun questioning the purpose and meaning of her life as a lawyer before the panic episodes manifested themselves. After ten years in her chosen profession, she was discovering the hidden costs—the fierce rivalry, the lack of loyalty, the greed, and the treadmill-like existence—of the driven corporate world. But Kim was conflicted. On the other side of the ledger were the assets of that life—the money, the security, the excitement, and the social prestige—that compelled her forward despite the stress. "I worry that I don't have enough money to stop yet," Kim told me. "Sometimes my concerns about money feel like an addiction. If I really want to fly off to Hawaii for the weekend, I can. But, of course, I never do. So the freedom that I believe money gives me is only there in fantasy. Also in my professional circle, money defines the social hierarchy. I'm fearful that without a high income—without the security of money—I will be diminished, that somehow my social status will erode."

"ONCE YOU'RE on the treadmill in a competitive organization it's not easy to quit," Bystritsky had told me during our conversation. "Kim's dilemma is commonplace. Human beings, like all primates, are sensitive particularly to changes in social rank. Even for those who *choose* to step aside from a demanding position, there's a sense of failure. In fact, the social criticism is overt. The rumor goes around that the guy couldn't make it: that he crashed. Even when changing jobs within a corporation, this sometimes happens. So in fear of losing face, the individual does nothing. The treadmill runs faster and the stress increases, until some decisive event occurs and the alarm bells sound. Then the anxiety breaks through, as in Kim's case, or illness intervenes."

Humans, by choice, live in hierarchically organized social groups. As Kim described in her struggles with JP, competition and tests of endurance are the means through which such social hierarchies develop and are maintained. It's an experience that begins early in life. Initially it is the parents who keep the child's needs in balance with those of the siblings and of the parents. Self-interest is innate and universal in human interaction—and nonreciprocal altruism is rare—but with practice and parental oversight complex social behaviors of dominance and submission become ingrained. Also through these experiences are built the secondary emotions of pride and shame—in distinction to the primary emotions of fear, anger, joy, and attachment—that become the powerful modifiers of self-interest and social interaction in adult life. Once in place, a stable social ranking within the family, or a group, facilitates cooperative behavior among members—who individually would be of unequal strength and have limited access to resources—thus blunting individual greed and facilitating the survival of all.

However, the key to an individual achieving this cooperative advantage is the *stability and cohesion* of the social group to which they belong. Hence when JP became angry and withdrew his support of Kim, she felt suddenly alone and forced to rely on her own resources. That the confrontation was close in time to her father's illness compounded the stress. The stability of the two social hierarchies that she had long taken for granted—that of her family and that organized around her special relationship with JP and his team—had been called into question. In fact, in the time-pressured bustle of America's workplace, Kim's denouement with JP is an example of an increasingly common occurrence.

In America's demand-based and time-driven commercial world, competition is replacing collaboration and social concern. The self-serving celebrity, with the "winner-takes-all" mind-set of JP Moran, is replacing the generative leader, as might be exemplified by the humanitarian posture of Kim's father. It is a shift that offers significant commercial advantage, as is apparent in America's global dominance. But it also has the drawback of fostering personal greed—as was evident in the wake of the telecommunications bubble—and of generating stress and anxiety by eroding the bonds of mutual support and social sentiment (to return to the familiar phrasing of Adam Smith) that are essential to human happiness.

As Robert Putnam has detailed in *Bowling Alone*, his analysis of the social habits of contemporary Americans, during the last decades of the twentieth century there was a marked shift away from civic and social engagement—be that with a political party, the church, the Parent Teachers Association, or even the family—toward the pursuit of individual self-interest. In contemporary American culture we now introduce children to stress and competition at an early age. The responsibility for providing education in socialization and family life, however, is all too commonly delegated to a time-starved, overworked single parent. Competition at all levels and all ages has become a key school agenda. As a result, many children are overscheduled and chronically fatigued with too few hours in bed and truncated sleep, leaving too little time for the complex task of nurturing individual curiosity and the development of collaborative social skills.

In Alexander Bystritsky's opinion this cultural shift, if it is sustained, portends a new generation of highly competitive but socially inept Americans. The growing social ineptitude has been facilitated, he believes, by the growth of a virtual world that, despite its electronic "connectedness," in reality increases isolation and social unease. A fast typist working on a computer keyboard can hold a conversation with somebody across the globe that he or she is unlikely ever to meet. The World Wide Web is a form of intimate communication, but it provides little practice at social interaction with real people or in the development of broader social skills. While during the bubble years the Internet provided upward social mobility through the commercial system for many young people, its cultural contribution is a pseudoreality of virtual social groups and narrow technical competence. "So I believe it is for complex reasons that anxiety and social phobia are rising in America," Bystritsky told me. "On the one hand, the traditional strength of the family and of the communities in which we once learned social skills has been diminished, while on the other, in our blind technical genius, we have created an electronic world that is depersonalized and driven by commercial competition."

"Freedom and happiness are delicate things," Bystritsky continued, "and the pendulum may have swung too far in the laissez-faire direction. When it comes to finding the right balance, unbridled competition in a migrant culture of inherently poor social cohesion can be as stifling to a sense of individual freedom and to happiness as is social rigidity."

As an émigré from the Soviet Union, Bystritsky has experienced the extremes of the pendulum's swing. Before glasnost, Bystritsky had gained a reputation as a satirical poet and lyricist. He first discovered his talent as a medical student when working in student theater, but as his reputation grew, the critical nature of his satire soon gave him greater visibility than was healthy in Russia at the time. Hence, despite winning a national medal in science, he was denied his dream of a Ph.D. in pharmacology and of studying to become a psychiatrist. Such were the circumstances leading to his migration.

"In many European societies and certainly in Russia, where freedom and mobility until recently were not options, life was simpler," Bystritsky reflected. "Everybody knew the rules of engagement. You were going to take over your father's store, the marketplace was essentially the local village, and everybody knew what would happen. Thus, if you avoided trouble, you enjoyed a stable, fruitful life, and if you fell into conflict with the elders, you moved on to the next village. However, if you chose to stay, society expected no less of you, and no more of you, than was socially defined by the position of your family in the social hierarchy. Your freedoms were determined by family tradition. For some of us that was stifling but for the majority life was rigid, simple, and stable.

"By contrast, in America's migrant culture everything is unstable and socially mobile," Bystritsky continued. "When I arrived here from Russia, the foremost feeling I had was one of freedom. That happened in an instant, but I soon realized that cultural expectations still exist. They're different, but from the standpoint of personal choice they can be similarly constraining. The whole point of coming to America is to compete as an individual, not to perform in relation to the expectations of your family or of the community. The open expectation is that everyone will compete and seek independence. To stand aside is considered aberrant. That's the migrant impulse expressed in its rigid cultural maturity. You move out of the family complex when you're eighteen, you often pay for your own education, and it is the cultural expectation that you will succeed financially, move beyond the social position of your parents, and pay back later. That's what the Carnegies, the Morgans, and the Vanderbilts were all about—and what Bill Gates is about today. That's the American model."

In America, Bystritsky had observed, the responsibility of living life to its fullest is both a privilege and a burden. The upward social mobility that is integral to the American model explicitly promises increased material well-being to each new generation, but achieving that prosperity is necessarily associated with considerable competition and chronic stress, which some individuals prefer to avoid. As the merchant has become dominant in American society, however, and as measures of personal achievement alternative to money have declined in social significance, the options for standing aside from the "mad race to riches" have diminished. In America it is the cultural imperative that one strives to maximize one's financial success (something that for many migrants is America's most exciting challenge). But the reverse is also true: potentially all achievement can be improved upon, given resolve and greater effort. Thus America's cultural message is simultaneously both positive and negative. Success is a relative construct. Prosperity's pursuit demands a single-minded, lifelong commitment. In the promised land, enough is never enough.

It is this competitive quest for prosperity that drives America's insatiable appetite for time. As the commercial demands of the Fast New World increase, so does our hunger for time. To feed that hunger, as did Kim Phan, we chip away at sleep and at our social and family investments, until the alarm bell rings and we wake to discover that work has become synonymous with life. Then there are decisions to be made. Some modify their pursuit, hoping to find a new balance that is meaningful to them, while others continue their climb toward the illusory relief of some distant plateau, when all will be accomplished. Fortunately for the latter group, medicine now has the tools to modify the ancient alarm, to turn the system down. There are advantages and disadvantages to such a plan. Anybody who experiences panic can now receive a prescription for an SSRI (a selective serotonin reuptake inhibitor) that quiets the bells and potentially offers a fresh platform for performance. Daily function may improve but questions remain: In our helter-skelter pursuit are we creating our own market for psychotropic drugs? In the absence of taking steps to buffer the stress and strain of the Fast New World, is merely resetting the threshold of our ancient alarms a sensible long-term strategy?

It is in keeping with the imperial nature of human self-deception that we seek to ignore the persistent biological tether that marks our evolution. But the instinctual mechanisms of survival—for self-preservation, for kinship, and for social intimacy—still shape the meaning of human existence today, much as they did for our ancestors one hundred thousand years ago. We may choose to override these adaptive human instincts to better exploit the opportunities presented by our technologically advanced society, but it is a difficult path, and for those unaware, there comes a day of reckoning, for ultimately it is the affections of kinship and family that give meaning to existence.

"It's a time trade," Kim had said to me at one of our later meetings. "I see that now. I have traded my personal and family time for affluence and financial security. The anxiety was just a warning, and now I must decide. Is the dream I'm living no more than a Disney roller-coaster ride for adults?" Kim had waved her hand at the office window, drawing my attention to the sunshine beyond. "Look at this land. How wonderful it is. America has given me everything that I hoped for, and more. I dreamed in Vietnam of survival but never that I would be a successful international attorney closing deals worth billions of dollars." She looked back at me and smiled. "Now the question in my mind is whether I can survive the American dream, whether I'm equipped for the Darwinian existence that I have chosen. That's the ultimate irony, isn't it."

PART III

MORE IS NOT ENOUGH: PROSPERITY RECONSIDERED

I listened and marveled at the feebleness of human reason.
I was poor, and now, look, I am rich: if only prosperity, while
affecting my conduct, would leave my judgment free.

Alexis de Tocqueville
Democracy in America, 1835

Chapter Seven

DREAMS FOR SALE: OF CULTURE AND COMMERCE

The dream lives on, promising so much in the matter of American living. It also threatens to become an anti-dream, an American nightmare. Memory, then, must come to our aid; for while the recovery of the past can traumatize, it can also heal. A culture failing to internalize some understanding of its past . . . has no focus on the promise and dangers of the present.

Kevin Starr
Americans and the California Dream 1850–1915, 1973

TO PROSPER, THE DICTIONARY tells us, is to flourish, to thrive, to enjoy good fortune and well-being. Just how that well-being is realized, however, varies among individuals and between cultures. That freedom, tolerance, equality, and justice in human affairs are fundamental to prosperity is generally agreed. Americans, long privileged to live in a democracy dedicated to the defense of such liberties, look beyond these elemental assurances to other definitions. When it comes to prosperity, true to the migrant heritage, Americans are dreamers.

The American dream is unique in contemporary culture. While the American Constitution is grounded in the Enlightenment and draws on a faith in human reason, the American dream is part of the émigré package, integral to the never-ending search for El Dorado. Kim Phan had dreams, as do each of us and doubtlessly all other people in the world, but no culture has institutionalized the dream as the guiding vision for social progress as America has done. The predominant imagery of the dream has shifted as the national identity has evolved—a Christian commonwealth embracing a biblical vision of heaven on earth; the claims of manifest destiny that drove America's western expansion and conquest; Martin Luther King's enduring dream of equality for all citizens; and an unfolding strategy for global leadership, built on military and commercial hegemony—but throughout the decades the dream's unswerving message has been for America to grasp the future as its own and to make it prosperous.

In this Utopian journey, technological advance has been America's consistent and reliable companion. It is a visceral union. In novel technology the American instinctively sees the challenge of a new frontier, and smells too the commercial opportunity that such challenge may afford. Thus for the American dreamer, technology and the marketplace are inextricably intertwined with prosperity and social progress.

"The American," Alexis de Tocqueville observed during his visit in 1831, "lives in a land of wonders; in his mind the idea of newness is closely linked with that of advancement. Nowhere does he see any limit placed by nature on human endeavor." But with our invention of the Fast New World we have learned that there are limits—within the mortal self. In 1831, before the ruminations of Charles Darwin instructed us to the contrary, mankind was considered sovereign among God's creations. Today, regardless of one's views—creationist or otherwise—that we overlap in our biology with other creatures and are yoked in our physiology to the experience of our forebears on this planet is irrefutable. We may choose to ignore evidence of melting polar ice caps, diminishing supplies of clean water, and holes in the ozone layer, deeming them the preoccupation of cranks or harmless environmental shifts within a larger planetary cycle. But it is difficult to deny the accumulating data indicating that America's manic pursuit, and the frenzied life we lead every day, are damaging to individual and civic health.

The evidence is now clear. The examples that I presented in Part II of this book—that an overindulgence in self and celebrity seeds greed and social mania, that a reduction in exercise and a high-calorie diet seeds obesity, and that time-hunger and demand-driven environments seed anxiety—confirm a growing mismatch in American life between who we are as evolved creatures and the social environment that we have built for ourselves. As a nation driven by the workaholic migrant temperament, we have discovered first what those who live in other industrialized nations are just beginning to learn: when it comes to technical innovation, human ingenuity is capable of building environments that are so addictive to our ancient instinct for self-reward that we can make ourselves sick—pushing the physiology of mind and body to the limits of its tolerance, and beyond. This is the American paradox—the paradox of prosperity.

Today America's guiding images are predominantly concerned with commercial dominance, focused through the powerful lenses of technology and the international marketplace. Guided by this vision of the future, in our consumer culture prosperity and material wealth have achieved compelling equivalence. But does that equivalence embrace the broader definitions of the prosperity that enables a society to flourish and the individual to thrive? Do America's guiding images now deceive? Our paradoxical experience of prosperity has begun to raise questions in the minds of many Americans. Does the growing personal strain of life in the Fast New World portend a disruption in America's social fabric that threatens to erode the human capital on which the future vitality of our nation depends? Is our preoccupation in the global marketplace with selling our own particular brand of turbocapitalism, at any cost, distorting America's cultural image in the eyes of other nations? In our commercial success have we achieved what the Founding Fathers had in mind as the New Order of the Ages, and if so, why are many citizens anxious and unhappy? These and similar questions now abound.

Momentarily the future vision of this great nation has become clouded, but for many Americans one thing is crystal clear: seeking more of what we have is not enough.

So what is to be done? To refocus our vision and to revitalize the American dream, I believe we must revisit the fundamental question: what does it take for civil society to thrive? Alone, neither technology nor commerce can provide a guiding philosophy through which a complex society can live and prosper. While markets are essential to a vibrant culture, channeling as they do self-interest and envy toward the common human need, not all human needs flow through the marketplace. Markets are tools just as technology is a tool. Their purpose is to serve prosperity, not to be its embodiment. The history of technology and of its market application is littered with examples of unintended consequence. So we must ask, what is it that we seek with our innovative technologies? How is the Fast New World changing traditional market practice? How as individuals can we learn to live in harmony with those changes? And how can we in our collective wisdom, knowing what we now know about neurobiology and human behavior, restructure our commercial enterprise to foster a prosperous and balanced civil order that will better sustain the health and happiness of all Americans? These are some of the questions that I will explore in the three remaining chapters of this book.

I BEGIN MY exploration by seeking to understand American commerce from a European perspective. There is much we can learn about ourselves from the opinions of others. Europeans have always been mixed in their feelings toward America, and particularly so since the United States emerged as the world's only superpower. After September 11, 2001, when terrorist attacks violently inducted Americans into ordinary membership among the world's peoples, there was a unified outpouring of sympathy, but it did not last. With each demonstration of U.S. power—be that the flaunting of international agreements on nuclear arms and greenhouse gases, impatience with the deliberations of the United Nations in international affairs, or the penetration of American entrepreneurship ever deeper into other cultures—the accusations of arrogance and commercial hegemony increased until the Iraq crisis and the war that followed, during 2003, when they were at their height. But it would be a mistake to accept this acrimony at face value, for Europe is not monolithic. Significant differences of opinion—both positive and negative—exist among European nations toward America and American culture, and they are informative.

So I was to learn firsthand during the summer of 1999 when I visited Poznań, Poland, at the invitation of Professor Janusz Rybakowski of the Karol Marcinkowski University. Centered on a great slab of alluvial plain fed by a knot of mighty rivers rolling to the Baltic Sea, the city of Poznań has been an enclave of trade and agriculture since medieval times. It was in the tenth century, on the banks of the Warta River, that the Polan tribes first forged a dominion that would become the sovereign state of Poland. Unfortunately, as the history of the region affirms, it is a landscape equally suited to the marching of armies as to the growing of crops. The story of the Polish people is one of upheaval and struggle— beset by Slavians to the East and Teutons to the West—and it has been erased from the map more than once by those hungry, powerful neighbors. But Poland's story is also one of freedom and triumph, and it was the persistent solidarity of the Polish people that ultimately helped penetrate, in 1989, the rusting armor of Soviet Communism.

My visit to Poznań coincided with the tenth anniversary of the free elections that had returned democracy to Poland and cleared the way to the opening of the Berlin Wall just three months later. The visit coincided too with the final days of a glorious summer. For three weeks there had been no rain in Poznań, despite it being early September. This was unheard of and seen as good fortune, for under bright skies and fluffy clouds an abundant harvest was near completion. So on the Sunday that I first took my jet-age ritual exercise of a morning run, I found a city dozing contentedly amid a quilt of brightly colored fields.

I find an old pair of running shoes indispensable to time-zone travel. When I first arrive in some distant place, the virtual world of laptop and cell phone is not for me. Without physical exercise to recalibrate the clocks of my bewildered brain, such nomadic tools are but discomforting reminders of a fogged intelligence. Rather my interest lies in exploring the surroundings. In the early morning light, as the muscles stretch with a run through quiet streets, so does my mind relax. The route from my hotel into the old town that Sunday morning took me across Ostrów Tumski, or Cathedral Island, a little finger of land between the Warta and Cybina Rivers. There, it seemed, stood the whole history of Christian Poland, a land where ninety percent of the population attend church each week. The bishop's palace, a monastery, the Church of the Holy Virgin, the tombs of kings, and the Gothic basilica of the cathedral itself—the first stones of which were laid in 968—established this little peninsula, Professor Rybakowski had informed me, as the oldest place of worship in Catholic Poland.

The timing of my run could have been better. Mass must have ended just as I approached the cathedral precinct, for suddenly the great doors were flung open and immediately I was caught up in a vigorous stream of communicants heading for their breakfast. Feeling self-conscious, I broke from the path and headed for the trees, only to find myself pursued by half a dozen laughing teenage boys, each dressed in T-shirt, jeans, and baseball cap. "American, American," they shouted, obviously finding something hysterically funny. I grinned and nodded, hoping that running shorts were acceptable attire within the sanctity of Cathedral Island. Then one boy pulled ahead, and after slapping his shoes as he ran—a trick remarkable in the agility it displayed—he pointed eagerly to my feet. Finally I understood. We were all wearing the same brand of sneakers.

Sneakers, jeans, and baseball caps were not the only emblems of Pax Americana that I was to encounter on my run through Poznań that Sunday morning. Once I started paying attention, the symbols of American marketing began popping up everywhere. One particularly memorable image appeared only minutes after my encounter at the cathedral. Crossing the Warta bridge, with the spires of the city ahead, my eye was drawn to a beautiful mural, painted in brown and sepia tones on the side of a massive warehouse that overlooked the river. It could be seen from a considerable distance and depicted the skyline of Poznań as the city must have been before the destructive power of tanks and artillery, during the battles of World War II, permanently scarred its medieval face. My immediate attention, however, was drawn not to the spire of some ancient church, but to the bright red moon that rose majestically above it. Further yet, I realized as I drew closer, it was not the moon itself that had focused my attention but the image of the Coca-Cola bottle that stood within it. Such is the power of the familiar symbol when we are first in strange surroundings.

For Americans who travel abroad, experiences such as mine in Poznań are commonplace. Beginning in the decade of the 1990s, following the collapse of the Soviet Union and China's doctrinal embrace of market economics, American commerce has rapidly extended its global reach to penetrate some of the world's most remote and sacred places. Even in Beijing's ancient Forbidden City, the 5 million Chinese who each year enter the Palace of Heavenly Purity must now pass the brand logo of Starbucks coffee. American fresh-glazed donuts and decaf lattes have established themselves at the symbolic center of the tea-drinking universe. Such American icons—with Coca-Cola, McDonald's, and Disney being the leaders—are a familiar part of urban landscapes across the world. America has become synonymous in many countries with a universal, youth-driven, "pop" culture of Hollywood blockbusters, the Internet, Nike sneakers, and music video. And for many Europeans on the receiving end of this hegemony, the coming of a McDonald's restaurant represents the Trojan horse of America's insidious commercial imperialism.

Not so in Poland.

"In Poland we love all things American," said my student guide, Jaroslaw Majchrzak, later that afternoon when I described to him the cathedral incident. "What many young people wear are not real American clothes, for they are expensive and much prized, but good imitations." Most Poles see commercial sponsorship in a positive light—as evidence of their new democracy, rather than as a symbol of cynical mercantile exploitation—and thus corporate logos appear everywhere. Theater productions, classical music concerts, and other major cultural events proudly sport brand names. During my week in Poznań the majority of the movies I saw advertised were American movies, the music in the restaurants was American music, and every young person I met spoke near-perfect English. Fast food had become the "in thing." Three years earlier, after the American Consulate closed for "lack of money," the five McDonald's restaurants then in the city—a new McDonald's was opening somewhere in Poland every week—were endearingly nicknamed the "U.S. embassies."

Many Poles consider laissez-faire economics to be the ultimate declaration of freedom and take a triumphalist view of America's commercial display. Some believe that without the American-led globalization of commerce, perestroika and the roundtable discussions that led to free elections in Poland might never have succeeded. In the struggle for freedom, Solidarity used leaflets and books. There were no other weapons. Many took to the streets after witnessing peaceful demonstrations on television or listening to the radio. In the end bloodshed was avoided and vital liberties were restored to Poland and other Eastern European countries largely because the Soviet-backed regimes could not stand apart from the scrutiny of the multimedia and the material success of the market-based economies.

Thus, when George W. Bush made his first trip to Europe as America's president in June 2001, he pointedly stopped in Warsaw to praise the new capitalist spirit of the Polish people. In fact, in Poland, entrepreneurship had never been completely stamped out. The private sector had always accounted for 5 to 10 percent of economic activity, even during the communist years, and at the millennium there were more than 2 million registered businesses in Poland—one for every nineteen people. During the 1990s Poland had managed to avoid the recessions that plagued most of its central European neighbors and had acquired the reputation of being an "eagle" economy, with an average growth rate of over 5 percent a year. However, with imports outstripping exports, and with heavy corporate borrowing, the national debt was growing too. Nonetheless it had been a decade of great strides: infant mortality dropped, life expectancy rose, and the freedom to pursue individual initiative returned. The resurgence was clearly evident, even during my brief visit, from the number of new cars on the street, from the elegance of the citizenry, and from the extensive construction and refurbishing in the old town. Trade was flourishing again in Poznań, a city that in its medieval past had been at the hub of the commerce between Western Europe and Russia.

For Jaroslaw Majchrzak, and other young liberally minded Poles, the changes have brought excitement about their nation's future. After joining the European Union, I was told, Poland would strengthen ties with America, which has some 10 million citizens of Polish origin. But as Jaroslaw also had been eager to explain, his youthful passion for America should not mislead me. Poland's move to a free-market economy had not been all wine and roses. The sentiment for America was found largely in the cities. Fast food and trendy boutiques were rare in the countryside, where most Poles still lived and where horse-drawn carts could still outnumber cars. Although agriculture employed one-fifth of the national workforce, it accounted for only 4 percent of the gross national product and wages had fallen steadily for many rural workers. This had created what Jaroslaw described as an "elbow" society, where the commercially successful pushed aside the weak.

With the growing gap between rich and poor, and an insecurity of employment, many individuals, especially older persons, had begun to question the loss of a predictable order. Whereas under communism, poverty in Poland had been masked by rigid uniformity, its presence now stood evident. The surge in free-market capitalism has been devastating for many older persons attempting to survive on the equivalent of $200 a month (but with the cost of essential goods, now driven by the market, little different from the rest of Europe). A generation gap had been opened, and it was bitterly equated by some with the "Americanization" of Polish life. In the flush of liberty, social promises had been made but not kept. Such opinions troubled Jaroslaw. "Like America's revolution, ours was for freedom and a set of principles, not for a paradise," he suggested. "I accept commercial sponsorship because free trade is indivisible from a thriving democracy. For me, it's an American dream come true."

THE SIMPLE logic that freedom of choice in the marketplace is equivalent to democracy is a compelling message in Poland and other East European countries—the "New Europe"—where precious freedoms have only recently been retrieved. In the "old" European nations, however, longer established and more comfortable in their democratic ways, the invasion of the American merchants is viewed with suspicion by a growing number of activist citizens. Thus in the opinion of José Bové—the charismatic French sheep farmer who came to international attention during the summer of 1999 when he led the "deconstruction" of a McDonald's being built in his hometown—global commerce is not about democracy but about money. The international markets, Bové believes, are biased in favor of the massive financial resources of American corporations that are greedily intent on increasing their profits. Whereas democracy strives for one person–one vote, with globalization the operating reality has become one dollar–one vote.

To José Bové and the protagonists of this worldview, McDonald's is typical of American companies indulging a maniacal drive for global commercial domination under the banner of market freedom. In 2001, the McDonald's Corporation—the "largest and best known global food service retailer," as the company advertises itself—operated over 29,000 restaurants worldwide, more than double the number that had been in service only eight years earlier. (In Poland alone, in the five years between 1993 and 1998, the number of McDonald's restaurants increased from 10 to 130.) In keeping with the company's policy of international expansion as the key to greater profit—between 1996 and 2000 McDonald's delivered a total return on capital of 69 percent—this growth in new restaurants had occurred predominantly outside the United States. The "golden arches" have now established themselves in approximately 120 countries, with over $36 billion in worldwide sales. Indeed, McDonald's is so well entrenched across the globe that in 1986 the *Economist* magazine began using the price of a Big Mac hamburger as an index of relative value for the world's major currencies.

In the summer of 1999 McDonald's steamrollering globalization had arrived in José Bové's hometown of Millau, in the Aveyron region of southern France. As a sheep farmer, Bové had long considered McDonald's symbolic of an American fast-food invasion that threatened, one day, to force local merchants and small farmers, such as he, out of business. But now, as part of a larger squabble, that threat had become a reality. A refusal by the French to buy genetically modified American crops and hormone-fed beef had resulted in an American Customs surcharge—supported by the World Trade Organization (WTO)—that doubled the import cost of French luxury goods to the American market, including Roquefort cheese. Roquefort production is centered in the Aveyron region, and because the cheese is made from ewe's milk, the new U.S. import tariff threatened the livelihood of many local farmers and residents. The professional association of Roquefort producers lobbied the Ministry of Agriculture. It was to no avail: nothing could be done. France was powerless. And to add insult to injury, a new McDonald's was under construction in the heart of Millau. It was under these circumstances, in early August and just a few weeks prior to my visit to Poland, that the rising frustrations of José Bové and his fellow farmers finally bubbled over.

"Le mal bouffe" (lousy grub) became the rallying cry for a series of protests against McDonald's and the profiteers who dared flaunt the agrarian economy of French rural life. France, whose culture gave much to the founding of the United States, takes pride in being the embodiment of democracy. And in the exercise of that democracy, the French people have the right to eat any meat they choose, argued Bové, without being bullied by the market dominance of a handful of international junk-food chains that reduce personal choice in the local marketplace and threaten the liberty of livelihood.

In fact, America's commercial hegemony extends well beyond the food industry. The biggest U.S. exports are entertainment and brand marketing—based in California and New York, the home states of Hollywood and Madison Avenue—and these media now shape America's image in the farthest corners of the globe. The world's most popular television program, for example, is *Baywatch*, a surfing soap opera set in Los Angeles. America overwhelmingly controls the film market in Europe and would dominate television in France but for legislation dictating that 40 percent of TV programming must be domestic. Similarly, in January 2000, of the top 40 percent of companies traded on the Paris stock exchange, an average of 35 percent of the stock was held by American and British investors, suggesting to some that the Anglo-American drive for international free trade now imperils the individual liberty of the French nation. Amid growing public alarm that American values and American money are swamping France, even members of the French government have begun to speak of defending the national interest to preserve that which is distinctly and idiosyncratically French.

So what is it that the French wish to preserve? Can we learn something to our own advantage by better understanding their concerns about American culture and our commercial practice? As many French men and women see it, America's society is unabashedly materialistic, competitive, and commercially driven. It seduces through the power of marketing and the promise of pleasure, creating a mass culture of uniform style based on desire and ambition. The disquiet is not whether the French should be free to eat McDonald's hamburgers, watch blockbuster movies, or buy T-shirts from the Gap. As the fifth largest trader of goods and services in the world and a nation visited by more tourists than any other country, France is firmly in support of globalization. Rather the fear is that the financial dominance of the large multinational corporations will squeeze out local entrepreneurs, creating a lifestyle that depends on wage earnings from centralized "industrial" conglomerates rather than from community-based economies. Because such centralized monopolies are faceless and anonymous, the argument goes, they are destructive of a civil society—defined as a stable human community based on collaboration and mutual caring—replacing it with the competitive law of the jungle, where the biggest and most powerful dominate. Individual cooperation and creativity—the foundation of artistic expression, craftsmanship, and local market-based economies—are devalued in favor of mass production, shifting the cultural emphasis away from individual preference toward what Alexis de Tocqueville described as "an imperfect substitute" designed for a broad audience.

A poll taken in France in the year 2000 found that only 12 percent of respondents admire the United States, and that 46 percent are either critical or worried about its global intentions, with the overwhelming majority of those citizens surveyed (75 percent) wanting less American influence on the world's economic and financial affairs. While there are sour grapes here (French political opinion having lost out on occasion to the English-speaking world in international matters), such opinion polls should not be dismissed out of hand. The French know how to enjoy life. In another recent national survey, the declared rates of personal happiness with life in the French Republic, for both men and women, topped 90 percent and are the highest in Europe.

But even in the French mind there is ambivalence about the encroachment of American cultural values. The young, who believe in technology and the cross-cultural power of the Fast New World, find a seductive lure in the American invasion. And the French like hamburgers too. Even with the protests of José Bové and others, the number of McDonald's outlets in France continues to expand, reaping profits for their local owners in addition to the parent corporation. No Frenchman has ever been forced to buy a Big Mac. Nor have families been hijacked and taken at gunpoint to EuroDisney, the theme park just outside Paris. Despite a shaky start, Mickey and Minnie have learned the local language and the doors of the Magic Kingdom remain open, offering a warm welcome to dreamers of all ages.

The ambivalence in the French mind is not about the liberty of choice in France today. Rather it reflects the larger international debate about whether "Americanization" and the mass-marketing techniques of America's aggressive commercialism will confine future choice, distorting the preference of indigenous cultures. In large part, where you end up in that debate depends on where you begin. For the Poles, only recently released from the refrigerator of central planning, the return of the open market and an influx of branded goods provide welcome evidence of new freedoms and choice. In France, a seasoned multiparty social democracy where coalition and compromise are the norm, the invasion of American mass-marketing techniques is seen as diminishing choice by destroying local markets and individual initiative. In both instances, individual liberty is equated with the subjective desire of the consumer, but the assumptions made in reaching that conclusion are quite different. In the French mind, mass marketing where choice is distorted by intense commercial pressure aimed at expanding the customer base and increasing the profit margin is held distinct from commercial activity offering free individual choice to the consumer within a local market culture. It is the viability of these local economies—in the belief that they are the foundation of community life—that the French wish to preserve.

SO, ONE may ask, what explains the worldwide appeal of American mass-marketing techniques? Why do the French continue to buy Big Macs and to visit EuroDisney despite these national sentiments? The answer is a revalidation of Adam Smith—dressed now in baseball cap and jeans—and his insights into human instinctual behavior. The international juggernaut of America's commercial expansion is indifferent to the whims of democracy because it has discovered something universal and more powerful. Hollywood and Madison Avenue are tapping into a common human preference. While it is commercial dominance that drives the expansion of American "pop" culture across the world, it is also true that a majority of humans find the goods being sold attractive. Thus my Polish friends were correct when they suggested that it was not just a hunger for democracy but also the desire for consumer goods—for East Europeans to participate in the celebrated American freedom of shopping—that finally broke the Soviet hold. The success of pop culture in the global marketplace is founded on the same ancient reward-driven instincts of survival that Adam Smith rationalized in his economic thesis. The innate drives of curiosity and material self-interest remain ubiquitous, insatiable, and irrepressible.

It is no accident that Coca-Cola, McDonald's, and Disney are most identified with American pop culture across the globe, for they are each pioneers in the art of expanding consumer markets through the "branding" of instinctual desire and fantasy fulfillment. Classic Coca-Cola exploits the ancient human craving for stimulants (once cocaine, now caffeine), sugar, and spice (nutmeg) in its secret formula, promoted with advertising campaigns of youthful vigor and images of the good times. As a spokesman has unabashedly described the company's strategy, it is to put "soft drinks within arm's reach of desire." McDonald's similarly services primal craving, selling meat, fat, and salt under a branded name. It defends that name with consistency of product, "family fun," and lawyers if necessary, marketing particularly to children through Ronald McDonald House charities, clowns, playgrounds, cartoon characters, and those special golden arches.

Indeed, there is a peculiar euphoria associated with the fast-food experience. What Henry Ford did for the development of the cheap automobile, McDonald's has done for the restaurant. McDonald's has industrialized eating. Fast food, originally intended to mean fast service, has come to mean fast eating. McDonald's symbolizes speed. Fast food is designed to accommodate the Fast New World, where work is central. The average time spent in a fast-food restaurant in America is eleven minutes. Similarly, McDonald's insistence on clean kitchens and bathrooms has made it a symbol of purity throughout the world, and because of this high standard of hygiene, in many countries fast food is believed to be extremely healthy, more so than the local diet.

The consistency of the product denies reality. In the international fast-food business McDonald's is the legendary benchmark of standardization, ensuring that a Big Mac will taste exactly the same in Moscow as it does in Chicago. The hamburgers are uniform, a mere shadow of the original meat, just as José Bové has protested. Chicken McNuggets have neither the bones nor the skin of the original bird. The food is, as suggests Jean Baudrillard, the French philosopher of postmodernism, a *simulation* designed to reassure (while offering, of course, those essential ingredients of fat, salt, and sugar that were so coveted in our primitive past). Other American fast-food chains strive for similar consistency in their branding and marketing themes. Arthur Teacher's Fish and Chips is modeled on the Hollywood image of an English butler. Roy Rogers offers a restaurant that is a simulation of the cowboy's ranch house, as conceived in the golden age of the western film. In their successful serving up of pop American culture, fast-food restaurants have something in common with theme parks and malls. The goal is not only to satisfy hunger but also to entertain and reassure. Fast food has dreams for sale.

It is no surprise to learn that McDonald's and Coca-Cola have close business ties to Disney, the master of mass fantasy. Behind the union is the simple corporate strategy of doing what each company does best while collaborating to maintain global dominance. When McDonald's employees from around the world gather for their biannual convention, they often do so at Disney World in Florida. And Coca-Cola, as the sole vender of soft drinks at the Disney theme parks since 1955, provides the colas. In turn, Disney films—selling the dream come true—are promoted through McDonald's restaurants. Together these icons of American pop culture are selling reassurance and comfort in a stressful world—moments of fantasy in a friendly, tidy place where everything works as it should, where there are tasty things to eat and drink, and where happiness prevails.

Walt Disney remains the unrivaled architect of the reassuring fantasy. In his work as a Hollywood animator, Disney had studied what pleased people, and how reality could be molded to create the perfect place. An important prototype for Disneyland's Main Street U.S.A., which was then duplicated in the Disney theme parks built later in Florida, Tokyo, and Paris, was the midwestern town of Marceline, Missouri, where Disney spent much of his childhood. Everything about Disney's Main Street U.S.A. is harmonious. Although essentially the imitation of a suburban strip mall, it is not the familiar American commercial environment where individual merchants compete with neon signage for the attention of the citizen. No, this is America's fantasy of the perfect small community. On Main Street everything blends. Learning from his passion for model trains, Disney scaled back the buildings to be about five-eighths of their original size, thus giving a sense of intimacy, and peopled the village with characters from his animated films—Mickey Mouse, Minnie, Pinocchio, and Donald Duck—together with an army of smiling and energetic young people to aid the visitor. The Disney theme park also does something clever with time. The wristwatch, which stands witness to our enslavement by the manic society, becomes irrelevant. In Disneyland, time is dissolved. One does not live in the present, but either in the "simpler" past of frontier America or amid the expanding technology of Tomorrowland. The manic excitement of contemporary society is under one's personal control. The rewards of speed and the kinesthetic thrills of the roller coaster (necessary to offset mental boredom, another terror of the human species) are readily available but last only for a moment. The resulting world of Disney is manageable, comfortable, and pleasant; a place sweeter, gentler, and more appealing than is real life; a neighborly place where your dreams come true.

Disney's technology provides the antidote to the technical ingenuity that has built the Fast New World and quickened our lives. But the enormous success of Disney imagery across the world also ties back to the human fascination with novelty and a search for reassurance and happiness that long antedates the American dream. The carefully planned Chinese cities of dynastic times, the botanical gardens and great parks of entertainment built by European princes during the Renaissance and the Enlightenment—each in their own way were forerunners of the contemporary American theme park. Descartes, Montaigne, and the eminent philosophers of the age were enthralled by the toys they found in Tuscany, and later at Versailles, where Louis XIV amused his courtiers with gondolas, goldfish ponds, pulsating fountains, and an assortment of mechanical objects capable of surprise effects. His engineers, employing the new science of hydraulics, constructed animated birds, beasts, and even human figures for the amusement of the

Sun King's distinguished guests. Today's equivalent is the Disney Imagineering Workshop in Glendale, a sedate suburb of Los Angeles. There, some two thousand mechanics, designers, artists, architects, technicians, craftsmen, and sculptors—including the boffins who designed the interior of the Encounter Restaurant at the LA airport—work continuously to create the future of recreational reassurance. In constructing his parks, Louis XIV pursued the theme of paradise, drawing on the biblical constructs of Eden. But that was before Walt Disney imagined Mickey and Minnie Mouse, the couple destined to become the hosts to "the Happiest Place on Earth." For that achievement, Disney was named in 1936 to the French Legion of Honor, as the creator of "a new art form in which good is spread throughout the world."

Today that award might be considered ironic, given the anti-American sentiment that exists in France, and it is. What Disney had invented was not only the animated cartoon for which he received the award, but also the mass servicing of individual need as the insignia of a consumer society. When it comes to making people smile, Disney knew what he was about. Disney enterprises, in going just a little bit further in meeting the customer's desire, have made *Disney* one of the most powerful brand names on the planet. This attendance upon attracting and pleasing a mass customer base is the philosophy that McDonald's, Coca-Cola, Levi Strauss, Gap, Amazon.com, and the new Internet companies now emulate in their self-promotion. These American corporations have built a global market for themselves that transcends culture and creed by creating brand loyalty in the young. Through an alignment of instinctual human striving with the corporate interest, and shaping that desire with an addictive message, the individual is invited to sidestep—albeit briefly—the reality of an imperfect world. It is the American dream of plenty, homogenized and mass-produced.

AMERICA LEADS the world in creating the tools and enticements that nourish mass consumer demand through the reward of innate desire, but the sustaining roots of America's commercial success lie in the hard-core economics of the mass market itself. Beyond the branding of fizz and fantasy it is the continuous expansion of the market that permits profits to grow while costs are held down. But mass markets demand megacompanies, and while such corporations have improved the material standard of living for many people, their growth is crippling to local communities and the economic microcultures that José Bové seeks to protect in France.

Wal-Mart, the American retail giant, offers a powerful example. When Sam Walton opened his first store in Rogers, Arkansas, in 1962, his advertising slogan was the same as it is now: "We sell for less." Walton's special edge was that by mass purchasing he offered goods at prices lower than those that local variety and hardware stores needed to charge to stay in business. Forty years later Wal-Mart is a $200-billion-a-year enterprise accounting for over 6 percent of the retail spending in America (which in the year 2000 was approximately $2.3 trillion). In its dominance over the domestic market, each day Wal-Mart sells approximately 474,000 pairs of shoes, 52,000 pairs of jeans, 68,000 bras, and 110,000 pairs of women's underpants, an astounding achievement that would have been impossible before information-age technology and the globalization of trade.

Living with giants has broad social consequences. The service goal of Wal-Mart Stores is to "drive unnecessary costs out of businesses," and it achieves this by pushing its army of sixty-five-thousand suppliers to adopt lean practices. This has fostered a globalization of the production chain, where to meet the low wholesale prices Wal-Mart demands, many vendors subcontract with overseas agents running factories with unregulated, and sometimes highly questionable, working conditions. Similarly, Wal-Mart's domestic labor practices have come in for criticism. Fiercely opposed to union organization, Wal-Mart is the largest private employer in the United States, with more than 1 million full-time and part-time employees. Its down-home folksiness disguises the chain's subversion of small-town society and the dramatic changes in local employment that occur whenever it enters a community. In smaller towns some 25 percent of local retail shops commonly disappear when a new Wal-Mart opens nearby. This weakens the diversity and viability of the local market economy and of the community itself.

Also, size begets size. "Bigger is better" is the corporate mantra of the multinational company. Giants must become super giants if they are to survive in the competitive global markets, either by dominating a major market—as Wal-Mart has done in America—or through the acquisition of potential rivals and international competitors. Thus, pharmaceutical companies buy biotechnology firms, Daimler-Benz buys the Chrysler Corporation, Traveler's buys CitiBank, and so on, each for billions of dollars. In Eastern Europe many of the companies that have been purchased, privatized, and restructured, such as in the transportation and utilities industries, were previously in the public domain. But with few regulations governing the international movement of capital and with ambiguous definitions of monopoly, no industry has been immune to the merger mania. Hence superpower conglomerates with quasi-monopoly positions now dominate the food and agricultural business, banking, pharmaceuticals, media, telecommunications, and the auto industry. Some of the world's largest economies are now corporations with budgets higher than the gross national product of significant industrialized countries. The annual budget of General Motors, for example, is higher than the gross national product of Denmark, and Exxon's is larger than that of Norway. The powerful corporate voices that dominate the global marketplace are now concentrated within the boardrooms of a few hundred companies, about 40 percent of which are American. We have entered a new age of mercantilism.

The domination of today's international commerce by the megacorporation in many respects is the latest phase in the continued evolution of the mercantile trading that Adam Smith knew so well, and so abhorred, in the eighteenth century. For better than two hundred years, from the sixteenth century until the beginning of the Industrial Revolution, the feuding nation states of Europe and their merchant adventurers fought to establish trading empires and to dominate an expanding world market. Their methods differed, but the goals were similar to those of the megacorporations of today: to exploit the world's markets, natural resources, and labor pool to the advantage of their own dominion.

In the *new* mercantilism, the private diplomats of multinational corporations, investment houses, and policy think tanks have joined central bankers and ministers of government in the creation of a new commercial elite. Samuel Huntington, the Harvard political scientist, has called this powerful cosmopolitan group the "Davos" culture, after the World Economic Forum that is held each year in Davos, Switzerland. Started in 1971 by Klaus Schwab, a German intellectual with degrees in mechanical engineering and economics and a master's degree in public administration from Harvard, the World Economic Forum considers itself to be the major international venue for global economic strategy and elite consensus building. According to the forum's literature, each year business and political leaders, academic experts and media executives come together "to shape the global agenda in a unique atmosphere." Corporations must have annual sales of at least $1 billion, and banks $1 billion in capital, to be eligible for consideration. Each attendee pays some $40,000 for the week in Davos, except for those thirty or so national leaders who are guests. Together the companies represented account for approximately four-fifths of the world's industrial activity and "roughly seventy percent of the world's daily output of self-congratulation," as one London *Financial Times* correspondent humorously observed.

This new elite champions the power of the market and the wisdom of laissez-faire capitalism in shaping the future of all human societies. Much of their deliberation is focused on how to foster a safe commercial environment throughout the world. As the preeminent entrepreneurs of contemporary business, and of the art of political deal making, those who are of the Davos culture communicate in English, the language of globalization, and live in the Fast New World of computers, cellular phones, airline schedules, and international currency exchange. These are the new international nomads—those of the manic lifestyle—who set the frenetic pace of contemporary business and who through their commercial power drive the daily lives of billions of people across the world. Their loyalties and personal values, however, derive not from any traditional community or national identity but from the business ethos of capital markets. In the Davos culture, the expansionist dream of American commerce has been adopted as a state of mind.

In commerce America is now the workshop of the global imagination. As Microsoft software has invaded the world's computers, so have American commercial values invaded the world's business cultures. As the world's single superpower, America sets the terms on which the commercial world will be governed through the World Trade Organization and the International Monetary Fund. The United States seeks no empire comparable to that of Europe a century ago, for it has gained a commercial empire of the mind—a New Order of the Ages—where American-style consumerism is mankind's preferred pursuit.

This is exactly what worries many Europeans and an increasing number of Americans. With America's world dominance there is now dangerous confusion between the freedom of commercial choice and the broader democratic freedoms of tolerance, equality, and justice. For many—as for my young Polish guide Jaroslaw Majchrzak—the market and laissez-faire economics have become the ultimate expression of liberty, and the hero of that liberty is the business pioneer. But megacorporations and globalization are ill equipped to solve social inequality; indeed, without appropriate regulation they may worsen it by destroying local economies. As Klaus Schwab, founder of the World Economic Forum, and his associate Claude Smadja emphasized in 1996, globalization "tends to *de-link* the fate of the corporation with the fate of its employees," provoking a "backlash" that can threaten local economic activity and social stability. The anonymity of the international corporation must be broken and local economies nurtured if global capitalism is to benefit not just those who are corporate managers and investors but also the majority of the world's peoples. While international commerce must be protected, American-style marketeering is not the single answer to the ills of the world. "Only fools believe in the conscience of markets,"

George Soros has said. "Markets do not obey the law of reason, but rather the laws of desire."

To many foreign critics America's corporate stumbling following the Internet and telecommunications debacle of the late 1990s was a validation of Soros's viewpoint. Here was evidence that the American mania for work and money, fostering self-interest over social concern, was destructive of a balanced personal life and a caring society. To most Europeans, work and material possessions are not, in themselves, satisfying and life affirming. The idea that work alone—regardless of how well one is paid—provides meaning and self-fulfillment is seen as an American import, and not one to which most Europeans care to subscribe. Furthermore, an unbridled mania for money can be self-destructive and dangerous. Once excessive work begins, there is no escaping the consequences of the "hedonic" treadmill. Driven by desire and the prospect of material riches, time for the mundane things in life—for cooking and meal times, for friends, and for family play— becomes less available. Accept this Faustian contract, say the critics, and Europe will soon face the same trends in social disruption that are evident in American society.

It is already happening. Demand-driven, mass-market economies are growing in Europe and the trend toward longer working hours is becoming evident, particularly in the United Kingdom. The British work on average 8.7 hours a day, compared to 7.9 hours in France and 7.7 hours in Italy. Similarly, the British are moving closer to the American norm when it comes to vacations, with only twenty-eight public and annual holidays a year, whereas the French have forty-seven, the Germans forty-one, the Spanish forty-six, and the Italians forty-four days. For this extra effort, the British have a slightly higher disposable income than do the Germans or the French, but they also save less. Five percent of disposable income is put aside in England, as opposed to 15.8 percent in France, 15.1 percent in Germany, and 10 percent in Italy. And as the manic lifestyle takes hold in Britain, the diet is also changing. The average British household now spends approximately the same on snack foods as it does on fresh fruit and vegetables, with the fastest area of growth being in food-to-go such as cereal bars and snacks for children's lunch boxes.

Activist leaders such as José Bové point to these changing statistics and to the frenetic lifestyle of America's Fast New World and reject it as a mismatch destructive of the family and intimate friendship. Once a community is caught up in the anonymous web of mass markets, they argue, life changes and there is no retreat. Once you start eating at McDonald's, you stop cooking at home, and once you stop cooking at home, you stop buying local produce. It's all a vicious cycle and in the wrong direction. They note the demographics indicating that the gap between the rich and the poor in America is growing, and the evidence that wherever major franchises move in, local businesses are forced out until faceless international trade names replace the familiarity of local friendship. "Today money works by itself," says Bové, emphatically. "This has produced a new species of parasite: vampires thirsty for money. We reject the global model dictated by the American multinationals. The world is not for sale."

Is José Bové a Jeremiah, a protectionist Frenchman to be dismissed out of hand? Or is his protest reaching toward something of fundamental human importance—something beyond materialism—that is required to sustain a thriving and prosperous community, be that community in Aveyron or Michigan? When Bové and his farming friends were jailed for dismantling a McDonald's in their hometown, there was an outpouring of protest in France, then across Europe, and eventually from America. To many of the protesting citizens, Bové was no Jeremiah, but a David in combat with Goliath—a civic-minded man, passionate about genuine grassroots democracy and local diversity, who was bold enough to speak out in a world increasingly driven by corporate commercial interest.

There is irony here. The principles that José Bové stands for—self-expression, liberty of thought, and local economic autonomy—are the fundamental principles that Americans struggled to preserve in the fight for independence. These are the beliefs that shaped the early guiding images of the American dream. And similarly, they are the principles underlying Adam Smith's ideal of a market economy, one controlled by local sellers and buyers rather than by government regulation and mercantile giants. And perhaps the ultimate irony is that the commercial "Americanization" that is now so reviled in France grew out of American populist culture—the hopes and aspirations of ordinary American families living in small rural communities such as Marceline, Missouri. The roots of America's democracy and the nation's early images of success in the promised land draw heavily on a community-based, agrarian way of life not dissimilar to that which José Bové now seeks to protect. Such rural communities once nurtured a different American dream. And that is the focus of my next chapter.

Chapter Eight

THE ROOTS OF
HAPPINESS:
OF COMPASSION
AND COMMUNITY

The conditions of happiness . . . are to receive from
birth the best cultivation of our natural powers—physical, mental, moral, and practical—and to know how to
give this training to others.

Robert Owen (1771–1858)

FOR HUMANS, LIVING IN small groups is the natural order of
things. As social animals it is our preferred way of being, and something
with which we have had long experience—approximately 6 million
years, in fact. Our hominid ancestors lived in small communities composed of close relatives, much as the chimpanzee does today. And, as is
the case in such primate kinships, they depended on each other for protection, hunted and foraged together, shared food resources, and fought
with their neighbors. The optimum clustering for efficiency was somewhere between eight and twenty individuals, not greatly different in
number from a soccer team or a platoon of soldiers. Size was key. To be
effective the group needed to be large enough for its members to have
adopted a stable hierarchy, but small enough so that all idiosyncrasies of

communication, together with the temperament and talent of each individual, were common knowledge. Such familiarity and mutual attachment ensured safety and efficiency, regardless of the task in hand.

When the group got too large it would split in two, and inevitably fighting broke out—over territory, food, females, or something—but the challenge only served to stimulate further cunning and sophistication. Both the competition among groups, and the cooperation and rivalry within each group, had their creative value, teaching individuals new strategies in the art of survival. But it was working together as a unit that gave an edge and drove intelligence forward. Thus our forebears learned from each other through a process of competitive collaboration, and we still do.

The marketplace is a natural evolution of these practices. As we became aware of the rhythm of the seasons and began herding animals and sowing wild seed for easier gathering, nomadic wandering was replaced by village life, and during the years of success, scarcity was replaced by surplus. Local markets emerged as a natural consequence of this ingenuity—as practical extensions of the collaborative management of material resources—and capital markets grew similarly, around the prudent investment of surplus. Those practicing the most profitable customs in this economic competition were advantaged, and prevailed in the ongoing struggle between groups. The market thus became an indispensable cultural form where the fundamental principles of market practice—honesty, trust, competition, and fair exchange—were adopted as the preferred foundation of a liberal society. It was these principles that Adam Smith codified in his book *The Wealth of Nations*, first published in the year of American independence.

Markets are about more than money and material goods, for they provide the underpinning for community life, the bedrock on which social relationships are built and a forum where information is exchanged. The market offers a dynamic way of ordering human cooperation and channeling competitive behavior that goes beyond the limits of individual knowledge. In this regard a free-market economy is radically different from one centrally planned, for as we have learned from bitter experience, even the visionaries among us cannot ensure individual motivation or foresee the future. As a spontaneous evolution of group behavior, the beauty of the market is that it is an economic system driven by individual desire and ingenuity, and thus one responsive to the need and initiative of all participating members.

As I have emphasized, but it is important to do so again, it was this nurturing value of the free-market society that Adam Smith championed against the crushing influence of mercantilism in the late eighteenth century. And it was to protect their local markets from anonymous interference and destructive taxation that Americans went to war against the British in 1776. *In neither instance, however, was the market or the production of wealth considered to be an end in itself.* Rather both were seen as important mechanisms through which to sustain the intimate web of freedoms and relationships that are essential to the progress of a civil society. What now concerns José Bové and those of similar mind, including many Americans, is that the capitalist enterprise has become disconnected from the community activities and social liberties that gave it birth: that the profiteering of the turbocharged corporations of the Fast New World and the unbridled self-interest of those intent on building mass markets are destroying the local economies and the interpersonal networks that are vital to healthy communities. In our headlong pursuit of immediate material prosperity, we are neglecting the vital social infrastructure—the social capital of family and community—that shapes understanding and empathic behavior in youth, and sustains America's promise to future generations. Simply put, reward-driven markets do not work in the way that Adam Smith predicted and intended when their locus of control becomes detached from the communities they serve.

IN AMERICA the cultural transition from a socioeconomic order built on the comfort of a personal relationship with the butcher and the banker to an impersonal commercial world driven by automated credit card transactions and the ATM machine is now nearing completion. For the merchant and for those living at the manic edge, our technological

transformation has many advantages. Building close personal relationships, however, is not among them. The cultural influence of this transition is most clearly seen not in the urban centers where the changing
technology is immediately felt, but in the towns and villages of rural
America. In these remote areas—where for two centuries everyday existence has been inextricably woven with an agrarian economy—the
impact on community life has been profound.

That certainly is the opinion of Gordon and Fern Wilder, my fish-
farming neighbors in Plainfield, New Hampshire. Chartered in 1761,
the Plainfield Township sits at the middle of the western edge of New
Hampshire, divided from Vermont by the Connecticut River. With a
population of just over two thousand people—a census about a third
greater than in the early 1800s—it is a rural place spread out across two
villages, one of which is Plainfield itself. The other, Meriden, is home to
a private preparatory school, Kimball Union Academy. Increasingly,
Plainfield is a dormitory town for the urban area to its north, where the
Dartmouth-Hitchcock Medical Center and Dartmouth College are
found, and it was in the early 1970s when I was a professor at Dartmouth Medical School that my family and I first went to live in Plainfield. While our daughters were growing up, we farmed there on a
modest scale, and the village has rooted my migrant spirit ever since. It
is the place in America that I call home.

It was through our farming exploits and the 4-H that we met the
Wilder family. Gordon Wilder—nicknamed "Peanut" as a boy for reasons
that I have never understood, given his strength and stamina as a man—
helped me hay, shoed the horses, logged our land, and taught me many
things. When I was the executive dean of Dartmouth Medical School,
Fern Wilder was my assistant. The three Wilder boys, Mark, Shawn, and
Brad, went to school with Kate and Helen, our two daughters. We complained about taxes together, we disagreed occasionally about town politics, spoke up at the town meetings, and became firm friends. And
despite my peripatetic ways we have remained so ever since.

We stumbled into our discussion of the changing nature of community life and cultural values in America while together in the Wilders' liv-

ing room one darkening, late November afternoon. Peanut had just returned from a harrowing trip to Canada, hauling some three thousand pounds of live trout. At the hatchery in the plain of the St. Lawrence River an hour or so from Quebec City, it had been bitterly and unexpectedly cold—seven degrees below zero Fahrenheit, with a cutting wind—and the fuel line on Peanut's truck had frozen. With the trout already loaded, that was something of a crisis, as fish do not last long crowded together in a confined space without oxygenation. And to make matters worse, it was a Saturday afternoon.

"They're twenty or thirty years behind us up there," Peanut said. "The service stations are still locally owned businesses, and for me that's just as well. Without the spontaneous help that poured out from that community, I would have nothing now but the makings of a giant fish fry." Peanut had been shipping young trout from Canada for some years, to supplement his own production as the New England demand had risen. "At first they were suspicious of me," he said. "They'd tangled with Americans before and they were wary of our aggressive ways and the almighty dollar. But I worked hard at it. I learned a little French—they learned a little *more* English, I'm ashamed to say—and we got along." On that Saturday afternoon, people whom Peanut didn't even know had turned out to help. They had rigged up an independent power source for the truck's generator and then working together had managed to get Peanut's truck and its precious cargo under warm cover, moving out their own vehicles to accommodate it. "After about two hours' work and thirty-eight bucks for a new fuel filter, I was back on the road," said Peanut, "together with the warm feeling of having made several new friends for life."

Peanut would have done the same for others under similar circumstances; I knew that for sure. That past summer when a drought had threatened the Plainfield village wells, a system that supplies water to fifty or sixty homes, Peanut and his son Mark, who is a selectman in the town, had trucked water from a neighboring township. In all they had hauled forty-eight thousand gallons, enough to get the village system over the hump. There was no fanfare about that and Peanut would not have wanted any. I knew about it only because I had seen him up at the reservoir on several hot days, filling the tank on his fish truck.

For Peanut Wilder the most important ingredients in achieving personal contentment and meaning in life are self-respect, trust, and the friendship of living with others in a stable community. Peanut, who was born in 1942, grew up in Plainfield on the same piece of land that he still farms, although the place has gone through several transformations since those early days. When his father bought the farm in 1940, the kitchen had a dirt floor, and the running water came off the hill into a barrel. The Wilders lived together as an extended family, which included Peanut's paternal grandfather, who was a farrier and a fine horseman. Peanut admired his grandfather as a man of "fierce Yankee independence" and considers that he was cast from the same mold. That molding turned out to be important when, at the age of eighteen, Peanut had independence suddenly thrust on him after his father collapsed with a heart attack. "My father died on a Wednesday," Peanut told me, "and I was to depart for college on the Sunday." Realizing in his grief that he loved the woods and his way of life too much to leave the community, the necessary decision was clear to him. He would stay in Plainfield and become a farmer, ensuring that his mother and two younger siblings (Peanut is one of six children) would be well taken care of. "So," he said, "I changed my mind about college. I married Fern and we settled down here. We've never regretted it. We see ourselves in partnership with this land."

Peanut believes that his values stem from that partnership and from his experience growing up in a closely knit rural community. "On the farm, family life and our livelihood were one and the same," Peanut told me that afternoon, "much as they still are in the St. Lawrence valley today. The local people I grew up with were not quick to come forward—that Yankee hard shell thing—but just beneath that shell is where all the kindness is. At night there were few lights and you didn't see your neighbors. Each family had its independence, but if anything went wrong they were there for you." The Plainfield community in those days, as Peanut described it, was an extended social kinship—a community of independent collaborative groups—drawn together by economic necessity and tied in its activity to the seasons of the year. The family groups worked in union. If one farmer had a tractor with a bucket loader, then he was the one who helped load the manure in the spring. Those with spreaders would work along with him, moving from farm to farm until the chore was complete. Then during the harvest, the same neighbors would work together again, such that each good deed was repaid. And the community played together too, at the local fairs, at barn raisings and dances, and at family cookouts. "We fed ourselves predominantly from the land we had around us," Peanut said. "We all hunted. The deer meat supplemented the pig and the beef that we might slaughter in the fall. And on Sundays, for dinner, it was a chicken that wasn't laying eggs. Money was important but not central to everyday existence. The weekly grocery bill in the 1960s was little more than $10 for the whole family. We were closer to practical things. And nobody had heard of a dormitory town in those days."

The life Peanut was describing differs little from that of Adam Smith's day, or from the American experience of the early nineteenth century as portrayed by Alexis de Tocqueville, when the vast majority of the population lived close to the land. Such a life demands not only the investment of energy and initiative, but also an extraordinary range of skills. Peanut, for example, over the course of his career has run a dairy farm, worked as a machine-shop foreman, driven school buses, raised beef cattle, logged, built houses, shoed horses, hauled potatoes, and been a hunter's wilderness guide. Likewise Fern has nurtured three children and cared for aging parents, milked twice a day, helped hay the fields, been a 4-H leader, worked as an executive secretary and an accountant, and together with Peanut developed one of the most successful commercial fish farms in New England.

I offer these details not to romanticize rural life, for it can be just as dangerous and brutal as life in many urban areas (one of the Wilder boys, for example, lost his lower leg in a harvesting accident while growing up). Rather I do so to emphasize that for centuries a rural existence has been embedded in a community structure that is in harmony with our evolutionary experience of living in small groups, an ancient pattern of life where the commercial and social economies were intimately intertwined, and both self-interest and neighborly cooperation were rewarded. For all its hardships the agrarian lifestyle has worked well in supporting America's explicit promise of an evolving civil society, one where the rearing of children and the improvement of community are of paramount concern.

THE AGRARIAN culture that marked America's youth stands in stark contrast to the technology-driven, self-focused affluence of the social order in which we now find ourselves. In consequence, whether this new commercial experiment can sustain America's promise of a compassionate society dedicated to equal opportunity is a question that must be of serious concern to all citizens. I say this because, as a psychiatrist, it is evident that many of the behavioral qualities essential to individual survival in our novel habitat are corrosive to human social need. Particularly troubling is that the preoccupation with individual wealth and the manic demands that are promoted by our Fast New World are weakening the essential roles of family and community in shaping the cultural beliefs and empathic understanding that are vital to the health and happiness of future generations.

Human empathy—Adam Smith would have called it fellow feeling or social sympathy—functions as the immune system of a civil society, and family and community are the marrow from which that immunity springs. You will recall that it is empathic feeling and the social education we receive during our early rearing that in Smith's economic model molds self-interest to provide the counterbalance to greed in a market society. But unfortunately, in stark contrast to the instinctual reward-driven pathways that serve curiosity and self-interest, human empathy is a delicate commodity. The development of the capacity for empathy is critically entwined with emotion—both in the expression of one's own feelings in language and facial expression, and in the ability to read the emotions of others. The limbic system is the crucible of such emotional processing, but the experience of intimacy and the stability of the attachments one has in early years ultimately shape our capacity to understand the feelings of others. (Which explains why empathy cannot be learned by interaction with a laptop computer.) Human empathy is largely a learned behavior, much as is language.

And similar to the templates of brain activity that shape the acquisition of language, the development of empathic behavior has a permissive biology that must be organized by experience. Marco Iacoboni, a neurologist and colleague at the Neuropsychiatric Institute at the University of California in Los Angeles, has described this empathic learning process as guided imitation or *mirroring*. In brain imaging studies of normal human subjects, Iacoboni has demonstrated that a relay of collaborating centers within the frontal, parietal, and temporal cortex of the new brain facilitates empathic understanding of the feelings and actions of others. Working together, these centers can imitate and reconstruct—that is, "mirror"—within our own virtual world the feelings and body language of another with whom we are interacting. (Validate this for yourself: the next time you find yourself wrapped in animated conversation with a close friend, step back mentally for a moment and take note of your body posture. In all probability it will be in mirror resonance with that of your companion.) Thus, for each of us, the development of fellow feeling and our compassion for others is tied to learning and to reason rather than to instinct. It is empathy that transcends the interests of the "selfish" self, promoting shared values among individuals and shaping the collective behaviors we call culture. In short, empathic understanding provides the lifeblood—the psychic immune system—that is the humanity of the civil society. But over generations, a wellspring of healthy families and the nurturance of supportive, economically viable communities are required to sustain that lifeblood and to promote the rules of social conduct that we now loosely bundle together as "family values."

When Peanut and Fern Wilder were growing up, there was no talk of family values and how they might be preserved, for the principles of social conduct were embedded in everyday experience. These principles were handed down implicitly from one generation to the next as learned cultural practice. The human species has a unique capacity to learn from experience and to convey beliefs about that experience to subsequent generations. Together with the curiosity and cleverness of human intelligence—those qualities of ingenuity and self-interest that lead to innovation—our ability to mirror the experience of others and to learn from that experience provides the foundation for our cultural heritage. Culture is more than books and musty museums: it is a set of dynamic educational templates with agreed-upon meaning that provides social cohesion once a kinship or a community grows too large for the individual members to know each other personally. Through these educational templates we embrace and distinguish the extraordinary diversity of human social organization into kinships, tribes, clans, religious sects, political parties, business corporations, communities, nations, and so on, with each cultural clustering having its own unique adaptive value.

But in all societies, the natural order of the extended kinship, as a microculture within the larger community, is what plays a critical role in this educational process and in the development of empathy. For humans of all cultures, the kinship is the optimal educational environment. Learning is cooperative, fostered by mutual attachment and by traditions—those transgenerational beliefs—that the kinship holds in common. Through empathic understanding, familiarity within the group bridles competition and self-interest and harnesses them to mutual benefit, establishing a set of agreed-upon principles of social conduct—or virtues—to which the larger community also adheres. It is through this continuous process that cultural mores evolve, including the mores of fair market practice, as well as the qualities often referred to now as family values.

These microcultures provide an enriched form of inheritance, one where we acquire not only a genetic legacy from our parents but also their moral values and transmitted beliefs—and those of our relatives, friends, and the extended social order in which we are reared. Within a nurturing community this enriched inheritance equips an individual with an extraordinary resilience and flexibility—what behavioral scientists call *adaptability*—and the necessary confidence in adult life to cooperate with others, to overcome difficult circumstances, and to seek innovative solutions to complex problems. How this adaptability can work across generations to general economic and social advantage is well illustrated by Peanut's story of the development of his family's fish farm.

AS A YOUNG farmer, after his father's death, Peanut milked cows for a while. But as government regulations concerning dairy farming grew stricter during the 1960s, he realized that he needed some forty head to survive economically, whereas the family had the resources to sustain only twenty-five animals. Reluctantly, after extensive family debate, the Wilders sold the dairy herd and Peanut went to work at a local machine-manufacturing company, utilizing the practical engineering skills he had learned on the farm. He thrived there, rising rapidly to a position of responsibility, but he was not happy. Peanut's cultural heritage was to work the land. A decade went by. Then, with their three boys growing up, the Wilders decided to build a pond and to stock it with trout, for recreational fishing for themselves and for friends in the summer months. Much to Peanut's surprise, he found he couldn't buy live trout anywhere in the state of New Hampshire. So, being of ingenious mind, he decided to grow them himself. Purchasing five thousand eggs, he tried raising them in a mayonnaise jar in the basement. Thinking carefully about what fish must need—nutrients, obviously, plus a stable water temperature and oxygen—Peanut developed a Heath Robinson apparatus that maintained a constant temperature and pushed air through the water to oxygenate it. To his great pleasure the contraption worked and the trout hatched and grew. That spring Peanut stocked the family pond and, curious to learn more, began reading about fish farming.

Within months, sensing an economic opportunity and restless in his engineering job, Peanut decided with Fern's support to take the risk of returning to full-time farming, with the intention of developing a trout hatchery. There was abundant water on their old hill farm, and the cascade of the land lent itself well to a series of gravity-fed ponds for rearing the fish. Fern, it was agreed, would reactivate her talents as an executive secretary and seek outside employment to provide the family with health insurance while Peanut would shoe horses and log until the hatchery either became economically viable or failed. They estimated that it would take about three years to find out. In a flurry of activity, the retaining dam of the old millpond on the property was rebuilt. The University of New Hampshire and the Fish and Game Authority in the state were contacted for information and were enthusiastic about the Wilders' efforts. Other hatcheries were visited, and professional relationships were built across New England and Quebec. The hatchery buildings and concrete breeding tanks were constructed, and as prospects improved, Fern returned home to manage the finances of the business. Within a decade the Wilders were selling to the live market between two and three hundred thousand mature trout annually, stocking farm ponds and clubs for recreational fishing throughout the New England states.

In an era when family farms are in steep decline in America, the Wilders' achievement is extraordinary. (Between 1987 and 1992, America lost an average of 32,500 farms per year, about 80 percent of which were family run. A mere 50,000 mega farming operations now account for 75 percent of U.S. food production.) And yet Peanut Wilder is modest in his accomplishment, considering himself a fortunate man to have found a successful market niche from which he has been able to support his family and to educate his children. He is just lucky, Peanut says, that in rearing trout for a living, he has found a farming practice that can be supported by the land he loves, and for which there is a growing market.

As the hatchery has matured, the next generation—the Wilders' three sons—have watched, worked, and learned, just as Peanut did with his father and grandfather a generation before. In manhood the Wilder boys have found their own way, but the thread of the family's cultural influence is clearly evident. After getting his degree in animal science from the University of New Hampshire, Mark, the eldest—who, as his father describes it, "grew up on a bulldozer"—now owns the Plainfield Construction Company. Building ponds for people is what he enjoys most. Shawn has followed his father too, but into the engineering business,

while Brad, the youngest—"the one who never lost a family argument"—
studied law and has a general practice in an adjacent community, taking
much pro bono work. Mark also serves as a town selectman, as did his
grandfather before him. To Peanut this is the natural way of things: paying back is the fulfillment of a citizen's responsibility in a civil society.

The secret of the satisfaction to be found in farming, I suspect, is that
the practice of a rural way of life was of cultural significance long before
it became an economy. What worries people like Peanut Wilder is that
now we have flipped that experience on its head, and are moving rapidly
toward an economic model in America that has little cultural value other
than that of facilitating the accumulation of material goods. The market
is no longer a place where the average American can build personal relationships and learn about life. The producer and the consumer are now
divorced from each other, and they almost never meet or converse—
indeed, only rarely do they live on the same continent. Most of us have
only our time to sell, and for many Americans that is heavily mortgaged
well into the future. In the pursuit of efficiency and greater profit, the
Fast New World is rapidly depersonalizing even the most fundamental
elements of market exchange. From the apartment where I live in Los
Angeles, I can order my groceries by phone or by the Internet using my
credit card, and have them delivered to my door. No prices are discussed, no hand is touched, no smiles exchanged, no emotion is registered. And if I choose carefully, there will be little cooking needed; the
microwave will suffice. Families rarely eat together at home, let alone
cook together or wash the dishes—with both parents working, there
simply isn't time. Small wonder that to feel good about family "togetherness" we take the children to McDonald's. In a frenzy of material pursuit, little by little we have dismantled the microcultures of family,
market, and community that traditionally have been the spring training
grounds for family values, and that have built the social capital essential
to the health of each succeeding generation.

One of the things that has weakened the family is that it is no longer
the core of a productive unit—be that product economic, social, or
recreational. When Peanut Wilder was growing up, family life was tied

closely to all three, but as the focus of the economy has shifted to become corporate, multinational, and dangerously impersonal, the family has lost its central role in American life. And along with that loss, Peanut believes, has come the erosion of a sense of personal responsibility for oneself and for the community. "My grandfather believed that you could judge a man's character by the size of his woodpile," said Peanut during our conversation. "And it was true. Most of the responsible people in town had their woodpiles up by the fall, and big enough to get them through the winter. That was the mark of a man of good character. We would joke that the man who had a small woodpile must have been doing something else—playing, drinking, whatever. Not paying attention to his family anyway, or that woodpile would have been ready for winter."

Today, metaphorically, nobody cares about the woodpile. "I find few people who worry about tomorrow," Peanut told me. "Whether that's because they're too busy worrying about today, or because they're having a good time, I don't know. But I do know that few people feel it necessary to pay back to the community: most expect that somebody else will solve the problems when they arise. That never used to be the case. In the past it was a matter of self-reliance. But as members of a community we took care of each other." Beyond the extended family, Peanut explained, the most important people in the community were the minister, the doctor, and the banker. One of the things that Peanut had always appreciated about New England townships was that the people who lived in them ran them, and everybody knew who was responsible and who had integrity, regardless of their profession or status in life. So when Peanut was growing up, it was expected that the doctor would come to the house when he was needed. He was part of the family. The minister was considered the spiritual healer, and the whole family went to church on Sundays. It was a ritual. Everyone dressed up and ate dinner together afterward. The local banker frequently loaned money on a handshake. When Peanut's father had wanted to extend the farm by buying more acreage, his banker had advanced the money before the contract was signed, being confident that the loan would be repaid. "In those days short-term transactions were fostered by long-term friend-ships," said Peanut. "But now it is impossible to *find* a local bank, let alone to shake hands with a banker."

What has been lost—in Peanut's opinion, as he thinks about his sixty years of experience in the world—is the integration of personal need and social responsibility into a simple framework that is easily understood. The rural life provided that framework. After all, Peanut asks, what is learning to become an adult all about? Few believe that it is simply to achieve material wealth. Generally when one asks that question, some spiritual or social ideal is advanced. All cultures embrace both the symbolic and the practical. A culture must have its symbols to inspire—the flag, the Statue of Liberty, the Declaration of Independence—but they are *symbols*. Such icons stand for something of more practical importance—the ideals of freedom, truth, honesty, and responsibility that are a prescription for personal conduct, and that tie to the deeper reasons for being alive. As children grow, they develop goals, and those goals are shaped by what they see around them: the virtue of a devoted mother, the competence of a grandfather, and so on. It's not just knowing your grandfather that's important in shaping those goals, but knowing what he believed in and what he endured that made him the feisty, self-reliant Yankee that he was. "Machines do not teach prudence or generosity, people do that," Peanut said. "What was once community in America is in danger of becoming nostalgia, the stuff of Norman Rockwell paintings."

WERE THE old philosopher alive today, I believe Adam Smith would share Peanut Wilder's concerns about the changing nature of community life in America. And so should we. After all it is a cornerstone of Adam Smith's economic philosophy that sympathy toward others (empathic understanding) is essential in harnessing the twin engines of desire—self-interest and curiosity—such that the free market will work to the benefit of all those who participate. Building on that platform, Adam Smith contended that the market is an effective mechanism for encouraging honesty and self-control—the merchant who keeps his word stays in business—and thus it further helps channel self-interest toward socially acceptable goals. In a commercial society, Smith wrote in the *Wealth of Nations,* every man is "in some measure a merchant" and plays his role in shaping market behavior. Customer demand sets the standards for goods and services, the producers respond accordingly, and the cheaters in the marketplace are soon identified and kicked out.

But Smith did not contend that market forces alone created virtue or character. In Smith's time the mark of character was considered to be an awareness of social duty and the appropriate exercise of that duty. Smith firmly believed—just as Peanut Wilder expressed during our conversation—that the origins of a dutiful character lay in the family and in the community, rooted in the daily expectations and the informal rules to which we are exposed when growing up. Smith also recognized that in contrast to the instinctual drive of self-interest and survival, both the prudent management of one's own affairs and benevolence toward others are *learned* behaviors forged in the experience of, as he described it, "those friendships which are naturally contracted when the heart is most susceptible." Smith was describing, of course, the same capacity for imitative behavior that Marco Iacoboni has identified in his brain imaging experiments, and which Iacoboni now calls mirroring.

Thus there is common ground between the discoveries of modern neurobiology and Adam Smith's astute observations of over two centuries ago. It is through the experience of living, working, and learning in proximity with others that the moral virtues—the accepted cultural standards of conduct—are acquired. And it is against these cultural standards that we first engage in self-judgment until, as Smith explained it, there is seeded within each of us an "impartial spectator" (a conscience or social mirror) that monitors our behavior. Thus, through our relationships with others, Smith argued, we move from moral conformity to moral autonomy. When, in the pursuit of human affairs, these moral standards are obeyed, the result is a sense of satisfaction and personal happiness, and when they are broken, the experience is one of shame and social failure. Smith believed that while we each aspire to our own happiness above all else (the survival instinct again), people of virtue will strive in their dealings with others to go beyond self-interest to achieve self-respect and the trust of their neighbors. For Smith this give-and-take of community life is what transforms men and women into moral beings who then, with their reinvestment, sustain that community in a continuous cycle.

It was also the security of the moral constraint and social decency that Smith believed to be present in small communities that emboldened him to formulate his system of "natural liberty" whereby the competitive spirit of ordinary men (and women) could be released safely into the marketplace, to the benefit of all. Contrary to popular belief, Smith was not an advocate of unrestrained market competition. When Smith spoke of freedom from restraint, he was referring to the impersonal restraint of trade imposed by the import and export tariffs of his day. The liberty Smith advocated was not freedom from all control, but freedom to control one's own instinctual passions in the service of self and community. Liberty, in this sense, is conceived within the natural context of man as a social animal. Through the power of our extraordinary imagination, we may put ourselves in another's place, and once in that place, because of our own wish for sympathy, we discover empathy—the capacity to understand the joy and suffering of others. Hence, empathic understanding—the social sentiment of the impartial spectator—offers collective immunity against the avarice and envy that are the inevitable consequence of unbridled self-interest. Empathy, functioning as the immune system of the civil society, is vital to the healthy balance of a market economy. And that is precisely why I believe Adam Smith would share Peanut Wilder's concern, should the old philosopher visit America today. In our commercial success we are eroding the communities that traditionally have sustained our civil society.

WE HAVE spawned another American paradox. In economic terms the fundamental principles that Adam Smith systematized so clearly in his *Wealth of Nations*—the championing of entrepreneurial self-interest within the dynamic framework of the free market—have served America well and have brought consistent material improvement. But there is a darker side to this achievement. Despite the nation's growing wealth, few Americans are any happier. Material progress and happiness, it turns out, do not march hand in hand. There is correlation between per capita gross domestic product and the happiness of nations; however, that relationship disappears once justice is established and a certain standard of living is attained. Thus, on average, wealthy nations are happier than poor ones, but there is a cutoff point in income—equivalent on an international scale to around $10,000 per capita annually—after which happiness does not increase. Most Americans are already well above that income level. In America we are not as happy as we are rich.

America is the richest country in the world but ranks only in the middle range among nations when it comes to happiness. Despite driving bigger cars, living longer than our parents in larger houses with more plumbing and with more food than we can (or should) eat, we are no happier. Our avowed national intent notwithstanding, the pursuit of happiness through material possession has proved to be illusive. Indeed, surveys suggest that in pace with our growing affluence there has been a steady decline not only in our happiness but also in our satisfaction with marriage, with work and finance, and with the homes we live in. Material goods may be more important in America, where we have few other systems of establishing social rank than in some societies, but happiness does not aggregate with social status. Nor is happiness like wisdom: it does not accumulate with age. But the evidence does indicate that happiness—and general health—does *diminish* when the wealth of a nation is poorly distributed, when families and friendships wither, and when we lose the support of living in a cohesive community that is economically viable.

Ironically, considering our acquisitive behavior, it appears that Americans already understand these things. Americans agree that money and material possessions are not the major source of health and life satisfaction. In most surveys Americans put family and friendship, rather than money or material things, at the top of the list when asked what it is they seek in the good life. We intuitively understand that happiness comes from fellowship, but in our social and political behavior we fail to exercise that understanding. In consequence, community withers all too often in the face of commercial demand. Robert E. Lane, a professor of political science at Yale, in his book *The Loss of Happiness in Market Democracies*, has likened the decline of American community to a state of psychic malnutrition: "a kind of famine of warm interpersonal relations, of easy-to-reach neighbors, of encircling, inclusive memberships, and of solidary family life" amid a life of material abundance. I would agree but go further in my diagnostic description. Our psychic malnutrition is but a symptom. In the decline of community, America faces a growing deficiency of its cultural immune system—a disorder that without thoughtful remedy could threaten the very marrow of our great society. We have become the victims of our own success.

One thing is clear: the pursuit of happiness through the accumulation of material wealth is proving to be a blind alley. The purchase of luxury, Americans have discovered, does not substitute for neighbors in building happiness and security. It is intimacy, not materialism, that buffers the stress of everyday living. Meaning is found in the social bond. Attachment to others serves survival in infancy, and empathic understanding facilitates adaptation throughout life. Feelings of happiness are tied to intimacy and are dependent on the reinforcing presence of companions and friendship. The widowed and those alone in the world suffer higher rates of depression and die younger than those who live with a companion. And, in general, married people are happier than unmarried people—indeed, there is even some evidence that a lack of companionship spurs the urge to shop.

It is the rare human, it seems, who genuinely prefers to be alone. And yet the commercial and technological demands of the Fast New World have dramatically increased the time that many Americans spend each day in solitary activity or in the maintenance of their affairs: the long commute, the overload of information to be processed, and the hours before the computer screen all deprive us of time that could be spent with others. It is the familiar treadmill existence. As career mobility increases, we are less loyal to particular institutions. As residential areas move away from commercial centers, our mobility increases. As we become more oriented to our jobs than to our families, the divorce rate rises. The Internet is a new technology that unites the world, but it is a virtual world. Connections in cyberspace, while an advance on the passivity of television, do not provide the gratification of social intimacy. The human preference, when reaching out to touch someone, is to have that person be in the same room.

The good news is that America's loss of community is slowly commanding political attention and generating creative ideas. Take the state of Iowa as an example. At first glance it would seem that the migrant impulse in American culture runs antithetical to any preference for intimacy, but in fact, especially to the first-generation migrant, family solidarity is of great importance. Appropriately channeled and economically supported, this commitment to family in combination with the migrant's willingness to relocate, on the basis of work necessity or to pursue some commercial opportunity, ironically may help rejuvenate rural states that have lost population because of out-migration. That is the thinking behind a movement by a governor's commission in Iowa to encourage migrant families to relocate in the state by creating three hundred thousand new jobs designed specifically with immigrants and internal migrant workers in mind.

Approximately 1 million legal immigrants arrived in the United States each year during the 1990s, and probably another three to five hundred thousand entered illegally, either by smuggling themselves across the border or by overstaying their visa. It is estimated that some 9 million illegal aliens live permanently within America's borders, gainfully employed by willing American citizens. The cultural mix of contemporary immigrants is far greater than it was at the peak of the last great migration, at the close of the nineteenth century. Then, in New York City, an estimated five nationalities accounted for 80 percent of the immigrants, whereas now in that city twenty-two nationalities account for only 66 percent. The recent immigrants are also predominantly young (one-third of the members of migrant Latino families, for example, are under eighteen), and because of that, the median age of the

American population is falling, something demographically unusual among industrialized nations.

Immigrants are a boon to the U.S. economy, coming literally free of developmental cost and hungry for employment even at minimal wages. The educational profile of the migrant population is predictive of the diversity of that employment. Over 20 percent of migrant individuals have a postgraduate education (a percentage three times higher than that for native-born Americans), but another 20 percent have only minimal schooling (less than nine years), which is again higher than the percentage for those native-born. Immigrants with higher education enhance the scholarship of our universities and our technical prowess as a nation, while the illegal workers and those with little schooling take on the most menial of tasks. These unskilled workers provide a "floating human capital" in several segments of the American economy: in the hotels and restaurants, in the meatpacking industry, and in the garment factories. It is also the immigrant who baby-sits our children, who cleans our houses, and who landscapes our gardens—jobs that in many instances native-born citizens do not want.

The internal migratory patterns of native-born Americans and the demographic distribution of first-generation migrants tend to complement each other. In general, the internal migration of Americans is from the heartland of the Union—from the rural areas and the small towns of the Midwest—to the urban coastal centers, particularly those in the South and the Southwest. In consequence, the population of the rural Midwest is aging. Thus the stimulus behind the governor's commission in Iowa is that the average age of a full-time farmer in the state is now fifty-eight, and it is estimated that each year some 60 percent of Iowa's university graduates leave to settle elsewhere. Iowa's family-owned farms are in decline and the small towns that once served farmers are declining also. Slaughterhouses are taking up the slack in employment, and immigrant workers from Asia, Mexico, and Eastern Europe are providing the manpower, backfilling for the Iowa-born Americans who are moving out. A similar story is being told in other rural states, such as North Carolina, Arkansas, Nebraska, and Kentucky, which during the economic boom of the 1990s experienced a migrant influx of both Americans from the northern states and immigrants who were foreign-born.

Partially as a result of these demographic shifts, some see America becoming a nation of two cultures. The first is represented by the declining agrarian communities of the heartland that adhere closely to God, family, and the traditional virtues, while the second, driven by a cult of self and self-interest, thrives in the urban centers of the coasts. American nostalgia holds up the first—an embodiment of the self-reliance, integrity, and hard work that forged a great nation from the wilderness—as the popular ideal. (To burnish his image as a man of the people, for example, President George W. Bush is photographed cutting brush on his Texas ranch, dressed in jeans and a sweaty T-shirt.) The picture drawn is one of a moral dichotomy, where a decline in virtue and "family values" is at the root cause of any social upheaval that the nation suffers—from school violence to teen-age pregnancy.

I believe that such an analysis misses the mark. I suspect that at the root of America's social problems is a capricious and poorly distributed economy with shallow local roots—plus a growing disparity in the distribution of wealth—rather than a skewed morality. In the runaway power of our global commercial success, we have become blind to our failure to nurture the economies of small communities—be they urban or rural—and to foster the local markets that support the financial and moral well-being of those who live there. Deregulated capital markets by their very nature foster self-interest, and success brings increasing central control and reduced concern for the general economic welfare. With globalization and the worldwide distribution of U.S.-financed manufacturing, local economies in rural states are particularly vulnerable. Thus the closing of one IBM plant in Vermont can decimate the economy of several local communities with a single stroke. The notion that megacorporations provide trickle-down social benefit appears comparable to the contribution of material wealth to happiness: there is a cutoff point in the size of the corporation beyond which such benefits no longer accrue, indeed beyond which an erosion of earlier gains becomes apparent.

The worst poverty in America is not in the inner cities but in the coun-

tryside—in Texas, Mississippi, Kentucky, Arkansas, and places like California's Central Valley. In these rural communities people have barely 70
percent of the purchasing power of their urban counterparts, and one in
six children in the countryside are raised in poverty. Bank robberies
jumped by 82 percent in small towns between 1997 and 2002, and by
only 17 percent in the nation as a whole. Drug use, particularly amphetamines, is an increasing problem. The farming communities that Peanut
Wilder sees slipping away in New England are already dead in some of
these areas—areas where the agricultural industry is now so large that no
small farmer can sustain himself. Small businesses rapidly follow. Should
a Wal-Mart be built within driving distance, the local market economy
essentially disappears. In rural America the social fabric is tearing.

If we wish to strengthen the empathic virtues of honesty, trust, and
responsibility in America, we must restore the opportunity for meaningful labor to the individual communities that are the source of those
virtues. Such is the thinking of the enlightened state leadership in Iowa.
Migrants, whether they are internal migrants holding American citizenship or immigrants from abroad, bring energy and fresh ideas. Their restlessness is focused on improving themselves, their families, their
adopted community, and their respect within those communities. With
appropriate economic support in the early stages of their endeavor, the
evidence is that migrants can contribute significantly to the health of an
economy within a generation. Such an investment is in the great American tradition. Before 1776 each settler in Virginia in repayment for their
passage across the Atlantic was given a hundred acres. And after 1776
as President Jefferson, and later President Polk and the U.S. Army,
expanded the territories of the Union in "manifest destiny," land was
given out to settlers in forty-acre lots.

Whether Iowa's creative effort to rebuild its rural communities on the
bedrock of America's migrant heritage will prove successful is yet to be
decided, but the effort is in the right direction. In securing the health of
American society, we must look beyond the family to its supporting community, for it is there—in community—that the roots of happiness are
to be found. The phrase "family values" has become a moral lightning

rod in America. And yet the family plays just a part in the development of our social mores. An individual of virtue, as Adam Smith recognized, is built from the progressive union of many cultural forces, each pulling together. Moral values are empathic behaviors learned not just from parents and family, but also from the environment that sustains the family's livelihood. If we are to promote the civil society that Adam Smith and the Founding Fathers envisioned, we must nurture families and communities in the same way as we nurture markets—through investment.

That unregulated capitalist societies carry within themselves the potential for their own destruction is a suggestion that many philosophers and political scientists have made, Karl Marx, Joseph Schumpeter, and Daniel Bell among them. As Daniel Bell has observed, any economic system that stimulates hedonism and self-indulgence, but at the same time requires for its effective functioning self-discipline and deferred gratification is bound to have built-in contradictions. The potential that greed and self-interest will diminish social reinvestment is one of them. And such concerns grow as the control of commerce centralizes and exercises a global reach. Of parallel concern to some, as Bell points out in his book *The Cultural Contradictions of Capitalism*, is that "capitalist society, in its emphasis on accumulation, has made that activity an end in itself." I believe this is an unfair indictment. It is not the philosophy of capitalism that promotes material accumulation, but our lack of understanding of the biological and behavioral drives that underpin a market society and how those drives must be held in balance if the social and individual benefits are to be realized.

If as a culture America continues to reinforce self-interest at the expense of social reinvestment, then predictably our cultural-economic system will run away to greed. It need not be so. Working together, we have the knowledge to construct a society built on empathy, not envy. The choice is ours. There's nothing wrong with Adam Smith's American dream. Rather it is that in our migrant zeal for individual betterment, and in our technological ingenuity, we have distorted Smith's vision of what it takes to sustain an economically viable and healthy civil society.

Chapter Nine

FINDING BALANCE
IN THE AGE OF
THE MERCHANT:
OF SELF AND SOCIETY

They are as sick that surfeit with too much,
as they that starve with nothing.
It is no mean happiness, therefore,
To be seated in the mean.

William Shakespeare
The Merchant of Venice, 1596–98

"HAPPINESS AND PLEASURE, I'VE decided, are entirely different beasts," Tom said, raising his glass in a mock salute. "So here's to pleasure. Of the two it's by far the more attainable." It had been over a year since I had seen Tom—not since dinner with Anna and Marcel in Los Angeles—but he had lost none of his charm and provocative exuberance. On this occasion we were in New York: I was on my way back to Los Angeles from New England and Tom was up from Florida to see a banker and to pay off an important business loan—the loan that had helped start his new career as an entrepreneur developing rehabilitation centers for those suffering from stress disorder. Tom was in the mood to celebrate, and eager to tell me how he had changed his life.

For our luncheon rendezvous, at the Algonquin Hotel on West 44th Street in Manhattan, Tom could not have found a place of greater contrast to the Encounter Restaurant. Dark wood paneling, brass table lamps, Paisley fabrics, and wing-backed chairs evoked images of an earlier era and offered a studied retreat from the Fast New World. "Being here at the Algonquin is part of my effort to recenter myself," said Tom. "I came frequently to New York with my father in the 1960s, when he was a reporter for the *Boston Globe*. With his Irish heritage he loved the St. Patrick's Day parade and we always stayed here. Once I met Brendan Behan, the Irish playwright, right in this lobby. He was drunk, of course, but he made quite an impression on a lad of ten years, believe me. Which is really to my point," Tom said, taking his first sip of the wine. "Being deprived of personal happiness, Brendan Behan was into pleasure."

Tom had been thinking. As I was to learn that afternoon, he had been thinking a lot, and about difficult subjects. "What is happiness?" Tom had asked rhetorically, as Matilda the Algonquin cat strode imperiously by. "Is that cat happy? Is the amoeba happy, engaged in its simple dance with the environment in which it finds itself?" From his reflections, Tom suspected so. Happiness, he had concluded, emerged from balance, from finding harmonious fit with one's circumstances. Tom, in his fascination with biology, saw that harmony as reflective of an internal biochemistry and thus believed it was logical that the amoeba could enter a state that parallels human happiness by achieving optimum balance with its habitat. "There's probably no objective measure for such harmony," Tom said, "but I've discovered that by introspection you can tell when you're there."

The main problem with life in the Fast New World, Tom had decided, was that the demand-driven frenzy of that world crowded out an awareness of the present moment, making it difficult to achieve the inner sense of harmony and balance that we perceive as happiness. "I realize now that in my manic pursuit I was either preoccupied with past events and how I had handled them, or was juggling in my head some future scheme. Rarely did I concentrate on being in the present moment and appreciating what was going on around me. I was too busy and too important," Tom said. "In consequence, I was never able to sense whether I was happy or not. In fact, I never thought about it until I felt miserable. It's a bit like being hungry—unless you take time to think you never quite know what your appetite is until you're starving, and then the instinct is to grab the first thing that comes within reach. I'm convinced that is why fast food is popular with people who are living a frenetic life; they have no time to think. Eating french fries is pleasurable —just as I find that this wine gives me pleasure—but the pleasure is transient. To rekindle the feeling of pleasure you have to repeat the behavior that generated it. But that repetition does not equate with happiness. So I've concluded that pleasure and happiness are distinct. Pleasure has something to do with external reward and the dopamine circuits. Happiness, however, at least for those who like me are not depressed and can afford to pay the bills each month, is linked to *how one chooses to live in time, with oneself and with others.* I now realize— after slowing down enough to think about such things—that for years I have been confusing the two feelings."

The English language abets Tom's confusion: *happiness* in the *Oxford English Dictionary* is described as success or pleasant appropriateness, and *pleasure* as a sensation induced by that which is desirable. The distinction between the two words is much clearer in French, where *plaisir* (pleasure) has much the same definition as in English, but where *bonheur* (happiness) in literal translation means "good hour." Similarly in French, being happy—*heureux* (feminine) and *heureur* (masculine)—is phonetically evolved from the same Latin root of *oür*, meaning "hour." (We have something of the same derivation in the English language when we speak of "the good times" or of "having a good time.") Tom, in his reflection, had rediscovered that which is easily forgotten in the helter-skelter Fast New World. Fundamental to personal happiness is the emotional insight gained from living honestly in the moment.

Benjamin Franklin did not clarify the general confusion over the wise use of time when he advised the young tradesman that "time is money." A broader and more helpful aphorism to have given posterity would have been that "time is life." But Franklin, in offering his advice, was focused on commerce, where time is different. The delicate ribbons of inner experience that mark the ebb and flow of time in human biology are far removed from the precision of clock time and the "real" time of a technologically driven Fast New World. As I have emphasized in earlier chapters, human time is tied to ancient planetary experience, while clocks serve predominantly the necessary coordination of our commercial world. That world imposes a public drummer that can both disrupt the harmonic rhythms of inner time and disturb the integrated personal experience that is perceived as happiness.

"One of the neat things about this new business," Tom said, "is that I get to meet a whole range of people, psychologists and so forth, who have thought deeply about these issues. I'm learning and that always excites me. But most important, I'm *unlearning* some of the stuff that has driven me since childhood and that business school reinforced. I was brought up to believe that success and happiness were goals beyond myself—opportunities to be pursued. They would be mine only if I were smart enough and competitive enough to achieve them. Efficient time management was a key to that success. I've listened to countless consultants with the same message: efficiency means breaking time into smaller and smaller pieces until daily life is obsessively tied to a detailed continuously unfolding schedule. Now I'm learning that such schedules are not as efficient as they seem. Overscheduling is another form of personal debt. Rather than savoring the moment and using it efficiently, by being preoccupied with what comes next you mortgage the present to the future. So I'm discovering that efficiency and happiness have common roots. When I invest in what I'm doing in the moment—in this conversation or in reading a financial report—without being distracted by past or future, I find myself both efficient and happy. Most moments turn out to be like that when you pay attention. Most moments are comfortable moments, good moments, even happy moments, but I had lost the ability to focus on them. Happiness, once you're fed and clothed, has little to do with worldly goods. The real search goes on within the privacy of your own head. Finding personal happiness is an individual responsibility."

I agreed with Tom's line of reasoning and told him so. But, I pointed out, the time pressures, competition, and temptations of America's Fast New World have made such introspection increasingly hard to achieve. Technology and the marketplace are no longer invaders that can be shut out from the everyday world—they *are* the everyday world, unless one just happens to be hidden away in the lobby of the Algonquin Hotel. In America's ad culture we have invented a new public drummer, one far more powerful than being overscheduled. The average citizen is now relentlessly besieged with information that does little to inform beyond its commercial content. Promotional messages demand attention when we are placed on hold by the automatic telephone, they arrive unannounced in the fax machine, and they are found lurking at the start of the rented video. They are on e-mail, at the gym, on the grocery cart, on the parking meter, and at the sports arena, and have even invaded those bastions of established culture, the museum and the music hall. Advertising has become central to American culture, and the market is a continuous presence in every facet of life. The once individual streams of entertainment and commerce, and the activities of home and workplace, have converged in a confusing flood of demand, choice, and opportunity. As never before in history, the average American is now presented with an abundance of everything that fascinates, seduces, and intrudes. How under such circumstances, I asked Tom, does one live in the personal moment?

"It's not easy," Tom replied, "but I believe it's essential if one wants to find some sort of meaningful balance in this age of the merchant. The key is relearning to focus one's attention. The more demanding the commercial environment gets, the more essential it is to live in the moment, and to use that present moment effectively. It seems deceptively simple, but it works. I know: I've found the more I focus on the task at hand, the better are the choices I make. The alternative is to be overwhelmed and swept away by the maniacal excess that exists all around us—the excess of material goods, of food, of competition, and so on.

"In America," Tom continued, "we have confused finding happiness with the pursuit of pleasure. Mr. Jefferson did a great disservice when in writing the Declaration of Independence he changed the phrase 'life, liberty, and property'—as it was originally in the Bill of Rights—to 'life, liberty, and the pursuit of happiness.' It has confused us for two centuries. Changing the words didn't change the behavior. In the hope of finding happiness, Americans are still pursuing property. But as many citizens are learning, the acquisition of property does not equate with being happy. So, if the goal is to discover happiness, taking back one's personal time from the impersonal demands of the merchant is a place to start. When we welcome the enticements of the merchant and purchase more than we need, it is the reward of pleasure that we pursue, not happiness. In an affluent society like America, they are not synonymous. Happiness cannot be pursued. Happiness is something that wells up from inside."

Tom was now leaning toward me across the table, pressing home his argument. I was reminded of our first meeting in LA and found myself, once again, admiring his restless, enquiring spirit. Secure in my attention, Tom hurried on, eager to tell me of all that had happened over the past year. He had been pleased with the growth of his new project and its financial success, which was "well ahead of the business plan." But most exciting had been the affinity he had found with his partners, and the personal meaning he had discovered in the stress reduction programs they were developing together. Tom and his colleagues had started from the premise that the affluence of the Fast New World was unique in its human challenge. The ingenuity and seductive power of America's laissez-faire mass markets had created "a giant casino: the greatest pleasure-generating machine the world has ever seen." Unfortunately, however, while fascinating and seductive, this machine had no published instructions on its optimum use. "Everyone has had to figure it out for him or her self," said Tom, "and some people have never learned how to switch the thing off. As a nation we are just beginning to realize that living with extraordinary affluence is not like going to the gas station. There's no automatic shut-off when the gas tank is full. So our strategy is to help stressed-out individuals construct their own shut-off systems—to learn how to play the casino without getting hooked."

Tom admitted that much of the enthusiasm for his new career stemmed from the opportunity it offered to rethink his own approach to living in the fast lane. He had found great satisfaction from putting together something that he whimsically referred to as "the Rules of TOM," an acronym for "Toward Optimum Mindfulness." It was, Tom told me, "a personal survival practice for those at the manic edge," drawn from his own experience and the expertise of his new colleagues. When I wondered out loud whether "mindfulness" implied that he was working on a new career as a Zen master, Tom smiled and reminded me of the many years he had spent in Japan. "I believe that in times of overload there's a lot to be learned from the simplicity of Zen practice and meditation," he said, "but that was not my purpose here. I don't see this effort as an East versus West thing. Rather I've tried to set down some practical guidelines that foster living in the present moment—of being mindful of one's own goals and intentions. I suspect, in fact, that a good deal of what I have been thinking will be familiar to you from your counseling practice as a psychiatrist. My 'rules' are really a collection of simple principles that I have found personally helpful in refining what is relevant to survival in our demand-driven culture."

INDEED, TOM'S "rules for survival" do have much in common with psychotherapeutic principles. In managing excess stimulation, which is the core challenge of the Fast New World, the setting of clear personal priorities and the efficient use of time are essential strategies in sustaining health and well-being. Thus central in Tom's scheme is an appreciation of inner *time* and its wise management (mindfulness). He also highlighted during our conversation three other areas—*technology*, *appetite*, and *activity*—where he believed mindful awareness was important if anxiety, obesity, and other health complications were to be avoided under high-stress conditions. In practice, these categories overlap, but for ease of elaboration here, I take them each in turn.

Tom's cardinal rule is the wise management of **time**. The time we each have in the world is finite, and is the only marketable commodity that we truly own. It is also through the gift of personal time that we offer of ourselves that which others cannot repay, even in gratitude. Thus time is to be cherished and protected. Time is the new money. Life in the Fast New World, by demanding more time than we have available, reminds us of these truths and helps drive the discomfort that many Americans feel. In response to that discomfort, frustrated by our "lack" of personal time but also afraid of lost opportunity, we resort to "living by the clock" such that daily activity becomes fragmented and discon- nected, rather than a continuous unfolding experience.

Tom described the impact on family life as a common example. When overscheduled and caught up in a treadmill-like existence, family mem- bers no longer share a flow of time with each other. Frequently, in the family's fragmentation, members retreat to their own interests—playing video games, watching television, writing e-mails, working on the com- puter, talking on the telephone—such that the house is no longer a home but a way station to another world. Meals are not eaten together, running the household becomes a chore for individuals rather than a shared investment, and "family activities" become contrived rather than emerging from spontaneous interaction. In guilty awareness of this dis- integration of family life, parents frequently set aside "quality time" to "share" with the children—who are also heavily scheduled—only to find that when the magic moment arrives, mother has been delayed at the office or father has another business dinner.

Tom believes that through such "heroic" overscheduling, undertaken to accommodate all demands, efficiency—and ultimately fulfillment and happiness—is lost. When family members are pulled in so many dif- ferent directions, conflict among them is inevitable and the setting of meaningful priorities is compromised. The opportunity to live life in the moment and to enjoy close personal attachment is eroded. "If," Tom said, "the father of our family were to concentrate during his dinner meeting (his third of the week) on evaluating the real benefit of such discussions to his business goals—rather than repeatedly looking at his watch, stressed and guilty at not being home with his children—he might conclude that evening engagements are a poor investment of his precious time and decide to change his future priorities." Similarly, if the father willingly gives his full concentration when spending time with his son or daughter, the need to schedule "quality" time is removed, for every moment becomes of value. Based on this personal honesty, a new set of priorities emerges that serves as the template for future planning. And reciprocally, knowledge of what one seeks in the future helps shape the wise investment of time in the present. "Thus mindful awareness of the emotional value of the time we invest," said Tom, "makes priority setting easier and helps sow the seeds of genuine personal happiness."

The second category that had received Tom's close scrutiny is **technology**. In its commercial application, the technology of the Fast New World has the power to overload and addict, producing information far more rapidly than any human can process it. It is estimated, for example, that the average American is targeted by over three thousand advertising messages each day. So one of Tom's most important rules for surviving at the manic edge is that information and communications technology be controlled to service personal priorities. Technology, rather than intruding as a tyrant, is then recast as a valuable tool. While many technologies were introduced as "time savers"—such as voice mail, e-mail, online services, and fax machines—if not held consciously in check they become vehicles of intrusion that do not save but *consume* time, creating more stress than they relieve. And because communications technology is now mobile and targets the person rather than a place, that intrusion can be relentless, randomly inserting into one's life the priorities of others, both day and night.

If personal priorities are to prevail, then caller identification, unlisted telephone numbers, the screening of calls, private e-mail addresses, and simply ignoring incoming information until its review is convenient must become a way of life—at least until new technologies make possible the sorting and mechanical blocking of such harassment. "Fortunately, whereas new information was once rare and usually important, most of what we now receive in the deluge is of little value and can be disregarded," Tom said. "Although as I know from personal experience, given the insatiable curiosity of most human beings, ignoring incoming information is no easy task. Mindfulness and setting one's own priorities help, but it takes resolve and diligent practice."

Learning to appreciate the power of the natural **appetites** is another key strategy in Tom's program. "In an affluent society appetite is the gateway to both pleasure and disaster," Tom asserted. Appropriate to our meeting at the Algonquin, Tom had taken the appetite for good food to illustrate his point. Because the depriving environments in which we evolved offered little opportunity for overindulgence, we possess few natural internal constraints to eating. Thus when confronted by excess, we must learn to carefully observe the body signals available to us. As any gourmet will advise, the pleasure in eating is found in savoring the aroma, the taste, and the consistency of a meal, in eating it slowly and sharing those experiences with others. By being mindful in this way, not only are the delights of a fine meal enjoyed but also one is better able to monitor when satisfaction is complete. "McDonald's has fooled us into thinking that we no longer have time to indulge appetite in such a way," Tom said. "But eating anything quickly not only destroys the pleasure, it is also unhealthy. Only internal cues can provide the signal of when the stomach is full, and those signals are weak. When we eat quickly—which happens particularly when one's appetite is extreme— these delicate signaling systems are overwhelmed. We move quickly from extreme hunger to discomfort, appreciating none of the pleasures of a healthy appetite."

Ideally we eat when we are hungry and stop when we are full. That apparently simple task becomes more difficult when one is surrounded by abundance. In such circumstances it is essential to appreciate the internal cues of hunger to prevent the weight gain of excess consumption. "Eat whatever you wish when hungry—and do so for pleasure—but when you have the urge to eat without feeling hungry," said Tom, "then ask yourself why? Is it because the bread smells good in the shop you've just passed, or because you are feeling unhappy or anxious? Ask yourself, are you hungry for the bread that first appears on the table in the restaurant, or would you prefer to wait for the fish and vegetables that you have chosen for your main dish?" With few natural limits, either internal or external, when it comes to eating, one is necessarily one's own gatekeeper. "So the rule is eat slowly and mindfully," Tom concluded, "tasting everything. Then you will feel pleased and well served, not cheated, by your appetite."

A thoughtful approach to managing daily **activity** was Tom's last area of concern. Such an approach he had found consistently lacking in the lives of those who seek help for stress-related disorder. The Fast New World has few limits, and the increased activity it demands is an invitation to the accelerated and disorganizing effect of manic behavior. "I learned that the hard way, from my time as the world's most frequent flyer," Tom said, referring to that period of his career when he was an international business consultant. He now considered multitasking— thought to be a sign of competence and skill by many executives—to be a seductive illusion and an inefficient use of time. "We've fooled ourselves that the human brain can manage several tasks simultaneously," Tom said, "whereas what we are really doing is switching attention back and forth between them. That's not only exhausting, it's dangerous. So telephoning while driving can kill you—or somebody else—and eating and watching television at the same time is a guaranteed way to get fat." One activity at a time, mindfully engaged, is Tom's rule for this category.

Regular physical activity is also important in finding personal balance. Wisely planned and distributed throughout the day, physical exercise can provide a unifying thread in an otherwise fragmented schedule. Walk to work if possible. If that luxury is denied, as it is to most Americans, then take public transportation or park some distance from your workplace to ensure some morning exercise. Driving yourself is the poorest use of time. (And similarly try to avoid driving long distances with small children strapped into confining chairs. We know from animal experiments that the most stressful thing you can do to a young primate is to confine it, and such constraint guarantees that a period of hyperactivity will follow.) While at work, get out of the office to meet with others whenever feasible and enjoy the exercise that it affords. Take the stairs rather than the elevator. Use every opportunity to exercise during the day and you will need the gym less—and when you do work out, choose the time of the day that best fits your body rhythm.

"Plan travel realistically," Tom said, "and don't overschedule yourself. Then when you are caught in a traffic jam, it is not an emergency. Turn on the music, sit back, and enjoy the fact that you don't have much to do for the next hour. Relax when you can, and then when peak performance is demanded, that performance will be efficient and effective." Tom believes that those who are habitually late are trying to crowd in too much, a habit that serves only to escalate their mania. Similarly, in family life, it is important to seek moderation in scheduling children's extracurricular sports. Tennis, swimming, hockey, gymnastics, and soccer are not needed every week. Competition is innate, but the thoughtful management of one's own time is not. Start those lessons in youth, advises Tom, and preferably by example.

"Once you recognize that the merchant is in business to make money for himself—not to make you feel happy—then protecting yourself in our supercharged commercial society turns out to be largely a matter of common sense," Tom observed. "But without taking time out for reflection, such simple logic can be hard to find. When enjoying the excitement of the casino, it's tough to say no. In my own experience the little things that go on between people are the key to breaking the megalomania. When you pay attention to those, then reconnecting with the real world is easier. Think about it: we have 8,766 hours in a single year and my bet is that few people spend more than an hour each day talking with members of their family, or with people they love. That's less than five percent of the total time available. Is that prudent when it is in human closeness that true happiness is to be found? What prevents living in the moment with others is that the novelty of the world we've created is constantly pulling us somewhere else. But once you take that vital step of investing in other people by being honest with yourself, then it's smooth sailing from there. When you're happy within yourself, then it's easy to decide which pleasures to indulge."

Tom looked at his watch. The time for his meeting with the banker was near. "I got lucky," he said. "I spotted my mania, identified my discomfort, and was able to regain control of my life before depression set in. Now I've learned what fires my circuits and how to cope by staying in the mean, within my comfort range. I have a better sense of what I enjoy, of what I can do and of what others can do. I focus my energy; I distinguish between what makes me feel good and pays back and what doesn't. I listen to my emotions. I work hard to evaluate the moment and to stay in it. I avoid sensory overload. I turn off my cell phone when I go to dinner. In fact, I rarely use it when I'm not traveling. I don't help everybody immediately. I own my own distress and expect others to own theirs. I take care of myself. I no longer take red-eye flights. I exercise, but not excessively. I still indulge myself, but in moderation. I'm a risk taker still, but not when the odds of survival are poor. That something feels good, I've discovered, is no justification for mortgaging the future. So I no longer bet my livelihood on a project—only the remainder. In short, I've become a 'safe' risk taker. I sleep better that way.

"Finding balance," Tom continued, "is a matter of personal honesty. At first it was painful to look back—to realize that I was chasing goals I hadn't thought through and buying things I didn't need—and to own up to myself that I was hooked. Casino life is a rush, a surfeit of pleasure, and also an addiction. If you're not prepared, too much reward can kill you—with greed, gluttony, or alcoholism. It happened to Brendan Behan. That funny, bawdy, wild-haired genius loved New York and New York loved him. The greatest city in the world, Behan said—the place where you're least likely to get a bite from a wild sheep. Yes, New York adored him, aggrandized him, and eventually killed him. My father understood such things. 'My boy,' he would say to me in his wonderful Irish brogue, 'flattery is fine as long as you don't inhale.' I was going in the same direction—not from alcohol, but from a frenzy of celebrity and overwork—an addict of the technological age. As you put it to me once, I was hijacking my own brain circuits."

There were no regrets about the past, Tom assured me as he put on his coat. Nor should I conclude that he had had some messianic conversion. He did not consider doing something socially good as being an end in itself. "Business is business," Tom said. "The goal is to make a profit and theoretically how you achieve that is all the same, whether you're building guided missiles or rehab centers. But there's more to life than the market, so this new venture is a double payback. In helping build these programs I'm doing well by doing good, and I like that. So, I got lucky. I'm a happy man."

We shook hands. The tab was on the room bill, Tom advised me, so I should stay until I needed to leave for the airport. And with that he was gone.

I TOOK TOM at his word. The lobby of the Algonquin Hotel was quiet—Matilda, the cat, and I being the principal occupants—and it was raining outside. I had the luxury of time to spend. As I sat thinking about our conversation, it was clear to me that Tom had lost none of his creative skill as a turnaround artist. The difference was that now his extraordinary abilities were focused on taking care of himself, rather than on rescuing some imploding corporation. Recognizing that his workaholic ways were damaging to his health, he had pulled back from the manic edge and found a new viewpoint—a new balance—from which to order his priorities and to parcel his energy. In the best American tradition Tom had turned the page and was writing a new chapter in his life story.

Tom had retrieved his personal equilibrium not by changing the frenetic world around him but rather by modifying his approach to that world. In diagnosing himself as "an addict of the technological age," he had decided that he must impose self-constraint, much as an individual with manic depression, having suffered through several episodes of illness, finally accepts the need to regulate his or her daily activities as an essential step in controlling the illness and its destructive power. In that regard, I suspect Tom's story is a familiar one to the many Americans caught up in the world of work. In the excitement of material pursuit and the competitive struggle to succeed, the temptation is to accelerate and to overreach. As in the early phases of mania, the rewards of such frenzied engagement are initially compelling, even intoxicating, but over the long haul the frantic activity is unsustainable. Eventually the energy dissipates and the manic cycle turns down toward depression. It takes time to recognize this roller-coaster pattern and some never do, descending instead into a self-destructive vortex of stress and physical disability. Yes, Tom had been lucky. For Tom the visit to the Florida rehabilitation center had been an epiphany.

Once Tom had accepted that changing his lifestyle was his own responsibility, he worked hard, as was his habit. Analyzing how he spent his time and prioritizing what was most important, he achieved greater control over the demand-driven world to which he had become habituated. With conscious effort Tom bridled his restless instinct to exploit every opportunity that presented itself. He no longer responded automatically to all the business offers he received, but considered the merit of each against his new priorities. Only then, after having stepped back from the frenzy, was Tom able to bring his considerable intelligence into focus. His new "mindfulness"—behavioral adaptation through reasoning—helped promote a new modus operandi, a heightened awareness of mind and body that enabled him to live comfortably once again, within his physiological limits. Tom now engaged the world on his own terms and in his own time, and secure in this newfound balance, he felt happy.

Tom's story is important not only in its illustration of the limits of human adjustment, but also in its emphasis on why conscious correction is essential when those limits are exceeded. Just as we have the unique capacity as humans to change by ingenuity and to learn about the environment in which we live, so can we learn to adapt to such environments—but only up to a point. With each new wave of technical advance, we devise new ways to cope with what is demanded of us, later adopting those behaviors by cultural custom to establish a new social equilibrium. We call such accommodation "social progress," but when the adjustments demanded are rapid and profound, there can be hidden costs to both body and mind. The reason for this is that the physiology of all living creatures—at all levels of complexity, from the amoeba to the human—is dependent on active regulation to sustain equilibrium with the surroundings.

In ourselves these regulatory systems function largely automatically, and outside our conscious awareness, orchestrated by the ancient brain centers inherited from our reptilian and mammalian forebears. But such mechanisms were designed largely to manage acute stress, and they are easily overwhelmed by relentless challenge or "hijacked" by excessive enticements. This is what Americans are now discovering as we struggle to embrace, each in our own way, the novel demands of the Fast New World. But, make no mistake: this new habitat is here to stay. And if the next phase of the American experiment is to succeed, we must learn to adapt to it, not only as individuals but as a society. That adaptation will require thoughtful and diligent effort based on sound principles. While we may hope in fantasy for a breakthrough in science or a sudden genetic mutation that will facilitate rapid and painless accommodation to our new circumstances, in reality our tools are those already in our possession—and the same tools that Tom employed so successfully—namely, old-fashioned ingenuity guided by human reason and trial and error.

In making our adjustments, we do not have room for complacency. Tom, for example, was personally advantaged in making his successful accommodation: he worked for himself, had money, and was smart and had had a good education. The majority of Americans do not enjoy such privileges. For the average citizen the reward structure of contemporary American society does not make it easy to escape from the stress and strain of the Fast New World. As a nation we have become preoccupied with economic growth, and to that end we have embraced a seductive form of megamarketing that, while it may be good for commerce, continuously beckons each of us toward self-destructive, addictive behavior.

This fostering of consumer craving, the treadmill of work and spend, and the burden of accumulated debt carried by many citizens have promoted a curious mixture of frenzied individual striving and conformity to commercial pressure that erodes the precious freedom of personal time management, just as Tom had encountered. Indeed, although Tom enjoyed certain privileges in engineering his escape from our American mania, his experience of it in many ways parallels that of the American nation as a whole. In our collective striving for more, we have climbed ever higher toward our imagined paradise, only to look down from a pinnacle of opulence and find ourselves beset by a growing social crisis, the self-inflicted torment of greed, anxiety, and ill health that I documented in Part II of this book. We have built for ourselves an environment that in one and the same moment both seduces and destroys—an environment that is rapidly shifting the vital balance between self and society. There is no easy escape. It is the new reality. In America Tom's world is now our world—the world that each of us must face every day.

SO WHY, at the peak of America's commercial success, should our nation's social equilibrium be shifting so rapidly and so destructively? And what can be done about it? To answer the first question we must return once again to the philosophy of capitalism's patron saint—Adam Smith—and to the behavioral assumptions that underlie his vision of a self-regulating economic system that would efficiently create material wealth and equitably distribute goods and services without central planning. As you will recall, Smith's original conception grew from his study of human behavior and the social challenges of his times. In the eighteenth century, government tariffs, taxes, religious laws, and a misguided attachment to precious metals as the index of wealth bound down the economic activity of England's mercantile society. Amid this stagnation the energy and initiative of the individual (where Smith correctly believed the true wealth of a nation is to be found) lay relatively untapped. Thus Smith's prescription for economic vitality—based on the understanding of human behavior that he had set forth in *The Theory of Moral Sentiments*—was to free the individual from constraint and to reward personal initiative through the open marketplace. In resonance with Bernard de Mandeville's *Fable of the Bees*, Smith believed that private vices thus would become public benefits. Through the magic of the market, self-interest would be transformed into social fellowship, to the betterment of the larger community.

Whether Smith knew it or not, his prescription for a stable economic order is grounded in the dynamic principles of small-group behavior, principles that are now compromised by the growth of megacorporations and globalization. Thus implicit to Smith's vision was a market society composed principally of small independent merchants and their customers—markets similar in form to the farmers' markets and the ethnic neighborhoods that survive in some American cities, or to the rural communities championed by José Bové and Peanut Wilder. To enable the market to work its social magic, Smith favored private ownership, with capital being locally rooted. He distrusted large institutions—be they government or corporate—as forces that foster greed, distorting and suppressing the dynamic market exchange and social intimacy that are essential to fair dealing. Under these ideal conditions, Smith argued, the give-and-take of market practice would decrease cost and improve efficiency and through an "invisible hand" would translate self-interest into public benefit. The poor, in tending to the larger appetites of the rich, would be able to provide for themselves the necessities of food and shelter. For the rich the reward system would be balanced between the pleasure of self-gain and the civic pride of serving others. By these mechanisms the most powerful citizens would be limited in their greed. And with appropriate education in the virtues and cultural pleasures of life, the young would mature in liberty to enjoy the benefits of community. Through interdependence and initiative, individual citizens would flourish and the community with them.

In an agrarian age when workers enjoyed few fruits of their labor and even less material comfort, a model that made the individual rewards of the marketplace central to everyday life worked well both in stimulating economic growth and in supporting the stable social order that most humans prefer. But, confined as Smith was by an eighteenth-century vision of the civil society, the old philosopher failed to appreciate how growth in trade would change the conditions necessary for the altruistic performance of his economic model. With commercial expansion the market's effectiveness as an instrument for achieving social balance rapidly declines. This occurs because as businesses merge and increase in size, and as manufacturing and services become geographically remote from each other, the behavioral contingencies essential to promoting social stability in a market-regulated society—close personal relationships, tightly knit communities, local capital investment, and so on—are quickly eroded. Similarly, the fierce competition for personal profit and the disparate distribution of wealth, which inevitably occur as such social constraints diminish, encourage envy and greed. A transgenerational vicious cycle develops: as the intimate bonds of community and family life weaken, the powerful instinctual drives for reward and pleasure are no longer adequately regulated.

That culture and family environment shape the ultimate expression of our genetic predisposition is clear from recent research. Of intriguing pertinence here, for example, is the evidence from a long-term Finnish study that as family intimacy is lost and children are exposed to hostile challenge, those individuals carrying the repeat alleles of the DRD4 dopamine receptor gene—the receptor family associated with the brain's reward pathways—display greater impulsive and risk-taking behavior in adulthood. Hence, nature is shaped by nurture. As empathy withers and social fellowship falters, the fulcrum around which Smith's dynamic model oscillates shifts away from civic concern and the nurturance of community toward self-interest and servicing personal satisfaction. With unbridled economic growth Smith's free-market design for a balanced, self-regulating civil society becomes hijacked by competition and individual desire.

Thus, as a psychiatrist, I am not surprised by America's recent drift toward self-interest. It is the predictable response to affluence in a minimally regulated market-based society. (Or in the language of brain biology, it is predictable that during times of great abundance, unless the prudence of frontal lobe reasoning imposes collective constraint through cultural agreement, human social behavior will run away to greed as the brain's ancient centers of instinctual self-preservation engage in a frenzy of self-reward.) While this shift toward self-satisfaction is also evident in other affluent industrialized nations, American culture is well ahead of the curve. America's migrant temperament and the international growth of corporate power have played their part in tipping the social balance. The migrant's willingness to move for economic advantage and a mind-set of risk-taking and fierce independence aggressively promote commercial competition and foster a distrust of political authority, while the mass marketing of cheaply imported goods to the consumer seeks out and exploits the common denominators of individual desire. In consequence, by the late 1990s American business was distinctly self-centered and profit driven while the enticements to consumer spending had pushed personal debt to unprecedented levels. With increasing mobility the decline of local community as the economic and social hub of American life accelerated. Self-fulfillment, self-gain, self-expression, self-realization, and even self-help became the order of the day, with the goal of achieving a self that was satisfied for its own sake. A new commercial ecology had been created: short-term reward was now a more powerful motivation for the individual citizen than was social responsibility.

Probably the most visible evidence of this new ecology is the rapid growth in wealth and the "celebrity" status of many corporate executives. The scandals that came to light in the aftermath of the telecommunications bubble, surrounding the leadership of Enron, Global Crossing, and other corporate giants, drew public attention and much indignation. But these stories were just the flotsam on a current that now runs broad and deep in America's business culture. As an example, in 2003 Richard Grasso, the chairman of the New York Stock Exchange, resigned after it was revealed that he was to receive $188 million in accumulated benefits. The defenders of Grasso had argued vehemently that his compensation was in line with other corporate executives, which as his detractors were quick to point out was a scandal in itself. A movement that began with the theory that aligning executive pay with market performance through stock options would enhance a company's competitive edge has spawned a new commercial elite in America. In a frenzy of self-promotion, the checks and balances usually inherent in group behavior have broken down, with executive compensation being set by boards of directors—often well-paid CEOs in their own right and frequently close business colleagues—that are handpicked by the incumbent management. Through these mechanisms the celebrity leaders of American business—essentially free agents with little allegiance to any one corporation—have pushed executive salaries to unprecedented heights, often by the uncompromising restructuring of companies, with the release of thousands of employees and the reduction of benefits for many others. (Between 2001 and 2003, despite continued growth in the gross national product, America lost 3 million jobs.) This combination of aggressive enticements for business leadership, plus a policy of outsourcing and flexibility in the labor force has paid off handsomely for American commerce, helping the economy remain reasonably resilient despite bursting bubbles, terrorist attacks, and war. But it has also spawned a modern form of mercantilism where millions of Americans with little financial security and few retirement benefits find themselves working for multinational companies with little accountability. It is a discomforting fact that many Americans are working astonishingly hard but not sharing in the benefits of their increased effort. Between 1983 and 1998, 47 percent of the nation's total income was claimed by just 1 percent of Americans, while the bottom 80 percent of citizens claimed merely 12 percent. As a result America's inequity in wealth distribution is now greater than that of any other industrialized nation. America has become a "champagne glass" society dominated by a mercantile elite.

DOES ANY of this matter? I believe so. Nostalgia and political persuasion, however, play no part in my concern. What does is my growing awareness, as a practicing psychiatrist and a behavioral scientist, that American culture is becoming detached from some fundamental truths about human behavior. As Tom proclaimed during our luncheon, pleasure and happiness are indeed distinct. Together with life and liberty, pleasure is of the individual self. Happiness, on the other hand, is found for most of us within a social context and in the relationships that we have with others. In the *pursuit* of happiness, freedom and opportunity are essential, but if we wish to *secure* happiness—and to protect the national health—then vibrant local communities and an equitable society are imperative.

So what is to be done? How is personal happiness secured in a migrant society where stable communities are hard to find and where consumerism has become the primary exercise of individual freedom? Well, one option is to follow Tom's path and to exercise one's freedom in a different way, stepping aside from the treadmill and embracing a simpler existence. And, in fact, mindfulness works, as many Americans are discovering. And so do other alternative lifestyles—such as the Seeds of Simplicity movement that is enjoying healthy growth in California, Seattle, and across the country—if it is personal tranquility that one is seeking. But where does that leave the commitment to the larger culture? What responsibility do we have to each other and to future generations when it comes to sustaining the great American experiment?

First we must give credit where credit is due. In fact, in America the pursuit of self-gain has been so successful in building the capital enterprise that the potential for mass affluence—among 280 million people, no less—has been achieved for the first time in history. This is an extraordinary accomplishment. Many Americans now enjoy privileges once reserved only for the rich and they have left scarcity behind, without a second thought. The complexities of today's marketplace may no longer reflect the social circumstances of the eighteenth century, but human curiosity and self-interest—Smith's twin engines of economic growth—remain in fine fettle. Over two hundred years people have not changed. In our compulsion to "truck, barter, and exchange" we are still motivated to maximize gain and to minimize risk. The genius of the capitalist enterprise is affirmed. Over the same time frame, however, the social infrastructure that Smith took for granted has not faired as well in America—as I have documented—and it is here that we must focus our collective ingenuity, toward a humane agenda of revitalization.

To sustain a civil society we must share with each other. In the abstract such sharing is not an attractive idea, especially for those of the migrant mind-set. And as society grows more complex, and we spend more of our lives among strangers, the notion grows more alien. Diversity erodes the common culture. Acts of sharing flow more easily and more generously when values are shared and when the recipients of the social benefits seem like us. As kinships fragment and communities decline, social programs become impersonal and fall easily to the bottom of the political agenda. And yet in many respects, the dramatic shift away from social concern and toward competitive self-interest that occurred during the closing decades of the twentieth century is a novelty in American society. While, from the beginning, America's migrant culture has favored the individual and entrepreneurship, nevertheless the intimacy of community was essential to survival during the developmental years of the Union. Alexis de Tocqueville, for example, was enormously impressed during his visit to America in 1831 by the "use which the Americans make [in civil life] of associations . . . that have no political object." "Among democratic peoples," Tocqueville wrote in *Democracy in America*, "all the citizens are independent and weak. They would all therefore find themselves helpless if they did not learn to help each other voluntarily. [To that end] . . . Americans of all ages, of all stations of life, and of all types of disposition are forever forming associations."

Even amid the frenzy of the Fast New World our fundamental need for intimacy is clearly displayed, both in the media and in our technology. Across the nation television programming serves to blunt our hunger for friendship and support. Obvious examples are the growing popularity of the gospel channels and of "reality" television. Here is life with a Hollywood ending, where the game is to watch others fall in love or compete for survival, with the opportunity to phase out before anything bad happens. Similarly, sitcoms serve as a replacement for friends—one popular show even carries that title—and they come complete with a "laugh-track" audience, for we hate to feel that we are watching alone. And, of course, there is the frequently professed hope that the Internet will somehow heal the centrifugal spin of globalization and knit us back together as one giant community. But nothing can duplicate the intimacy of personal attachment. It is the empathic understanding of friends and family, and the social networks of community that act as vital buffers when we are challenged by uncertainty and stressful circumstance. Technology, financial success, and material goods are a pale substitute for such support. Kim Phan, confident though she was in her professional achievements, thought first of her family when she found herself alone and anxious in a Paris hospital. Our intimate attachments not only secure the roots of our humanity and that of future generations, but also provide the behavioral safeguards required to endure the demand-driven environments of the Fast New World.

Inadvertently, with our emphasis on materialism and profit in America, we have invested primarily in the self and allowed our society's infrastructure of "psychic support" to deteriorate. And yet indices of social and behavioral unrest, such as school violence or the number of young people in prison, suggest that our cultural need for sustainable, tightly knit communities—for the social anchors that can successfully instill empathic understanding and civic concern across generations—has never been greater. Such indices of social disruption emphasize that from the standpoint of our moral development as a nation, we cannot divorce our economic life from our family and community life. The integrated communities that my friend Peanut Wilder remembers from his youth have been rendered economically obsolete by the march of commerce toward homogenized mass consumption. As a cultural form, they will never return. It is toward finding viable alternatives that we must now apply our considerable ingenuity. Local communities require local businesses that pay local taxes to provide local employment, thus to maintain an infrastructure of local services. It is a misunderstanding of culture to assume that the social sentiments of an earlier age will remain secure when relentless competition, mass markets, and unbridled self-interest are busily dismantling the community framework that once nurtured those sentiments, and the happiness of the people that created them. Ironically, the same tools and technologies that have enabled America to achieve Adam Smith's "universal opulence" have also compromised the social anchors that the old philosopher took for granted.

The "invisible hand"—Smith's metaphor for the unanticipated conse-quences of market action—has been at work in unintended ways.

Somewhere along the road to affluence, caught up in the excitement of material opportunity and a virtual world of electronic wizardry, Amer-ica has lost sight of the purpose of the journey. The marketplace is inte-gral to the civil society. But is it purposeful that many citizens under the stress of market competition have mortgaged their future to debt and slowly relinquished the vital freedom of how to spend their time? I sus-pect not. In the two decades leading up to the millennium, the Ameri-can economy, with an average annual growth rate of around 3.3 percent, grew significantly faster than did that of Europe, at 2.3 percent. Produc-tivity per hour, however, is comparable for the European and American worker. Thus, in large part, working longer hours accounts for America's greater economic growth. Thanks to that industry, we Americans enjoy bigger paychecks, more possessions, and probably fewer taxes than do our European friends, but there are trade-offs in the social realm. In addition to the now familiar examples—that we Americans are fatter, more anxious, enjoy less free time, and have less job security—41 mil-lion citizens among us have poor access to America's multiple health care systems, and the quality of education a child receives varies signif-icantly with his or her family income.

In America's time of affluence, the faith that the profits of commer-cial growth will trickle down to sustain the nation's social infrastructure is emerging as a fatal misconception. Ayn Rand's doctrine of rational self-interest equating wealth with happiness is in retreat, but in blind perseveration we struggle on. The examples are legion. Despite evidence that humans are prone to addiction and confused by abundance, as a culture we persist in exploiting desire and competition as the principle engines of "progress," offering little reward for social responsibility. In times of budget shortfall, governors and state legislators turn to enhanc-ing gambling revenues, and as federal deficits mount, personal tax cuts that largely benefit the wealthy are recommended to spur a sluggish economy. In the interest of commercial gain, we exploit the restlessness and self-searching of the teenager, rather than investing in the schools that will shape the adolescent experience and provide the skills vital to the exercise of a lifetime of freedom. In a collective denial of aging—at the other end of the life cycle—we employ all available technologies to simulate youth, misunderstanding that the secret to immortality lies not in the individual but in the society we leave behind. The thread that runs through each of these examples is that in our economic philosophy we ignore what we know about human behavior and adhere tenaciously to a dangerous misreading of Adam Smith's prescription for a sustainable civil society. We persist in promoting the self-interest and competition of the marketplace, not as the valuable tool that it is, but as an end in itself—as an ideology.

THE AMERICAN experiment is entering a new and critical phase. At times in human history certain cultural groups have risen to dominance by virtue of geography, natural resources, or political purpose. Americans exercise that cultural dominance today, in part because of the unique temperament of restless assertion that flows from the nation's migrant self-selection. In little more than two centuries the American people have overcome every constraint to build a society of unprecedented commercial abundance. This extraordinary achievement is the product of extraordinary ambition nurtured by a land of extraordinary opportunity. Now, in the time of America's hegemony, it is tempting to lapse into complacency—to be blinkered in our vision of the future by our own mythology—and to believe unquestionably that American society is the next step in the evolution of human culture. After all, if we dominate the globe, is that not evidence that we have devised the best society in the history of the world? And does it not follow, therefore, that America's competitive, market-driven social reality must be mankind's preferred state of being?

But, in a nation built on the freedom to question and a foundation of self-examination, commercial success is only one dimension of civil society. Thus we Americans must ask, to what purpose is our manic striving? Why do we live this way in a land where we are free to choose? Have we fallen victim to the illusion that only more of what we have can be better? It is time to follow Tom's example, time for each of us to stand back and exercise our freedom of speech and reason—to think hard about who we are and what we want our society to become over the next hundred years. What is clear is that while the frenzied excitement and the potential reward of the Fast New World may be intoxicating, it is doing little for the health of the average American citizen. And certainly the evidence is in that unbridled reinforcement of self-indulgence will not promote the balanced society that Adam Smith and the Enlighten-ment thinkers had hoped to inspire; nor was it the creation of a new form of mercantilism that our forebears had in mind when they broke with King George.

Central to the Enlightenment was the goal of extending scientific inquiry—observation and experiment—to human nature and to society, thus to better understand the roots of the human condition. To do so does not substitute science for humanity, but the wise use of science can help us understand who we are as evolved creatures of this planet, and where our happiness is rooted. Thus our discovery that the chal-lenges of the Fast New World have a disorganizing power over our phys-iological and mental well-being is knowledge too dangerous to ignore, much as were the climate shifts that our ancestors faced in the Rift Val-ley many centuries ago. But America is not the Rift Valley. The demand-ing circumstances in which we find ourselves come not from the stirrings of nature but are of our own making, and thus it is within our power to change them. And thanks to science we are forearmed in mak-ing those changes. As we become more knowledgeable of the limits that our physical inheritance imposes on us, we are in a better position to order our lives accordingly. When neurobiology reminds us that as a species we are pleasure seekers and prone to addiction—especially when faced with an abundance of food, information, or choice—it is useful knowledge. Similarly, it is valuable to learn that our humanity— the empathy and tenderness that bring happiness—while deeply rooted in our nature requires a sympathetic culture in which to be expressed.

AMERICA HAS yet to solve the conundrum of transforming self-interest into social fellowship, but it is now within our understanding and within the nation's economic power to do so. In its migrant heritage America has received great gifts—the talents of curiosity, ingenuity, and a heightened awareness that destiny is in large part a matter of personal responsibility being among them. I was reminded of that heritage when late in the afternoon after my luncheon with Tom in New York, I slipped out of the Algonquin Hotel to buy some reading material before heading to the airport. The rain was abating, giving way to a watery sun that was washing the familiar facades of 44th Street in a tint of pale yellow, as I made my way amid the urgent city bustle. Threading through the colorful confetti of umbrellas—marshaled by citizens in business costumes, damp T-shirts, parkas, sneakers, and storm boots—I was impressed once again with America's motley crew. Within the collective face of the crowd—in the broad forehead of Africa, the hooded eyes of the Orient, the sharp facial features of Europe, and the high cheekbones of those who came first to this continent—was the living evidence of our nation's émigré roots.

Arriving at the newsstand on the corner of Sixth Avenue, I was greeted by the headline that the Bill and Melinda Gates Foundation had given $51.2 million to help start sixty-seven small high schools within New York City's public school system. "In helping poor and minority students to prepare for college," Bill Gates of Microsoft fame was quoted as saying, "the answer is not smaller classes but smaller high schools . . . a school that has cohesiveness, [where] when a kid walks down a hall and encounters an adult that adult will know their name . . . and be able to talk to them about their progress." The moment seemed a fitting coda for my discussions with Tom, and to my afternoon of reflection. The king of the virtual world—and the richest man on the planet—had decided that more of the same is not enough. When it came to social sentiment, Bill Gates was thinking small.

The merry-go-round of modern life is not going to stop. Hence it is imperative that we use our intelligence and our technology to celebrate rather than to chain our humanity. Finding an optimum balance between self and society in this age of the merchant is for each of us a matter of personal responsibility. Such responsibility cannot be contracted out to others—be they governments or corporations. But as we orchestrate the collective voice in the setting of social priority, it is in our own self-interest to take note of what drives human behavior. In America today, our personal priorities seem clear, but what are our social priorities and how do they each meld with the other? As "The New Colossus," will we remain the "beacon of hope" for the disadvantaged peoples of the world? Or are we in danger, as Tom suggested, of standing apart as an aberrant breed—the first addicts of a technological age—forever in pursuit of some illusory state of greater material perfection?

Perfection does not exist in nature. That commerce and technical achievement will ultimately yield perfection is a human construct. Nature is infinitely more pragmatic. In nature it's all a matter of dynamic fit—of living creatures achieving balance with their surroundings. And what is true for the individual is also true for the social group. Building America's pleasure dome of mass affluence took two hundred years. Now comes the more difficult task of transforming those pleasures into "mass happiness," of forging from the affluence of commercial success a balanced and equitable society. For the restless creativity of America's migrant culture, it is a novel challenge and a worthy frontier.

NOTES

Frontispiece

Alexis de Tocqueville: Both quotations are from Tocqueville's *Democracy in America*, translated by George Lawrence (New York: Anchor Books, 1969). "The doctrine of self-interest . . ." is from Vol. II, Part II, Chapter 8, p. 525; and "Providence did not make mankind entirely free . . ." is from Vol. II, Part IV, Chapter 8, p. 705.

Introduction: THE MANIC SOCIETY

1 Ronald Reagan: Ronald Reagan launched his political career with his speech "A Time for Choosing" in 1964, harking back to what he saw as America's rendezvous with destiny. Quoted by Anders Stephanson in *Manifest Destiny, American Expansion and the Empire of Right* (New York: Hill and Wang, 1995), pp. 127–128.
2 George Carlin: From a New Year's message circulating on the Internet, under George Carlin's name, in January 2002.
3 A declining satisfaction with life in America: Data, circa 1980, from 23 countries (principally European) ranked the United States tenth in happiness. After 1980 the proportion of Americans who believed that "the lot of the average man is getting worse" rose steadily to reach approximately two-thirds of those surveyed in 1994. See *The Loss of Happiness in Market Democracies*, by Robert E. Lane (New Haven: Yale University Press, 2000), p. 26–31.
9 "like a game of chance . . .": Alexis de Tocqueville's many insightful obser-

vations on the habits, behavior, and temperament of Americans made during his visit in 1831 and recorded in *Democracy in America* (first published in 1835) suggest that the risk taking, optimism, and self-interest that are so evident today have changed little over two centuries. This quotation is from Vol. I, Part II, Chapter 10, p. 404.

Part I
THE AMERICAN TEMPERAMENT:
A MANIA FOR PROSPERITY

19 Alexis de Tocqueville: From *Democracy in America*, translated by George Lawrence Vol. I, Part II, Chapter 9, p. 281. Here Tocqueville is describing the continuous movement of the American population—both immigration and internal migration—that he observed. He writes in prelude to my quotation here: "The European arriving in the United States comes without friends and often without resources; in order to live he is obliged to hire out his resources, and he seldom goes beyond the great industrial zone stretching along the ocean. One cannot clear the wilderness without capital or credit. . . . It is therefore Americans who are continually leaving their birthplace and going forth to win vast far off domains. This double movement of immigration never halts."

Chapter One: ADAM SMITH'S AMERICAN DREAM

21 Bernard de Mandeville: Mandeville (1670–1733) was a Dutch physician who lived in England. These lines are from a satirical poem which was first published in book form in 1714, and revised in 1723 (*The Fable of the Bees: or Private Vices, Publick Benefits* (reprinted by Oxford University Press, 2001). In the book Mandeville championed the ideology of self-interest, suggesting that avarice, pride, and a lust for luxury had public benefit as a stimulus to economic growth. It was the forerunner of what became known during Ronald Reagan's term as president as the "trickle-down" effect, where consumption by the rich provides nourishment for the less fortunate. For a discussion of how Enlightenment intellectuals in Britain and France sought to rationalize the pursuit of material prosperity as a worthy political goal, see "Self-Love and Self-Command," in *Adam Smith, In His Time and Ours: Designing the Decent Society*, by Jerry Z. Muller (Princeton, NJ: Princeton University Press, 1993).

23 *Martha Stewart Living*: This magazine, part of the Martha Stewart Living Omnimedia empire, provides advice to the ultimate homemaker. For a lively review of Martha Stewart, the American domestic icon, see "Everywoman.com: Getting out of the House with Martha Stewart," by Joan Didion, *New Yorker*, February 21 and 28, 2000. Apparently Martha has all the manic qualifications for success, sleeping only 4 hours each night and utilizing the time saved to groom her six cats and garden by flashlight. In the summer of 2002, amid the corporate and financial scandals that broke after the bubble collapsed, Martha and her empire fell under a cloud when she was investigated for possible insider trading ("Cooking Martha's Goose," *Economist*, September 14, 2002). Two years later Stewart was convicted of lying about her reasons for the sale of a biotechnology stock ("Stewart Found Guilty of Lying in Sale of Stock," *New York Times*, March 6, 2004), and her television show *Martha Stewart Living* was withdrawn by CBS.

23 Seventy-eight percent of Americans still believe: Quoted in "Ambition and Its Enemies," by Robert J. Samuelson, *Newsweek*, August 23, 1999.

23 riches won and lost: For a concise and amusing, if opinionated, review of such excesses, see *A Short History of Financial Euphoria*, by John Kenneth Galbraith (New York: Penguin Books, 1994). Also *Money, Greed, and Risk: Why Financial Crises and Crashes Happen*, by Charles R. Morris (New York: Times Books, Random House, 1999).

24 havens of lifetime employment: See "The Future of Work: Career Evolution," *Economist*, January 9, 2000, and "In the Options Age, Rising Pay (and Risk)," *New York Times*, April 2, 2000.

24 the quest for economic prosperity: Driven by competitive desire and self-interest, Americans are fascinated by the many possibilities of the Fast New World, and we accelerate our activity to take advantage of it. We deprive ourselves of sleep, never miss a call on the cell phone, neglect our families, and work all hours in fear of missing some golden opportunity. Lured on by the delightful toys that our new technology produces, we buy the latest car, house, or gadget, going into debt if necessary, for in the enthusiasm of the manic rush we give little thought to future consequences. As debt increases, so do the number of hours that we must work to pay off that debt. And as the cycle of technological innovation quickens (there are lots of clever people out there thinking up new attractive toys and tasty goodies that will have a great market and make them rich), we buy more and the manic cycle, a positive feedback loop, accelerates further until either we fall by the wayside exhausted or the money runs out (i.e., there's no more time or equity to borrow against) and the economy crashes.

This cycle occurs to a greater or lesser degree in all market economies, but it is particularly exaggerated in the United States where the migrant mind-set (of survival) heightens competition and self-interest. With the coming of instant communication and rapid transportation in the closing decades of the twentieth century, the natural constraints of time and place were removed and the Fast New World was born, and with it America's manic cycle of desire, debt, and frenzy.

THE MANIC CYCLE

A FEEDBACK LOOP OF POSITIVE REINFORCEMENT

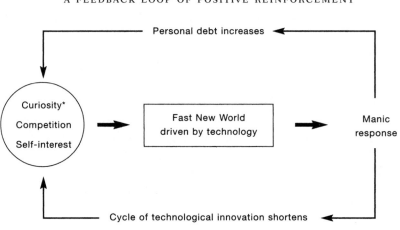

*Behaviors associated with activation of the dopamine reward pathways (see Chapters Three and Four for details).

24 the average hour of American effort: Technology has driven most of the gain. The number of hours worked per individual fell from a high of 70–80 hours in the latter part of the nineteenth century to around 40 hours in the mid-twentieth century. Productivity has multiplied three times since World War II but the number of hours worked has also increased. (Productivity is used here as the output of goods and services per hour worked in the market economy.) See *The Overworked American: The Unexpected Decline of Leisure*, by Juliet Schor (New York: Basic Books, 1992), pp. 43–84.

25 Americans enjoyed the longest period of wealth creation: For background articles to the boom of the late 1990s, see "Sizzling US Growth Confirmed," *International Herald Tribune*, June 28, 1997; "America Bubbles Over," *Economist*, April 18, 1998; "Too Triumphalist by Half," *Economist*, April 25, 1998; and "America's Economy, What a Peculiar Cycle," *Economist*, March 10, 2001. The rise in purchasing power was real at all levels of America's consumer society. Some comparisons are informative. It took approximately 20 minutes to earn enough money for a Hershey bar in 1900 and only 2 minutes in 1997. Similarly, in 1908 a Model T Ford cost 4,696 work hours to purchase, while in 1997 a Ford Taurus cost only 1,365 hours of labor. The cost of a movie ticket, however, remained relatively stable, at 19 minutes of labor ("Every Second Counts Even More," *New York Times*, June 28, 1998).

25 median income . . . rose from $48,008 to $51,681: Derived from the U.S. Census Bureau, 1992–1997, and quoted from "Ambition and Its Enemies," by Robert J. Samuelson, *Newsweek*, August 23, 1999. For details taken from the census of 2000 regarding the rise and distribution of personal income during the 1990s, the growing mobility of the American workforce, the increased time spent in commuting, and the growth in median house size, see "Census Data Show Sharp Increase in Living Standard," *New York Times*, August 6, 2001.

25 Patrick J. Kiger: "Too Much of Everything: A Consumer Culture That Just Can't Stop," by Patrick J. Kiger, Los Angeles Times Magazine, June 9, 2002.

25 the median size of a newly constructed American house: See "Gilt Complex," *New York Times*, November 7, 1999; and "Too Much of Everything: A Consumer Culture That Just Can't Stop," by Patrick J Kiger, *Los Angeles Times Magazine*, June 9, 2002.

26 government borrowing . . . runaway personal debt: In 1980 the U.S. national debt was $930 billion, but by 2003 it had multiplied almost seven times to $6.5 trillion. Added to that, the total household debt in 2001 was $7.6 trillion (quoted in "Sinking Fast," by Jeff Gates, *Utne*, July–August 2003, p. 59). The government debt was bimodally distributed over the two decades, with large deficits accumulating in the 1980s and again after 2000. In 2000 the United States had a general government budget surplus (state and federal combined) of 1.4 percent of gross domestic product (GDP), but by 2003 that surplus had become a deficit of approximately 6 percent of GDP. See "The Rising Tide of Red Ink," *Economist*, August 23, 2003. For background discussion, see also, "Who're You Gonna Call after the Next Bust?" *New York Times*, August 22, 1999; and "Companies' Big Debts Now Carry Big Risks," by Gretchen Morgenson, *New York Times*, October 7, 2001. Also, "Party's Over: A Survey of Corporate Finance," *Economist*, January 27, 2001; and "A Decade of Deficits," *Economist*, June 22, 2000. Of even greater concern is that American debt has been fueling the world's economy. Since 1995 almost 60 percent in the cumulative growth in the world's economy has come from America. With the nation's enormous appetite for spending, domestic demand in America has risen twice as fast as the rest of the rich world. As a result, whereas in 1980 America was the world's biggest creditor, by 2003 it was the world's largest debtor, with the indebtedness of American consumers growing twice as fast as their incomes. See "Flying on One Engine: A Survey of the World Economy," *Economist*, September 20, 2003.

26 The average rate of personal savings fell: See "Net Dearth: Today's Highly Leveraged Consumers Will Pose Danger in a US Downturn," by Edward M. Syring Jr., *Barron's*, May 24, 2001. Also see "In the Balance: America's Downturn Has Done Little to Remove the Country's Serious Economic Imbalances," *Economist*, July 14, 2001.

27 Juliet Schor: Professor Schor is a leading critic of the consumer society. The details of her analysis can be found in her books *The Overworked American: The Unexpected Decline of Leisure* (New York: Basic Books, 1992) and *The Overspent American: Upscaling, Downshifting, and the New Consumer* (New York: Basic Books, 1998). For a concise summary of Schor's ideas, see "The New Politics of

Consumption: Why Americans Want So Much More Than They Need," *Boston Review*, Summer 1999; and "What's Wrong with Consumer Society? Competitive Spending and the New Consumerism," in *Consuming Desires*, edited by Roger Rosenblatt (Washington, D.C.: Allan Press, 1999).

28 a Scottish professor of moral philosophy named Adam Smith: Adam Smith (1723–1790) was one of the most distinguished men of letters of the eighteenth century. His father, who died before Adam was born, was a lawyer and the Comptroller of Customs in Kirkcaldy, a post similar to that which Smith held—the Commissioner of Customs in Scotland—at the end of his life. Smith was first and foremost a student of human behavior. His fame was secured by *The Theory of Moral Sentiments*, which was published first in 1759 and continuously revised until his death. *An Inquiry into the Nature and Causes of the Wealth of Nations*, published in 1776, grew out of that interest and was a systematic study of the effects on human progress of laws, institutions, and the environment—what we might consider today as a discourse on evolutionary sociology rather than a formal treatise on economics. In addition to the original texts, my discussion of Smith's life and ideas, the philosophy of the Enlightenment, and mercantilism and the economic circumstances of the eighteenth century are drawn from several sources, including *Adam Smith: The Man and His Works*, by E. G. West (Indianapolis: Liberty Press, 1976); and *The House of Adam Smith*, by Eli Ginsberg (New York: Columbia University Press, 1934). Of the many books that have been written about Smith, his life, and his writings, for a concise review and analysis, I recommend *Adam Smith in His Time and Ours: Designing the Decent Society*, by Jerry Z. Muller (Princeton, NJ: Princeton University Press, 1993).

29 human instinctual desire: Throughout *American Mania* I use *instinct* and *instinctual* to describe behaviors that have a strongly inherited component. It is important to note, however, that there has been much debate about the patterns of "instinctual" behavior—those behaviors innately present at birth in primates and humans. We know, for example, that "lower" animals such as fish and birds have complex patterns of courting, nest building, and sexual behavior that are innately programmed and can be expressed without the animal having witnessed such behaviors in fellow creatures. But in higher animals such as primates, and in humans, instinctual behavior is more complex. While primed by the inherited biology, the behavior is drawn out by a facilitating environment, and the ultimate behavioral expression is a function of the interaction. Thus the songbird modifies and perfects its innate song by listening to a tutor, and human language is much the same. What we call *self-interest*—the drive for self-preservation—embraces a complex series of innate behavioral templates, all of which are designed to preserve the individual from harm. It is this constellation of drives that Adam Smith called "self-love," and which he believed could be harnessed and shaped by the give-and-take of the market to forge a stable and equitable social order. For a discussion of instinct in lower animals, primates, and humans, see *The Human*

Agenda: How to Be at Home in the Universe without Magic, by Roderic Gorney (New York: Simon and Schuster, 1972), pp. 63–65.

29 Darwin developed his ideas about natural selection: Charles Darwin, whose wife was a member of the Wedgwood pottery manufacturing family, was a heavy investor in industry. He had many books on economy and manufacturing in his library and was familiar with the specialized workforce as a means of increasing productivity. Indeed, he considered Smith's "division of labor" as the engine of civilization. For discussion, see *Darwin: The Life of a Tortured Evolutionist,* by Adrian Desmond and James Moore (New York: W. W. Norton, 1991), p. 421.

30 "Give me that which I want": Quotation is from *An Inquiry into the Nature and Causes of the Wealth of Nations,* 8th ed. (London: Strahan and Cadell, 1796), Book I, Chapter II, p. 21. (Smith's *Wealth of Nations,* first published in 1776, was written over a 10-year period and has been repeatedly edited and republished.)

30 Smith writes on the subject of the pocket watch: Smith's discussion of gadgets and of the human frailty for such instruments, particularly watches, is taken from *The Theory of Moral Sentiments* (Indianapolis: Liberty Classics Edition, 1969), Part IV, Chapter 1, p. 299.

31 "keeps in continual motion the industry of mankind": Ibid., p. 303.

31 "Mankind is disposed to make parade": Ibid., Part I, Chapter 2, p. 112.

32 "the number of people whose industry": *Wealth of Nations,* Book I, Chapter I, p. 17.

32 In his day Smith found a ready history: For an excellent review of the history of financial speculation and its relationship to the development of the free-market economy, see *Devil Take the Hindmost: A History of Financial Speculation,* by Edward Chancellor (New York, Farrar, Straus and Giroux, 1999). The material describing the Dutch influence on English banking practices will be found in Chapter 2 ("Stock Jobbing in Change Alley"). I am also indebted here to Mr. Chancellor for his detailed analysis of the South Sea Bubble and for the quotation from Sir Isaac Newton. Other information was gathered from John Galbraith's book *A Short History of Financial Euphoria* and from *The Extraordinary Popular Delusions and Madness of Crowds,* by Charles McKay (New York: Random House, 1980), originally published in 1841 as *Memoirs of Extraordinary Popular Delusions.*

34 Thomas Hobbes, the influential English philosopher: Hobbs was a man of strident opinion, antagonizing many during his lifetime. Hobbs argued, "Man is a selfish animal by nature, at constant war with other men. Without arts and letters and society, we are in danger of a violent death and live solitary, poor, nasty, brutish and short lives" (from *Leviathan,* published in 1651). Adam Smith had a more charitable view of the human race.

35 "The man whom we naturally love the most": *Theory of Moral Sentiments* Part III, Chapter 3, p. 254.

37 gap between the wealthiest Americans and everyone else: The statistical material in this discussion of income distribution and debt was drawn from news articles appearing both before and during the collapse of the "new economy" bubble, including "Wall Street Follies," *New Yorker*, September 13, 1999; "Gap between Rich and Poor Found Substantially Wider," *New York Times*, September 5, 1999; "Working Families Strain to Live Middle Class Life," *New York Times*, September 10, 2000; "Calculating One Kind of Middle Class," by Tom Zeller, *New York Times*, October 29, 2000; "With Bull Market under Siege Some Worry about Its Legacy" by Floyd Norris, *New York Times*, March 18, 2001; "Mired in Debt and Seeking a Path Out," by Peter Kilborn, *New York Times*, April 1, 2001; "To Save or Spend," by Alex Berenson, *New York Times*, April 1, 2001; "For the Boss, Happy Days Are Still Here; Chiefs' Pay Rises Even as Portfolios Fall," *New York Times*, April 1, 2001; "Making Sure the Rich Stay Rich, Even in Crisis," by Geraldine Fabrikant, *New York Times*, October 7, 2001; "Grounded by an Income Gap: Inequality Just Keeps Growing in the US," *New York Times*, December 15, 2001; "Housing Less Affordable as Rent-Wage Gap Widens," by Diane Wedner, *Los Angeles Times*, October 3, 2001. See also "America's Economy, What a Peculiar Cycle," *Economist*, March 10, 2001.

38 America's "champagne glass" society: At the millennium, approximately 20 percent of Americans controlled 91 percent of the nation's wealth ("Net Dearth: Today's Highly Leveraged Consumers Will Pose Danger in a US Downturn," by Edward M. Syring Jr., *Barron's*, May 24, 2001.

38 Shrink the population of the world: This is drawn from statistics circulating the Internet. The calculation is originally attributed to Philip Harter at the Stanford University Medical School. The data on America's three richest citizens is drawn from "Kofi Annan's Astonishing Facts," by Barbara Crossette, *New York Times*, September 27, 1998. The 1998 report of the UN Development Program featured the comparative consumption of the world's goods and services by different nations. For example, of the world's 225 richest individuals, 60 are Americans, with total assets of $311 billion. Of the 4.4 billion people in developing countries, three-fifths lack access to sewers, clean water, and adequate housing. Twenty percent have no access to modern health services of any kind. America spends $8 billion a year on cosmetics, $3 billion more than the estimated cost of providing basic education to everyone in the world. Europeans spend $6 billion a year on ice cream, $2 billion more than is required to provide clean water to the world's population. America and the European nations together spend $17 billion a year on pet food, $4 billion more than the estimated annual cost of providing basic health and nutrition worldwide.

39 Charles Ponzi: In America during the 1920s Ponzi, already a convicted felon, became famous when during the Florida real estate boom he paid handsome dividends to investors by using the money obtained from later investors. The scheme collapsed when the revenue flow from new buyers dried up, largely because it was discovered that Ponzi's "beachfront" lots were 15 to 60 miles from the coast. See John Kenneth Galbraith, *A Short History of Financial Euphoria* (New York: Penguin Books, 1990), p. 72–73.

39 For these "average" American families, debt: These data of the comparative debt burden of rich and middle-class households are taken from "Very Expensive Belts Tighten, but Just a Notch," by Blaine Harden, *New York Times*, April 1, 2001.

40 half of America's households have a net worth: See "Net Dearth: Today's Highly Leveraged Consumers Will Pose Danger in a US Downturn," by Edward M. Syring Jr., *Barron's*, May 24, 2001.

40 College students, for example, are particular targets: "Credit Worthy? Be Credit Wary Too," Abby Ellin, *New York Times*, July 21 2002.

40 buying dreams on credit is an American invention: For a history of the growth of consumerism in America, read *Land of Desire: Merchants, Power, and the Rise of a New American Culture,* by William Leach (New York: Pantheon Books, 1993).

41 Thorstein Veblen: Inspired by the Gilded Age, a term coined by Mark Twain, Thorstein Veblen's social satire *The Theory of the Leisure Class* was published in 1899, defining not only an era but also a way of life. The book saw a resurgence in popularity when the consumption of the 1990s was at its height. Veblen's is a social analysis with an evolutionary bent (one of the first) suggesting a conflict between the instinctual drive for more and social equality. *The Theory of the Leisured Class* was recently republished (New York: Penguin Books, 1994). The quotation is taken from p. 74.

42 F. Scott Fitzgerald: The decade of manic exuberance that preceded the Great Depression is now largely forgotten. But it was during those Gatsby years that technology first entered the minds and homes of ordinary American citizens, and the merchant redefined the American Dream. *The Great Gatsby*, published in 1925, satires that shift in vision. The full quotation, which appears on p. 159, is as follows: "Gatsby believed in the green light, the orgiastic future that year by year recedes before us. It eluded us then, but that's no matter—tomorrow we will run faster, stretch out our arms further. . . . And one fine morning—"

42 Harris Collingwood . . . the "sink-or-swim" economy: See "The Sink-or-Swim Economy," by Harrison Collingwood, *New York Times Magazine*, June 8, 2003. Also "Recession Is Over; Jobs Aren't Trickling Down," by Daniel Altman, *New York Times*, July 18, 2003.

43 "idiosyncratic volatility": Defined in "The Sink-or-Swim Economy," by Harrison Collingwood (*New York Times Magazine*, June 8, 2003), as "local level [economic] volatility that affects individual firms but doesn't show up in the big picture statistics."

43 only 21 percent of California workers: California is the classic example of how America's social mania can drive a roller-coaster economy and drive job insecurity. During the 1990s, after its worst recession in half a century and with the creation of 400,000 new jobs, California became the national leader in the percentage change of employment. ("The West Is Best Again," *Economist*, August 9, 1999). An earlier boom, led by a defense buildup in the 1980s, had collapsed after the fall of the Berlin Wall. The high technology of the new economy was principally based in California and the state's fortunes rose with it. Thus, while the state's economy is diversified, the 1990s growth was based largely on temporary jobs, with computers and filmmaking being the drivers of the economic expansion (for details, see "Job Boom Brings Insecurity," Raymond G. Macleod, *San Francisco Chronicle*, May 25, 1999; "LA's Growing Pay Gap Looms as Political Issue," by Jim Newton, *Los Angeles Times*, September 7, 1999). After the bubble burst, state tax revenues were hard hit by an electricity crisis (following deregulation), which may have been driven in large part by the sharp business practices of Enron and other energy corporations that later failed ("How Did They Value Stocks? Count the Absurd Ways," by Gretchen Morgenson, *New York Times*, March 18, 2001). Subsequently as the general economy slowed and the new economy collapsed, California went rapidly from a $9 billion surplus in 2000 to a $35 billion deficit in 2003, dramatically threatening education, health, and other state services ("Latest Blow to the State: The Incredible Shrinking Private Sector; The Figures Show That a Quick Fix Will Not Correct the $35 Billion Budget Gap," by David Friedman, *Los Angeles Times*, March 9, 2003; and "State Reflects Its People in Living Beyond Its Means," by George Skelton, *Los Angeles Times*, March 17, 2003).

43 the number of bankruptcies declared in America: See "Net Dearth: Today's Highly Leveraged Consumers Will Pose Danger in a US Downturn," by Edward M. Syring Jr., *Barron's*, May 24, 2001. Debt collection in America has become a big industry, minting a few millionaires of its own. Also see "Debt and the Salesman," by Phillip Gourevitch, *New Yorker*, July 30 2001.

44 Between 2001 and 2003, approximately 3 million jobs were lost from the American economy: For summary, see "Defying Forecast, Job Losses Mount for a 22nd Month," by Louis Uchitelle, *New York Times*, September 6, 2003.

44 Women, including women with young children: American social policy (or the lack of it), in comparison to many other countries, burdens the family in other ways besides temporary jobs and low benefits (see "When Waaa Turns to Why: Mom and Dad Both Work? Sure. But What to Tell the Children?" *New York Times*, November 11, 1997). The average length of paid maternal leave in the United States, for example, is 6 weeks, in contrast to approximately 18 weeks in Britain, Italy, and Denmark; 30 weeks in Germany; and 52 weeks in Sweden. Only in the United States and the United Kingdom is there *no* paternity leave.

45 Americans are workaholics: Americans have always had difficulty enjoying leisure, but this worsened in the 1990s. See "Holidays; A Great Time to Work," *Economist*, July 24, 1999; and "Workplace Demands Taking up More Weekends," by Stephanie Armour, *USA Today*, April 24, 1998.

46 "Though North America is not yet so rich as England": *Wealth of Nations*, Book I, Chapter VIII, p. 107.

46 "life, liberty and the pursuit of happiness": Those interested in the political forces surrounding the changes made by Jefferson in the Declaration of Independence, and that gave us the hallowed phrase "the pursuit of happiness," are recommended to read *Miracle at Philadelphia*, by Catherine Drinker Bowen (Boston: Little, Brown, Company, 1966); see particularly Chapter 6, "Life, Liberty and Property."

48 As Sigmund Freud observed in his essay: *Civilization and Its Discontents*, by Sigmund Freud (New York: W. W. Norton, 1961), p. 49.

Chapter Two: CURIOSITY AND THE PROMISED LAND

49 Emma Lazarus: The sonnet "The New Colossus" by Emma Lazarus (1849–1887) is inscribed on the pedestal of the Statue of Liberty, the 150-foot-tall maiden from France who commands the entrance to New York City Harbor and once welcomed immigrants to the United States. Lazarus, an American poet and essayist born in New York City, was an impassioned spokeswoman for Judaism. Her famous poem was inspired by the Russian persecution of Eastern European Jews in the 1880s. Over this period approximately one-third of all the Jews in Eastern Europe emigrated, with the overwhelming majority coming to the United States and most settling in New York City, principally in the Lower East Side of Manhattan. While four-fifths of this massive immigration came from Czarist Russia, it also included those who had lived in Poland and Lithuania before those lands were adsorbed by Russian expansion.

50 Ellis Island: The immigration facilities at Ellis Island opened in 1892 and for the next 62 years served as the principle gateway through which immigrants entered the United States. Originally some 3 acres in size, the name of the island comes from its first owners, a farming family, who sold it to the federal government in 1808 for $10,000. It was fortified during the 1812 war with Britain and was a naval magazine until its conversion into an immigration center. After closure in 1954 the facilities fell into disrepair, and after several fantastical schemes for its use, as a resort hotel among others, it was restored as a national museum in the 1980s. For a brief history, see *The Other New York Islands: A Historical Companion*, by Sharon Seitz and Stuart Miller (Woodstock, VT: Countryman Press, 1996).

50 migrant people in the world today: See *Migrations and Cultures: A World View*, by Thomas Sowell (New York: Basic Books, 1996). Also some details in this paragraph are taken from "A Nation of Immigrants," *Economist*, December 31, 1999.

53 maverick: The term derives from Samuel A. Maverick (1803–1870), a Texas

engineer who owned but did not brand cattle. His name has come into the English language to mean an unorthodox or independent-minded person.

53 Professor Lynn Fairbanks: The Fairbanks family genealogy is published
privately. See *The Fairbanks Family in America 1455–1897*, by Lorenzo Sayles Fairbanks (Orem, UT: Carl Rogers and Stephen Crabtree, 1980).

54 the oldest frame dwelling in America: The Jonathan Fairbanks house
is considered by Abbot Lowell Cummings, professor of American decorative arts
at Yale University, to be one of the most significant historic structures now standing in the United States. Its importance lies not only in it being the oldest house
in New England, but also in its architecture. No other New England dwelling of
the mid-seventeenth century has survived in such unspoiled condition. The Fairbanks House is open to the public from May to October of each year. Those interested should contact the Curator, Fairbanks House, 511 East Street, Dedham,
MA 02026, USA.

**56 "For Jonathan to leave England and his family of origin was
risky":** Lynn Fairbanks suspected that in addition to Jonathan's family situation,
there had been political considerations determining his migration. Jonathan had
been born around 1600, and thus his youth coincided with the decline of England's Elizabethan splendor. The struggles between those who denounced the doctrines of the Anglican Church and James Stuart of Scotland (who had succeeded
to the English throne in 1603) had sown fear and suspicion throughout the country. In the hysteria that followed the abortive gunpowder plot of 1605, both
Catholics and the reform-minded Puritans—threatening as they did the sovereign
power of the king—fell under attack. Mutual disaffection followed, and by 1630,
when Jonathan was weighing the benefits and drawbacks of leaving England, the
Puritan and Catholic exodus was in full swing. King Charles I, who had assumed
the English throne and was later to lose his head in the struggles with Parliament,
had become desperate for money and was busily selling off knighthoods and business monopolies to swell his treasury. New taxes on material goods, including wool
(which was Jonathan's livelihood), a stamp duty on cards, and a ship tax to build
the navy, were making the life of a merchant progressively uncomfortable. Short
of civil war, Jonathan thought it unlikely that the king would embrace greater liberties for ordinary men. All this, plus the knowledge that it was his elder half-
brother, not Jonathan, who would inherit his father's estates, made the decision to
leave comparatively easy. With the newly formed Massachusetts Bay Company
offering land for settlement in America, the opportunities of the New World
looked exceedingly attractive, despite the hazards of an Atlantic crossing. For a
comprehensive and colorful account, written only a century or so later, see *The
History of England from the Invasion of Julius Caesar to the Revolution in 1688*, by
David Hume, who was a close friend of Adam Smith. The volume relevant to the
period when the English migration to America began in earnest is number 9, of
the 1779 edition printed in Basel by J.J. Tourneisen.

57 studies of migrant populations: There are only a few studies of migrants that focus specifically on temperament and the behavioral characteristics of successful adaptation, but most general studies make some reference to it. A comprehensive behavioral analysis can be found in *Adaptation of Immigrants: Individual Differences and Determinants*, by William A. Scott and Ruth Scott (New York: Pergamon Press, 1989). The Scotts work at the Australian National University in Canberra, and thus Australian migration features heavily in their book. However, they also review studies conducted in Canada, the United Kingdom and the United States, focusing on individual differences in adaptation to the migrant experience. I have drawn heavily on their review in the material presented here. In addition, *Migration and Residential Mobility: Macro and Micro Approaches*, by Martin Cadwallader (Madison, WI: University of Wisconsin Press, 1992), is a valuable resource, especially with its focus on migration within the United States, and the individual preferences that trigger such internal migration. Worthy of perusal is *Migration, Migration History, History: Old Paradigms and New Perspectives*, edited by Jan Lucassen and Leo Lucassen (New York: Peter Lang, 1997). Of particular relevance is the chapter by Pieter C. Emma, "Was Migration Beneficial?"

58 "In Europe we habitually regard a restless spirit": Quotation is from *Democracy in America*, by Alexis de Tocqueville, translated by George Lawrence (New York: Anchor Books, 1969), Vol. I, Part II, Chapter 9, p. 284.

58 the metaphor of the "navigator": Tocqueville was fascinated by the determination he witnessed in the American people. The navigator metaphor is part of his "considerations concerning the causes of the commercial greatness of the United States" (*Democracy in America*, Vol. I, Part II, Chapter 10, p. 402). He muses that "nature destines the Americans to be a great seagoing people: the extent of their coasts; depths of their harbors; size of their rivers. However, the commercial superiority of the Anglo-Americans should be attributed much less to physical causes than to intellectual and moral ones." For an interesting discussion of the influence of American wilderness on the mind of the European settler, see the introductory chapters of *The Lost World of Thomas Jefferson*, by Daniel J. Boorstin (Chicago: University of Chicago Press, 1993).

59 The story really begins some 200 million years ago: For a concise but complete compendium of information about human evolution, see *How Humans Evolve*, by Robert Boyd and Joan Silk (New York: W. W. Norton, 1997). Two books, *The Making of Mankind*, by Richard E. Leakey (New York, Elsevier-Dutton, 1981), and *Origins Reconsidered: In Search of What Makes Us Human*, by Richard Leakey and Roger Lewin (New York: Anchor Books, 1992), are not as comprehensive as Boyd and Silk's reference but have the advantage of describing the quest for human origins through the experience and accomplishments of one of the leading archaeologists of the twentieth century.

60 Rick Potts: See *Humanity's Descent: The Consequences of Ecological Instability*, by Rick Potts (New York: William Morrow, 1996). A summary of his ideas regarding human evolution can also be found in the comprehensive article "Why Are We Human," *Washington Post*, April 14, 1999.

61 genetic sleuthing: The principles that lie behind the discoveries in "genetic archaeology" rest on sampling the genetic signatures of individuals from different nationalities and assembling a comprehensive map of the migratory patterns and genetic variation within the human species. The analysis rests on a set of well-established scientific principles. During conception the genetic material from the mother and the father is commingled to produce a unique individual. However, small energy-producing subunits called *mitochondria*, which are present in every cell of the body, are passed exclusively from mother to daughter. Constructed from an analysis of the relatively simple genetics of these mitochondrial units from blood samples given by women from across the world, a human family tree identifies "Mitochondrial Eve" as a woman living in North Africa approximately 200,000 years ago. More recently, in a similar worldwide sampling, an analysis of the male Y chromosome (which passes exclusively from father to son) has determined that the "Adam" of our species is also of African origin. The article "Mitochondrial DNA and Human Evolution," by R. Can, A. S. King, and A. Wilson (*Nature*, 325: 31–36, 1987) launched an intense debate (see *Science*, 14: 873, 1992). For a comprehensive discussion of mitochondrial analysis, see "The Mother of All Humans?" in *African Exodus, The Origins of Modern Humanity*, by Christopher Stringer and Robin McKie (New York, Henry Holt, 1997), pp. 115–148. Also see "Y Chromosome Shows That Adam Was an African," *Science*, 278: 567–569, 1997. The tracking of the Y chromosome was a combination of work from scientists at Stanford University and the University of Arizona. For a comprehensive description, see *Genes, Peoples, and Languages*, by Luigi Luca Cavalli-Sforza (New York: Farrar, Straus and Giroux, 2000). For a short summary, see "To People the World, Start with 500, Gene Studies Show," by Nicholas Wade, *New York Times*, November 11, 1997.

61 This evolutionary layering is reflected in the anatomy: For a more detailed discussion of the evolution of the human brain, see "The Legacy of the Lizard," in *A Mood Apart: The Thinker's Guide to Emotion and Its Disorder*, by Peter C. Whybrow (New York: Harper Perennial, 1998). Paul MacLean first proposed the concept of a "triune" brain to understand the mix of primitive and evolved behavior in humans, in *The Triune Brain in Evolution* (New York: Plenum Press, 1990). MacLean's research, spanning 30 years, led to the general acceptance of the limbic system as the anatomical home of emotion. For those interested in the evolution of human behavior, it is a text worth exploring, being full of anatomical and research details while adding a philosophical, sometimes whimsical view of the complexity of human development. For a brief essay by Paul MacLean on his basic concepts and ideas, see *Human Evolution: Biosocial Perspectives*, edited by S. L. Washburn and E. R. McCown (Menlo Park, CA: Benjamin Cummings, 1978), pp. 33–57.

62 elite sets of neuronal pathways: The messengers employed by these elite superhighways are collectively known as the *biogenic amines*, and the neurons that produce them cluster together in a discrete region of the brain called the *brain stem*. This is the old lizard brain. From these clusters the neurons extend their long highway trunks, the *axons*, to virtually all areas of the brain, suggesting that the importance of the amine-containing neurons is to simultaneously coordinate and modulate the activity of widely spread brain areas.

In the *norepinephrine* system, the fundamental region in which these neurons originate is called the *locus coeruleus*, a cluster of approximately 3,000 cells that lies deep in the old brain. There are two such centers, one on each side of the brain stem. The neurons from these centers extend their axons into the cerebellum (important in balance), the cerebral cortex, the thalamus (the information exchange center for the brain), the hippocampus (short-term memory), and the hypothalamus (overseeing the hormones of the body). Together these projections from the local coeruleus are called the "ascending reticular activating system."

The *serotonin* system also arises from an area deep in the brain stem called the *raphe* (*raphe* is a French word meaning "seam"). The axons of these serotonin neurons project upward into the new brain, running side by side with the norepinephrine neurons in the ascending reticular activating system. These systems complement each other and work together, with norepinephrine being the "energizing system" and the serotonin system "dampening" activity. In the maintenance of sleep, for example, serotonin is important, but the initiation of sleep requires collaboration between the two systems.

The *dopamine* neurons are close cousins to the norepinephrine system. Dopamine neurons begin in four prominent nuclei, again in the old brain, which together contain approximately 7,000 neurons. Neurons extending from the arcuate nucleus are important in the maintenance of the motor systems of the brain and also in the hedonic "reward" pathway connecting the brain stem with the nucleus accumbens at the base of the new brain.

Scientists catalogue neuronal systems by the type of messenger that is used in intercellular communication. At the vast majority of brain synapses, the messengers are simple molecules known as *amino acids*. Thus the messenger glutamine *excites* local neuronal activity, while glycine and γ-aminobutyric acid (GABA) *inhibit* it. The balance between activation and inhibition—the yin-yang of millions of local cell networks—then ultimately determines the baseline level of our behavior. For a comprehensive, although technical book providing an excellent and dynamic understanding of neurotransmission, neuroanatomy, pharmacology, and the genetic basis for behavior, see *The Molecular Foundations of Psychiatry*, by Stephen Hyman and Eric Nestler (Washington, D.C.: American Psychiatric Press, 1993).

64 the dopamine superhighways . . . sustain our curiosity: See "Getting Formal with Dopamine and Reward," by W. Schultz *Neuron*, 38: 241–263, 2002.

65 Some speculate that eating meat . . . facilitated brain growth:
Most primates subsist on fruits, leaves, and insects, and no primate hunts large
game. In contrast, residual groups of human foragers rely heavily on meat and are
sophisticated hunters. For discussion, see *How Humans Evolve*, by Robert Boyd
and Joan Silk (New York: W. W. Norton, 1997), pp. 396–403.

66 the ancestors of some Russians: This is the work of Professor Hizri
Amirkhanov, chief of paleolithic archaeology at the Institute of Archaeology in
Moscow. A short summary of the work can be found in "Why Live in Russia?
Maybe Mammoths Were the Lure," *New York Times*, March 31, 1998.

67 growing evidence: "Risk Taking by Juvenile Vervet Monkeys," by L. A. Fairbanks, *Behavior*, 124: 57–72, 1993; and "Maternal Protectiveness and Response
to the Unfamiliar in Vervet Monkeys," by L. A. Fairbanks and M. T. McGuire,
American Journal of Primatology, 30: 119–129, 1993.

67 *Curious George syndrome*: The creators of Curious George, the ingenious
little monkey whose adventures feature in a series of colorfully illustrated children's stories, were themselves migrants. Hans Rey was born in Hamburg, Germany, around 1900, and as a child lived close to the Hagenbeck Zoo, where he
spent much of his free time. A Jew, he left Germany in 1923 for South America,
where he met Margaret Rey, an artist and illustrator. The couple later lived in Paris
but fled the Nazi occupation in June 1940 and came to the United States, where
Houghton Mifflin publishes the Curious George books. This cheerful and durable
little monkey has a knack for falling into trouble but takes everything in stride, as
did his creators.

68 variations in curiosity and impulsivity: See "Individual Differences in
Response to a Stranger: Social Impulsivity as a Dimension of Temperament in
Vervet Monkeys," by L. A. Fairbanks, *Journal of Comparative Psychology*, 115:
22–28, 2001.

**68 the serotonin breakdown product 5-hydroxyindoleacetic acid (5-
HIAA):** "Social Impulsivity Inversely Correlated with CSF 5-HIAA and Fluoxe-
tine Exposure in Vervet Monkeys," by L. A. Fairbanks, W. P. Melaga, M. J.
Jorgensen, J. R. Kaplan, and M. T. McGuire, *Neuropsychopharmacology*, 24:
370–378, 2001.

68 genetically "preprogrammed" for migratory behavior: The research
regarding the biology of migratory behavior in rhesus monkeys living on Cayo San-
tiago was reported in "Delayed Dispersal and Elevated Monoaminergic Activity in
Free Ranging Rhesus Monkeys," J. R. Kaplan, M. B. Fontenot, J. Berard, J.
Manuck, and J. J. Mann, *American Journal of Primatology*, 35: 229–234, 1995.
The hamadryas studies can be found in "Cerebral Spinal Fluid, Monoaminergic
Metabolites Differ in Wild Anubis and Hybrid (*anubis hamadryas*) Baboons: Pos-
sible Relationship to Life History and Behavior," by J. R. Kaplan, J. Phillips-
Conroy, M. B. Fontenot, C. J. Jolly, L. A. Fairbanks, and J. J. Mann,
Neuropsychopharmacology, 20: 517–524, 1999.

69 Rarely does migration involve: Quotation is from *Migrations and Cultures: A World View*, by Thomas Sowell (New York: Basic Books, 1996), p. 3.

70 While migrants often begin their new life earning less: Social advancement and economic success are characteristic of the first-generation migrant, especially those who arrive already educated or skilled. In the initial years of immigration those with little education usually earn less than the general population of the country they enter, and can consume a disproportionate share of the welfare support system. However, over a generation there is a major net increment to the receiving country. Those of higher education immediately begin to generate profits for their adopted lands and enjoy a higher income than average. See Chapter 12 in *Modern Labor Economics*, by Ronald G. Ehrenberg and Robert F. Smith (New York: HarperCollins, 1994). Also "What Price the Huddled Masses," *Economist*, November 29, 1997; and "The Benefits of Migrants," *Economist*, March 31, 2001. An analysis of the situation in southern California can be found in "Immigration: The New Ethnic Entrepreneurs," *Los Angeles Times*, September 12, 1999; and "A Minority Worth Cultivating," *Economist*, April 25, 1998. The number of Latino-owned businesses in Los Angeles County has risen from essentially zero in 1972 to 200,000 in 1997. Nationally the 2000 census reported that the Hispanic population, the most rapidly growing contemporary migrant group in America, grew 58 percent in the decade of the 1990s (to 35.3 million). See "Portrait of a Nation," *New York Times*, April 1, 2001; and "Motivation, Focus Send Foreign-Born Students Soaring," by Patrick Walsh, *USA Today*, August 25, 2003. A similar phenomenon of migrant influx and rapid economic success is occurring in Great Britain. For an analysis, see "Employment: A New Mix," *Economist*, September 26, 1998. In 1998, with the freedom of movement created by the European Common Market, one person in nine in the labor market in London was from Europe.

Chapter Three: THE FREEDOM TO STRIVE

75 the American International Group, Inc.: AIG is a provider of "insurance and financial services." This particular advertisement, accompanied by a picture of the first moonwalk, was run repeatedly during the summer of 2002, when the Internet frenzy was cresting.

75 Alexis de Tocqueville and Gustave de Beaumont: For an interesting retracing of the 17-state tour made by Tocqueville and Beaumont in 1831, see C-Span's *Traveling Tocqueville's America* (Baltimore: Johns Hopkins Press, 1998).

76 "We are close enough to the time": At the beginning of his book, in Chapter 2, Tocqueville draws the analogy of America's fledgling democracy with the development of a child: that only by understanding the "the first struggles he has had to endure . . . will you understand the passions which are to dominate his life." Quotation is from *Democracy in America*, by Alexis de Tocqueville, translated by George Lawrence (New York: Anchor Books, 1969), Vol. I, Part I, Chapter 2, p. 32.

76 "Most of the people in these nations: Ibid., Vol. II, Part I, Chapter 10, p. 462.

76 the city of Los Angeles: Much has been written about Los Angeles and its meteoric rise to become one of the world's most vibrant urban centers. Thus, among many sources, here I have drawn principally on *Ethnic Los Angeles*, edited by Roger Waldinger and Mehdi Bozorgmehr (New York: Russell Sage Foundation, 1996); and *City of Quartz: Excavating the Future in Los Angeles*, by Mike Davis (New York: Vintage Books, 1992).

77 *Blade Runner*: A film adaptation of the novel *Do Androids Dream of Electric Sheep?* by Phillip K. Dick (Garden City, NY: Doubleday, 1968). Ironically, according to Mike Davis in his book *Ecology of Fear* (New York: Henry Holt, 1998), this caricature of multiculturalism directed by Ridley Scott was to have been filmed in New York, before Warner Brothers complained about the cost of doing so.

80 *temperament* . . . in twins: "See Genes, Environment, and Personality," by T. Bouchard, *Science*, 264: 1700–1701, 1994.

80 Professor Robert Cloninger: For a summary of Cloninger's work, see "Temperament and Personality," by Robert Cloninger, *Current Opinion in Neurobiology*, 4: 266–273, 1994. And also "A Psychobiological Model of Temperament and Character," by R. Cloninger, *Archives of General Psychiatry*, 50: 975–990, 1993.

81 genetic differences in the dopamine reward system: Fundamental to everything genetic is the unique structure of deoxyribonucleic acid (DNA), where four small molecules known as *nucleotides*—adenine, cytosine, guanine, and thymine—are strung between two rigid helical strands. Imagine DNA as a long, thin, spiral staircase, with each step composed of two nucleotides. The linear sequencing of the ascending nucleotide steps then represents the genetic code, and an allele is a variation in the coded sequence of the nucleotides that represent one gene. The DNA spirals are spooled together in protective capsules known as *chromosomes*. The nucleus of every cell in the body contains 46 of these capsules, and together they safeguard the unique copy of the genetic information—the recipe book—that is required to construct a unique person. There are 22 pairs of chromosomes, with a different copy of each pair being inherited from each parent. Two additional chromosomes—the X and the Y—determine our sex, with females having two X chromosomes while males have an X and a Y, to provide each individual with a total of 46 chromosomes. As the brain's molecular structure has become better understood, scientists have realized that there are many receptor subtypes, and that the variants of each subtype are not spread evenly throughout the population. Nor are the patterns consistent across generations of the same family, as the genome of each new member will have been mixed and stirred at the time of reproduction. Nonetheless, knowing the pivotal role of dopamine in activity and reward, several scientific groups began searching for an association among objective measures of temperament, such as those of the Cloninger scale, and a genetically determined dopamine receptor variation. See "Dopamine and the Structure of Personality: Relation of Agonist-Induced Dopamine Activity to Positive Emotionality," by R. DePue, M. Luciana, P. Arbisi, P. Collins, and A. Leon, *Journal of Personality and Social Psychology*, 67: 485–498, 1994. Also "D2 and D4 Dopamine Receptor Polymorphisms and Personality," by E. P. Noble, T. Z. Ozkaragoz, T. L. Ritchie, X. Zhang, T. R. Belin, and R. S. Sparkes, *American Journal of Medical Genetics*, 81: 257–267, 1998. For a concise review of behavioral genetics, I recommend *Mood Genes: Hunting for the Origins of Mania and Depression*, by Samuel H. Barondes (New York: W. H. Freeman, 1998).

83 Encounter Restaurant and Bar: Housed in the landmark Theme Building at Los Angeles International Airport, this establishment was originally part of an overall $50 million Los Angeles "jet-age" terminal construction project that began in 1960. The building was completed in August 1961, at the cost of $2.2 million. The restaurant sits on giant 135-foot parabolic arches and was the first structure in the United States to utilize supporting steel arches of this design. In 1992, the Los Angeles City Council designated the Theme Building a cultural and historic monument, and in 1994, extensive renovations of the restaurant by Walt Disney Imagineering created the current space with its Star Wars–like atmosphere.

83 the Star Wars epic: The Star Wars trilogy, the first film of which was released in 1977, is a parable laced with legend and updated with the fantasy of science fiction. Its importance lies in being one of the first films to use computer-based photography. While many of the special effects are crude compared to the industry standards 20 years later, it expressed the early beginnings of the interplay between entertainment, the computer industry, and money. Two decades later, in the late 1990s, Lucas announced his intention to make three more movies that concentrated on the period preceding the Star Wars trilogy, and particularly the relationship between the young Obi-Wan Kenobi and Anakin Skywalker before his transformation into Darth Vader. This had induced a paroxysm of anticipation in the hope of a repeat bonanza of the earlier Star Wars success. The first Star Wars trilogy had been the father of the modern merchandising megadeal, and even before the first movie of the second trilogy was produced, Pepsi with its restaurant chains—Taco Bell, Pizza Hut, and Kentucky Fried Chicken—had paid $2 billion to carry Star Wars characters on its products for the next five years. For details of the making of Star Wars, see *Empire Building: The Remarkable Real-Life Story of Star Wars*, by Garry Jenkins (Secaucus, NJ: Citadel Press, Carrol Publishing Group, 1997). And for the technical effects, *Industrial Light and Magic: The Art of Special Effects*, by Thomas G. Smith (New York: Ballantine Books, 1986).

85 a common chemical pathway of reward: Our understanding of the pleasure systems in the brain, how the reward pathways work, and how they can become hijacked by "addicting" substances is a triumph of modern neuroscience. Summary articles include the October 3, 1997, edition of *Science*, which was devoted to the "Science of Substance Abuse" (see p. 35–69). And "Drugs of Abuse and the Brain," by Alan Leshner and George Koob, *Proceedings of the Association of American Physicians*, 111: 99–108, 1999. Popular articles on risk taking and extreme sports include "Success Is Like a Drug," by Stephen S. Fall, *New York Times Magazine*, November 23, 1997; "For Our Ancestors Risk Taking Was a Good Bet," *Time*, September 6, 1999; "Extreme Sports, Sensation Seeking, and the Brain," in "Men: The Scientific Truth about Their Work, Play, Health, and Passions," *Scientific American Quarterly*, 10 (No. 2, Summer): 56, 1999; "Addicted to Sex," *Fortune*, May 10, 1999, pp. 68–79.

86 "conceit which men have of their own abilities": Adam Smith considered conceit and self-deception the "fatal weakness of mankind." See *The Theory of Moral Sentiments* (Indianapolis: Liberty Classics Edition, 1969), Part III, Chapter 4, p. 263.

86 the mushrooming growth of gambling: A 1995 study conducted by the Iowa Department of Human Resources found that 5.4 percent of the state's population had a gambling problem requiring treatment, up from 1.7 percent before the state introduced legalized gambling (see "When the Wheels Won't Stop," *Economist*, December 13, 1997). Americans wagered more than $600 billion in 1997 on lotteries, horse racing, casino gambling, and bingo—more than they spent on groceries, and 50 percent more than they gambled just 5 years earlier. A review by Howard Schaffer, a psychologist at Harvard Medical School (quoted in the *Economist* article), of 120 gambling studies conducted over 20 years (reported in 1997) suggests that the prevalence of severe gambling disorders increased by 55 percent in American over the past two decades.

88 "the managers in the U.S. were greater risk takers": In support of Marcel's claim, see "Determinants of Managerial Risk: Exploring Personality and Cultural Inferences," by Steven Williams and Sunitha Narendran, *Journal of Social Psychology*, 139: 102, 1999.

90 Anna . . . had wandered far from her Iowa roots: In America there is a persistent internal migration of individuals, particularly of those who are young and well educated, from the rural Midwest to the urban centers of the East and Southwest. During the 1990s many midwestern counties, in a wide swath from Canada to Mexico, lost 10 percent or more of their population. Some 60 percent of Iowa's graduating university students leave the state and take jobs elsewhere, such that the number of working-age Iowans continues to fall. In part, rural America is a victim of its own success. Through industrialization, Iowa's farmers are now among the most productive in the world, but with mechanization there are fewer jobs available for young people. That plus a good system of education encourages those Iowans with a restless spirit to seek their fortunes elsewhere. See "Fare Thee Well, Iowa," *Economist*, August 18, 2001.

93 Ernest Noble: For a summary of Noble's work and the debate it sparked, see "The DRD-2 Gene in Psychiatric and Neurological Disorders and Its Phenotypes," by E. P. Noble, *Pharmacogenomics*, 1: 309–333, 2000.

95 the presence of receptor allele D4-7: The original publication was "Dopamine D4 Receptor (D4DR) Exon III Polymorphism Associated with the Human Personality Trait of Novelty Seeking," by Richard P. Ebstein, Olga Novick, Roberto Umansky, Beatrice Priel, Yamima Osher, Darren Blaine, Estelle R. Bennett, Lubov Nemanov, Miri Katz, and Robert H. Belmaker, *Nature Genetics*, 12 (January): 78–80, 1996. For a discussion of the DRD2 and DRD4 receptors stories, see also "D2 and D4 Dopamine Receptor Polymorphisms and Personality," by E. P. Noble, T. Z. Ozkaragoz, T. L. Ritchie, X. Zhang, T. R. Belin, and R. S. Sparkes, *American Journal of Medical Genetics*, 81: 257–267, 1998. The D4-7 receptor allele is also disproportionately represented in some studies, but not all, of the genetic screens of children who exhibit impulsivity and excitability: see "Evidence That the Dopamine D4 Receptor Is a Susceptibility Gene in Attention Deficit Hyperactivity Disorder," by S. L. Smalley, J. N. Bailey, C. G. Palmer, D. P. Cantwell, J. J. McGough, M. A. Del'Homme, J. R. Asarnow, J. A. Woodward, C. Ramsey, and S. F. Nelson, *Molecular Psychiatry*, 3: 427–430, 1998.

95 In genetically engineered mice: See the report "Dopamine D4 Receptor-Knock-Out Mice Exhibit Reduced Exploration of Novel Stimuli," by S. C. Dulawa, D. K. Grandy, M. J. Low, M. P. Paulus, and M. A. Geyer, *Journal of Neuroscience*, 19: 9550–9556, 1999.

97 if the D4-7 allele is truly a marker of [migrant] behaviors: "Population Frequencies of the A1 Allele at the Dopamine D2 Receptor Locus," by C. L. Barr and K. K. Kidd, *Biological Psychiatry*, 34: 204–209, 1993; "The Worldwide Distribution of Allele Frequencies at the Human Dopamine D4 Receptor Locus," by F. M. Chang, J. R. Kidd, K. J. Livak, A. J. Pakstis, and K. K. Kidd, *Human Genetics*, 98: 91–101, 1996; and "Population Migration and the Variation of Dopamine D4 Receptor (DRD4) Allele Frequencies around the Globe," by C. Chen, M. Burton, E. Greenberger, and J. Dmitrieva, *Evolution and Human Behavior*, 20: 309–324, 1999.

101 "Choose any American at random": The full quotation from Tocqueville is "Choose any American at random and he should be a man of burning desires, enterprising, adventurous, and above all an innovator. The same bent affects all he does—his politics, his religious doctrines, his theories of social economy, his domestic occupations—he carries it with him into the depths of the backwoods as well as into the city's business" (*Democracy in America*, Vol. I, Part II, Chapter 10, p. 404).

PART II
OVER THE TOP:
PROSPERITY'S PARADOX

103 Alexis de Tocqueville: From *Democracy in America*, by Alexis de Tocqueville, translated by George Lawrence (New York: Anchor Books, 1969), Vol. I, Part II, Chapter 9, p. 283. Tocqueville was fascinated by the restless searching that he found in the American character, and in his writing he returned to it repeatedly. "A restless spirit, immoderate desire for wealth, and an extreme love of independence. A passion stronger than love of life itself goads him on."

Chapter Four: AMERICA BUBBLES OVER

105 Milan Kundera: Kundera's novel *Slowness* (New York: HarperCollins, 1995), contrasting two tales of seduction set in the same French chateau, intertwined but separated in time by 200 years, is a meditation on contemporary life, memory, slowness, and the "demon of speed."

105 A typical supermarket in America: "Overworked Americans or Overwhelmed Americans? You Cannot Handle Everything," by Jeff Davidson, *Vital Speeches*, 59: 470–478, 1993 (New York: City News Publishing Company).

106 "a restless, burning, passion that increases with satisfaction": From *Democracy in America*, Vol. I, Part II, Chapter 9, p. 283. Here Alexis de Tocqueville is describing the continuous quest that he found typical of the American temperament. The context is his visit to Ohio, "an immense stretch of unclaimed wilderness . . . only founded fifty years ago. Nevertheless the population of Ohio has already started to move west. An almost limitless continent stretches before him (but) he seems in such a hurry not to arrive too late."

109 modest mechanical things have acquired power: For those interested in a lively history of the advance of technology, two books are recommended: *Mechanization Takes Command*, by Siegfried Giedion (New York: W. W. Norton, 1969); and *Technopoly: The Surrender of Culture to Technology*, by Neil Postman (New York: Vintage Books, 1992).

110 For centuries the speed of human communication: For a history of the communications revolution and how it has changed the way we live, see *The Death of Distance*, by Frances Cairncross (London: Orion Business Books, 1997). Also, for a brief summary of the telegraph and its seminal role in the development of the electronic age, see "Creation of the E-Nation," by Rosa Harris-Alder, *Canadian Geographic*, 115 (November–December): 40–58, 1995.

111 the computer: An early history of the digital computer, including the contributions of George Stibitz, can be found in *ENIAC: The Triumph and Tragedies of the World's First Computer*, by Scott McCartney (New York: Walker 1999). Pascal invented the first analogue computer in 1642, just 5 years after the crash of the tulip market in Holland. The most eccentric and perhaps most brilliant predigital computer builder was an Englishman named Charles Babbage, who in 1820 realized that what manufacturers of the Industrial Revolution needed to expand commerce was engineering standards, more accurate navigational charts, and a mechanical accounting system. Brilliant though it was, Babbage's prototype machine occupied a good-sized room and was too complex for the manufacturing technology of the day to reproduce. Nonetheless, he established the principles of "analytic engines," including the need for such machines to store information and to be programmed for a specific task. Babbage's ideas influenced the design of mechanical analogue computers well into the 1930s, when large data sets were organized largely by the use of punch cards. That was still the case when I began my own career as a scientist in the 1960s.

112 The Internet was born as a concept: Within the university community, the use of e-mail and networked access to individual libraries became standard practice during the 1980s, particularly in America. A "world wide web" of interconnected information centers was an idea dreamed up at the research think tank CERN, located just outside Geneva, Switzerland, by an idealist named Tim Berners-Lee. Berners-Lee envisioned the web as a collaborative tool for science. Later after the launching of Netscape took the web in a commercial direction, Berners-Lee moved to MIT, where he continued to develop operating standards for the web. Other important first steps were made at the University of Minnesota, where an interactive search program for the web called "Gopher" (the gopher, a digging rodent, is the mascot of the University of Minnesota) was first developed, and by a team of researchers at the National Center for Super Computer Applications (NCSA) at the University of Illinois. Marc Andreessen who worked with Jim Clark in the development of the web browser Netscape, was a graduate student at the University of Illinois when these fundamental programs— based on the web standards that had been created previously at CERN by Tim Berners-Lee—were written. For a history of the Internet and its early commercialization, see *A New, New Thing*, by Michael Lewis (New York: W. W. Norton, 2000); and the article "Internet Pioneers," *Economist*, December 18, 1999. Also see "Net Imperative: A Survey of Business of the Internet," *Economist*, June 26, 1999. The relationship between Netscape and AOL is well documented in, *AOL.com*, by Cara Swisher (New York: Random House, 1998), pp. 133–141.

112 Jim Clark, the wealthy founder of Silicon Graphics: See *A New, New Thing*, by Michael Lewis (New York: W. W. Norton, 2000).

112 "e-commerce" and the Internet: At the turn of the millennium it was estimated that 200 million people had Internet access, or 3 percent of the world's population. This activity was heavily weighted toward North America, which at that time had more computers than the rest of the world's nations put together. While many of the pioneering efforts had stemmed from abroad, it was the entre-

preneurial climate of America—venture capital, a deregulated business environment, and a culture that celebrates risk and getting rich—that fed the Internet's
commercial growth and the development of e-commerce. Seventy percent of the
information circulating on the web originated in America (and still does). With
less than 5 percent of the world's population, America was home to 50 percent of
the world's Internet users, and the proportion of the population online was double
that of Germany or Britain. Only Sweden, with a much smaller citizenry, matched
the level of computer penetration that existed in the United States. Southern Asia,
by contrast, which has 20 percent of the world's population, had only 1 percent of
its computer hardware. This polarization was due not only to the low income and
inadequate telecommunications infrastructure of many developing nations but
also to the complexities of language. English, while spoken by a minority of the
world's population, was the language of 80 percent of the web sites on the Internet. The Internet was, and remains, U.S. territory ("Net-Americana, Welcome to
the Internet: The First Global Colony," *New York Times*, January 9, 2000). The
data cited in Chapter 4 regarding the Internet were taken from various sources,
including the *Economist* survey ("Net Imperative: A Survey of Business of the
Internet," *Economist*, June 26, 1999) and the article "Social Inequality and the
World Wide Web," by Michael Conachy, August 17, 1999, available on the web at
www.wsws.org/articles/1999/aug1999/www-a17.shtml. Despite the world's economic downturn after the bursting of the dot-com bubble, the number of users
continued to grow. (See "Wired China: The Flies Swarm In," *Economist*, July 22,
2000, which describes the explosion of Internet and mobile phone use in China,
the latter having multiplied from 5 million in 1995 to over 57 million in 2000. In
China a national grid of fiber-optics will increase Internet usage rapidly, but
nonetheless in 2001 China and India lagged behind the rest of the world, with no
more than 10 percent of the population in China having telephone subscriptions
and a miniscule 3 percent in India. The e-commerce market in Asia is growing,
however, with an estimated market worth of $32 billion in 2003 ["Asia to Have 64
Million Net Users in Five Years," *Times of India*, July 22, 1999].)

113 a supercharged upgrade of the consumer society: The improving
road conditions that made mail order possible in the 1920s were largely due to the
simple invention of the road drag by a Missouri farmer named D. Ward King. The
King road drag consisted of two wooden rails that lay side by side and were
attached to each other by a series of wooden braces. Pulled along a muddy road,
this invention had the effect of smoothing out the ruts and creating a slight crown
that shed the rainwater to the sides of the road. An interesting article about the
effect of this simple machine and the development of e-commerce can be found
in "Annals of Retail: Clicks and Mortar," by Malcom Gladwell, *New Yorker*,
December 6, 1999.

114 Ray Kurtsweil . . . and like-minded techno-utopians: *The Age of
Spiritual Machines: When Computers Exceed Human Intelligence*, by Ray Kurzweil

(New York: Viking, 1999); and *Metaman: The Merging of Humans and Machines into a Global Superorganism*, by Gregory Stock (New York: Simon and Schuster, 1993).

115 the swings of emotion that occur in manic depression: For details of the manifestation of manic depression, see *A Mood Apart: The Thinker's Guide to Emotion and Its Disorder*, by Peter C. Whybrow (New York: HarperPerennial, 1998).

117 The annual survey of entering college freshmen: See "A Long Way from Flower Power," *Economist*, January 17, 1998. The survey was of nearly 350,000 students at 665 American colleges and universities. New students were "markedly less interested in social issues than their predecessors." Those interested in the natural environment and sustaining its quality fell from 34 percent in 1992 to 19 percent in 1997. And American youth apparently were not alone. Young people in Britain were also obsessed with their careers, getting rich being the most important objective for 34 percent of Britons interviewed in a European survey commissioned by the British Broadcasting Company and other media groups. In contrast, only 15 percent of Italians and 11 percent of Swedes considered riches to be important (see "British Children More Selfish," *Sunday Times* (London), March 8, 1998).

117 half the graduating classes from the Harvard: See "MBAs Are the Latest Net Gain," by Steven Wilmsen, *Boston Globe*, May 9, 1999.

118 young migrant adventurers from India and China: Between 1992 and 2001, 640,000 foreign workers, mostly from India and China, were admitted to America with the H1-B visa, which permits American companies to search oversees for "specialty occupations" required to sustain the American economy. After 6 years the holder of an H1-B visa can apply for U.S. citizenship. Unfortunately when the bubble burst and the economy turned down, the status of many of these migrants was called into question. (See "Byting More Than They Can Chew," *Economist*, July 7, 2001; and "The US Wants More Migrants to Plug IT Skills Gap," *Times* (London), September 29, 2000.)

118 Jeff Bezos: The details of Mr. Bezos's personal story were taken from *Time* magazine's "Person of the Year" article about him: *Time*, December 27, 1999, pp. 50–102; "The Fantasy World of Jeff Bezos," *Red Herring*, October 2000; "Is There Life in E-commerce?" *Economist*, February 3, 2001; and "Long Amazon.com Tale Still Written in Red Ink," by David Streitfeld, *Los Angeles Times*, July 21, 2001.

118 Stephen Case: For details of the America Online (AOL) "takeover" of Time Warner, see "America Online agrees to buy Time Warner for $165 Billion," *New York Times*, Tuesday, January 11, 2000; and "The Big Leap," *Economist*, January 15–21, 2000. The AOL–Time Warner merger gained front-page status in both of these publications and in many other newspapers around the world, but the marriage proved to be a difficult one. (See also "Is AOL's Bubble about to Burst?" Talk of the Town, *New Yorker*, January 24, 2000.) For follow-up stories, see

"Mousetrap," by James B. Stewart, *New Yorker*, July 31, 2000; and "Who's afraid of AOL Time Warner," *Economist*, January 26, 2002. Also "A Search for Harmony within a Feuding AOL," *New York Times*, July 21, 2002.

118 "nothing can be the same again": See "The Big Leap," *Economist*, January 15–21, 2000.

120 "More than ever achieving the American Dream": Data from "The Whine of '99: Everyone's Getting Rich But Me!" *Newsweek*, July 5, 1999. This article appeared as the Internet bubble was reaching its height. Forty-three percent of those surveyed by *Newsweek* felt that investing in Internet companies was the new ticket to wealth, and 41 percent of households owned stock. At the millennium, the United States boasted 300 billionaires and 5 million millionaires, with Silicon Valley adding 64 new millionaires each day ("Lexington: The Country-Club Vote," *Economist*, May 20, 2000). Day trading had become the new "gold rush": see "The Solitary Obsessions of a Day Trader," by Matthew Klam, *New York Times Magazine*, November 21, 1999; and "The Last Floor Show: What Will Become of the New York Stock Exchange," by Elizabeth Kolbert, *New Yorker*, March 20, 2000. The book *The Day Traders*, by Gregory J. Millman (New York: Random House, 1999), was advertised as including the "extreme investor's manual" for stock trading in "real time."

120 Priceline.com: For details of the Priceline story, and many others, plus the backdrop that made the Internet bubble possible, see *Dot.con: The Greatest Story Ever Sold*, by John Cassidy (New York: HarperCollins, 2002). See also the story of Mary Meeker, the 39-year-old investment banker who helped bring Priceline and many other dot-coms to market: "The Woman in the Bubble; How Mary Meeker helps Internet Entrepreneurs Become Very, Very Rich," by John Cassidy, *New Yorker*, April 26 and May 3, 1999.

121 "irrational exuberance": On December 5, 1996, Alan Greenspan, chairman of the Federal Reserve, in a now famous speech wondered whether "irrational exuberance" had infected the American stock market. The phrase later became the title of a book by a Yale University economics professor who had advised Greenspan. See *Irrational Exuberance*, by Robert J. Schiller (Princeton, NJ: Princeton University Press, 2000). Also "He Didn't Say It, but He Knew It," by Louis Uchitelle, *New York Times*, April 30, 2000.

121 "I have new ideas on a weekly basis": see "The Whine of '99: Everyone's Getting Rich But Me!" *Newsweek*, July 5, 1999.

121 "Andy Warhol with stock options": "In the Dot-com Doldrums," by Evgenia Peretz, *Vanity Fair*, March 2001.

122 "from praising Amazon to burying it": Quoted from "E-commerce: Too Few Pennies from Heaven," *Economist*, July 1, 2000.

122 As the economy slowed through the year 2000: Some observers predicted the downturn earlier than others ("Why Internet Shares Will Fall, *Economist*, January 30, 1999), but by the summer of 2000 it was clear that the bubble was bursting and an adjustment in public sentiment was underway. A year later the recession arrived. In 2000, 176 publicly traded companies filed for bankruptcy and that increased to 257 in 2001 (*Fortune*, February 18, 2002). A comprehensive account of the dot-com bubble's rise and collapse can be found in *Dot-con: The Greatest Story Ever Sold*, by John Cassidy (New York: HarperCollins, 2002).

123 The Wall Street analysts and investment banks: "Just Who Brought Those Duds to Market?" by Andrew Ross Sorkin, *New York Times*, April 15, 2001; and "Buy Was Cry, as Stock Bubble Burst," by Saul Hansell, *New York Times*, March 4, 2001.

123 clear evidence of unbridled self-interest: The issue of an earnings restatement is one of the great embarrassments a business corporation can suffer. In 2000 alone there were 156 restatements, compared to an average of 49 between 1990 and 1997. See "The Earnings Cult," by Harris Collingwood, *New York Times Magazine*, June 9, 2002; "Fallen Idols," *Economist*, May 4, 2002; "The Greed Cycle: How the Financial System Encouraged Corporations to Go Crazy," by John Cassidy, *New Yorker*, September 23, 2002.

123 Enron Corporation: For summary of the Enron debacle, see "Enron Buffed Image to Shine Even as It Rotted from Within," by Kurt Eichenwald with Diana B. Henriques, *New York Times*, February 10, 2002; and "Enron's Awards to Executives Outrage Laid-Off Employees," by Mitchelle Pacelle, *Wall Street Journal*, January 29, 2002.

124 Gary Winnick, the CEO of Global Crossing: Details are taken from "The Emperor of Greed," by Julie Creswell with Nomi Prins, *Fortune*, June 24, 2002.

125 1987 film *Wall Street*: Quoted in "Is Greed Good? Only if It Is Properly Governed," in "Capitalism and Its Troubles," *Economist*, Supplement, May 18, 2002.

126 the president's critics were swift to point out: "Another Bad Week for George Bush," *Economist*, "Special Report: Bush and Big Business," July 13, 2002.

126 In 1985 the highest-paid CEO in the land: Data on salaries taken from "System Failure," *Fortune*, June 24, 2002.

127 Edward Chancellor: I drew information from two articles: "Perverse Incentives," by Edward Chancellor, *Prospect*, June 2002; and "Millennial Market," by Edward Chancellor, *Prospect*, November 2001.

127 "infectious greed": Testimony given by Alan Greenspan before the Committee on Banking, Housing, and Urban Affairs, U.S. Senate, July 16, 2002.

127 "For the most part this stuff was hiding in plain sight": See "The Long Boom's Ugly Side: Winners, Losers, and Liars," *New York Times*, May 12, 2002.

Chapter Five: A GROWING BURDEN

131 M. F. K. Fisher: One of the world's finest food writers, M. F. K. Fisher grew up in California and wrote 26 books packed with wisdom and wicked wit. This quotation is taken from the first line of an essay entitled, "Set-piece for a Fishing Party," which originally appeared in the book *Serve It Forth* and was published with others under the collective title *The Art of Eating* (New York: Simon and Schuster, 1990).

132 In the decades since John F. Kennedy: The population statistics and time spent in travel are quoted from "Overworked Americans or Overwhelmed Americans? You Cannot Handle Everything," by Jeff Davidson, *Vital Speeches*, 59: 470–478, 1993 (New York: City News Publishing Company). John Adams has given the name *hypermobility* to the increase in mobility facilitated by modern transportation (see "Hypermobility," *Prospect*, March 2000). Adams (an Englishman) points out the strong correlation between societies most physically mobile and the heavy use of all forms of telecommunication. Americans own the lion's share of cars in the world and the most per capita, and the trends in Britain are in the same direction. Adams estimates that in 1950 the average Briton traveled 5 miles a day; in 2000 it was 28 miles a day and it is projected to double again by 2025.

133 the unlimited supply of energy-rich, cheap fast food: The extraordinary nature of the American diet is the subject of an increasing number of books and articles. The most comprehensive about the fast-food industry is *Fast-Food Nation: The Dark Side of the All-American Meal*, by Eric Schlosser (New York: Houghton Mifflin, 2001). See also "That Other National Expansion," *Economist*, December 20, 1997; and "Come on In: The Great Food Debate," *Economist*, August 31, 2002. The details of cost per calorie of fast foods can be found in "Can Fast Food Titans Thrive on Healthy Fare?" *USA Today*, September 30, 2002. For review of the scientific studies being conducted, see "Environmental Contributions to the Obesity Epidemic," by James O. Hill and John C. Peters, *Science*, Special Section, "Regulation of Body Weight," 280: 1363–1369, 1998.

134 The statistics are alarming: A detailed analysis of the obesity pandemic in America was released in January 2001, during the tenure of Dr. David Satcher as surgeon general. "The Surgeon General's Call to Action: To Prevent and Decrease Overweight and Obesity" is available from the U.S. Government Printing Office, Mail Stop SSOP, Washington, D.C. 20401-0001. The stock number is 017-001-00551-7. The dimensions of the problem and the statistics can be found in this publication.

134 Kelly Brownell: Dr. Brownell, who is the director of Yale University's Center for Eating and Weight Disorders, was quoted widely after a presentation made at the American Psychological Association's annual convention in 2001. See the article "Fast-Food Culture Serves up Super-size Americans," by Bridget Murray,

Monitor on Psychology, 32: 11–12, 2001; and "Flap over Fast-Food Ads: Do They Target Obese Kids?" *Philadelphia Inquirer*, March 20, 2002. A study of 3,000 infants and toddlers conducted between March and July 2002 by Mathematica Policy Research of Princeton, New Jersey, found that french fries are the most commonly consumed vegetable for toddlers by the age of 15 months, and that one-third of children 19 to 24 months old eat no fruit. The study, which was conducted for the Gerber Products Company, estimated the median daily intake for that age group was 1,220 calories, some 30 percent above the estimated requirement of 950 calories. (See Supplement to the *Journal of the American Dietetic Association*, January 2004.)

135 Mayans from Guatemala: While poverty, together with the malnutrition that accompanies it, remains a major problem across the world, it is also clear that the "Western" diet does not necessarily offer a health advantage, especially when introduced quickly. Studies by Barry Bogin of the Department of Behavioral Science at the University of Minnesota suggest that Mayans migrating from Guatemala to the United States rapidly become obese on the American diet (see "Plasticity, Political Economy, and Physical Growth Status of Guatemala Maya Children Living in the U.S.," *American Journal of Physical Anthropology*, 102: 17–33, 1997). For details of the problems of obesity and diabetes throughout the Americas, see "Diabetes in the Americas," *Epidemiological Bulletin*, June 2001. For a remarkable case history of an individual struck down by the Western diet in his own culture, see "Requiem for an Overachiever: In the Fast Lane of Africa, the Good Guys Finish Dead," by Robert M. Sapolsky, *Sciences*, Essays and Comment, January-February, 1997, pp. 15–19.

135 regular physical exercise has a protective effect: See "The Effect of Graded Levels of Exercise on Energy Intake and Balance in Free-Living Women," by R. J. Stubbs, A. Sepp, D. A. Hughes, A. M. Johnstone, N. King, G. Horgan, and J. E. Bhindell, *International Journal of Obesity*, 26: 866–869, 2002.

136 McDonald's prides itself: With Ronald McDonald and special happy meals for children, the McDonald's Corporation is in the forefront of offering family fun rather than just food at their restaurants. However, this marketing principle of catching children early and socializing them to the taste and atmosphere of McDonald's is one of the most criticized facets of the fast-food industry. Kelly Brownell, a strident critic, believes that this seductive advertising drives much of the childhood obesity in America. For discussion, see "Flap over Fast-Food Ads: Do They Target Obese U.S. Kids?" by Lini S. Kadaba, *Philadelphia Inquirer*, March 20, 2002. The evidence that obese children tend to grow up as obese adults is well summarized in "The Child Is Father of the Man," in *The Hungry Gene: The Science of Fat and the Future of Thin*, by Ellen Ruppel Shell (New York: Atlantic Monthly Press, 2002); and "The Trouble with Fries: Fast Food Is Killing Us. Can It Be Fixed?" by Malcolm Gladwell, *New Yorker*, March 5, 2001.

137 During the 1960s and the 1970s: The figures here, assigned to Katherine Flegal, who is an epidemiologist at the National Center for Health Statistics, were quoted by Gary Taubes in his article, "What If It's All Been a Big Fat Lie?" *New York Times Magazine,* July 7, 2002. The exponential rise in obesity began in the 1980s and continued into the 1990s, and thus was coincident in time with the move to high-density carbohydrates as a substitute for fat calories in the diet.

139 The archaeological evidence: Here I have drawn on the neglected work of Drs. S. B. Eaton, M. Shustack, and M. Konner from Emory University, who in the 1980s wrote an important book, *The Paleolithic Prescription: A Program of Diet and Exercise and a Design for Living* (New York: Harper and Row, 1988). In that book, and also in the article "Paleolithic Nutrition: A Consideration of Its Nature and Current Implications," by S. B. Eaton and M. Konner (*New England Journal of Medicine,* 312: 283–289, 1985), the authors put forward a compelling case for modern nutrition being at odds with the physiological programming of our ancestors. My reference to the dietary practices of the still existing hunting and gathering tribes comes from their work.

140 the phenomenon of "lactase persistence": See "Identification of a Variant Associated with Adult-Type Hypolactasia," by N. S. Enattah, T. Sahi, E. Savilahti, J. D. Terwilliger, L. Peltonen, and I. Jarvela, *Nature Genetics,* 30: 233–237, 2002. For background in the genetic diversity of lactase tolerance, see "Lactase Haplotype Diversity in the Old World," by E. J. Hollox, M. Poulter, M. Zvarik, V. Ferak, A. Krause, T. Jenkins, N. Saha, A. I. Kozlov, and D. M. Swallow, *American Journal of Human Genetics,* 68: 160–172, 2001.

141 in many contemporary European societies: Data reported in "Weight Increases Worldwide?" by Gary Taubes, *Science,* 280: 1368, 1998.

142 the native peoples of the Americas: The information here is taken from *Native Americans in the Twentieth Century,* by James S. Olsen and Raymond Wilson (Provo, UT: Brigham Young University Press, 1984).

143 The Pima people: Information about the Pima people was obtained from the *Encyclopedia of Native American Tribes,* by Carl Waldman (New York: Checkmark Books, 1999). The area the Pima once lived in extended from central Mexico north to Arizona, the people being related to the Aztecs. The Arizona settlers arrived some 2,000 years ago and maintained an agrarian culture. They had a long-standing hostility with the Apache and the Yuma, who raided them frequently. They did not use the horse, fighting always on foot with the bow and arrow, the club, and the shield. During the eighteenth century when the first Spanish missionaries arrived, the Pima were welcoming and many were converted to Catholicism. When their way of life changed in the early twentieth century and the culture began to disintegrate, it came to national attention that they had a high rate of diabetes. In 1965, the National Institute of Diabetes and Digestive and Kidney Disease began a prospective series of studies in which the Pima actively collaborated to determine the origin of the diabetes. These studies and many details of the Pima culture can be accessed at the web site www.niddk.nih.gov, from which information is also referenced here. See also "The Pima Paradox: Can We Learn How to Lose Weight from One of the Most Obese People in the World?" by Malcolm Gladwell, *New Yorker*, February 2, 1998.

144 Nauru Islanders in the West Pacific: Nauru is a small island, some 8 square miles, with a population of 11,300 people, derived originally from migrants from Asia making their way down the chain of islands called Micronesia. Europeans first discovered the island in 1798 when Captain John Fern was sailing from New Zealand. One hundred years later, a British prospecting company determined that Nauru was almost solid phosphate, and for the past 100 years the mining of that phosphate has made the Nauru Islanders extremely rich. From phosphate mining, they enjoy an extraordinarily high per capita income of close to $8,000, and they import everything they want in the way of food and technology. Along with those riches has come a Western diet and the same problems experienced by the Pima Indians. Exposed to a high-fat, high-carbohydrate diet, the Nauru Islanders are now the fattest people in the world. In some estimates, 100 percent of the males are obese (see "The Metabolic Syndrome: From Inherited Survival Trait to a Health Care Problem," by S. Colagiuri and J. C. Brand, *Experimental Clinical Endocrinology and Diabetes*, 105: (Supplement 2): 54–60 1997).

144 series of studies undertaken by the Pima people: The evidence that insulin concentrations in the Pima people were normal but elevated in those with type II diabetes, thus indicating insulin resistance, was discovered during the long series of studies undertaken during the 1960s and 1970s by the National Institutes of Health (see "Impaired Glucose Tolerance in Pima Indians," by S. Lillioja, *Diabetic Medicine*, 13 (Supplement 6): 127–132, 1996). The comparative studies between the Arizona Indians and those living in Sonora, Mexico, can be found in the report "The Pima Indians in Sonora, Mexico," M. E. Valencia, P. H. Bennett, E. Ravussin, J. Esparza, C. Fox, and L. O. Schulz. *Nutritional Review*, 57 (Supplement 5): 55–57, 1999. For a general review of the role of carbohydrates in insulin resistance, see "Type 2 Diabetes among the Pima Indians of Arizona: An Epidemic Attributable to Environmental Change?" by P. H. Bennett, *Nutritional Reviews*, 57 (Supplement 5): 51–54, 1999; and "Diabetes Mellitus in American Pima Indians," P. H. Bennett, *Lancet*, 2: 125–128, 1971.

146 Pima children born to mothers with diabetes: The study showing that intrauterine exposure to diabetes increases the risk in later life is reported in "Intrauterine Exposure to Diabetes Conveys Risks for Type 2 Diabetes and Obesity: A Study of Discordant Sibships," by D. Dabelea, R. L Hanson, R. S. Lindsay, D. J. Pettitt, G. Imperatore, M. M. Gabir, J. Roumain, P. H. Bennett, and W. C. Knowler, *Diabetes*, 49: 2208–2211, 2000. Just how a mother's diet can permanently alter the genetic expression of her offspring was elucidated in 2003 by a study of "yellow" mice, an animal that carries a genetic predisposition to obesity, diabetes, and cancer. However, when pregnant yellow mice were fed a modest balanced diet and vitamins rich in methyl groups (vitamin B_{12}, folic acid, choline, and betaine), the mothers produced normal offspring; methylation chemically inhibited the gene that induces overeating in adult life. This field of study, called *epigenetics*, is the gateway to a better understanding of how environment may interact with genetic inheritance to alter the expression of a gene's activity, without changing the basic gene inheritance itself (see "Transposable Elements: Targets for Early Nutritional Effects on Epigenetic Gene Regulation," by R. A. Waterland, and R. L. Jirtle, *Molecular and Cellular Biology*, 23: 5293–5300, 2003. For summary, see "How Nutrition Affects Our Genes," by Sandra Blakeslee, *International Herald Tribune*, October 9, 2003.)

147 Obesity is becoming a problem worldwide: For detail of the trends, see "The Fat of the Lands," *Economist*, February 23, 2002; and "Spoilt for Choice," *Economist*, December 13, 2003. Obesity is no longer just a Western disease; it is becoming a problem in the developing world too. Countries such as South Africa and Egypt have rates of obesity that rival America and Western Europe. Some countries such as India have bimodal distribution, with some one-third of their population malnourished and 10 percent overweight and obese.

147 Tom Wadden: See "Obesity: Responding to the Global Epidemic," by T. A. Wadden, K. D. Brownell, and G. D. Foster, *Journal of Clinical Psychology*, 70: 510–525, 2002.

148 the artificial flavors: Eric Schlosser, in his book *Fast-Food Nation: The Dark Side of the All-American Meal* (New York: Houghton Mifflin, 2001), goes into detail regarding the role of the flavor industry in America's fast-food binge. A shorter version can be found in his article "Why McDonald's Fries Taste So Good: A Trip to Northern New Jersey, the Home of Natural Flavors," *Atlantic Monthly*, January 2001.

150 Jay Kaplan: See "Influence of Dietary Lipids on Agonistic and Affiliative Behavior in *Macaca fascicularis*," by J. R. Kaplan, M. B. Fontenot, S. B. Manuck, and M. F. Muldoon, *American Journal of Primatology*, 38: 333–347, 1996; "Cholesterol Meets Darwin: Public Health and Evolutionary Implications of the Cholesterol-Serotonin Hypothesis," by J. R. Kaplan, K. P. Klein, and S. B. Manuck, *Evolutionary Anthropology*, 6: 28–37, 1997; and "Monkeys, Aggression, and the Pathobiology of Atherosclerosis," by J. R. Kaplan and S. B. Manuck, *Aggressive Behavior*, 24: 323–334, 1998.

151 thrifty genes: The thrifty-gene hypothesis was originally proposed by James Neel, a geneticist and evolutionary biologist at the University of Michigan Medical School (see "Diabetes Mellitus: A Thrifty Genotype Rendered Detrimental by Progress?" by J. V. Neel, *American Journal of Human Genetics*, 14: 353–362, 1962).

152 This comparative approach: For an excellent review of the thrifty-gene hypothesis and the comparative study of primates and humans in determining which genes have been conserved, see "The Thrifty-Genotype Hypothesis and Its Implications for the Study of Complex Genetic Disorders in Man," by A. M. Sharma, *Journal of Molecular Medicine*, 76: 568–571, 1998.

152 Diligently we eat what is placed before us: Abundance and increasing portion size have played their parts in the obesity epidemic. Humans tend to eat the food placed before them, and Americans are no exception. In a study of undergraduates, David Levitsky of Cornell University showed categorically that the greater the quantity of food served, the more they ate (personal communication and "Putting Behavior Back into Feeding Behavior," by D. A. Levitsky, *Appetite*, 38: 143–148, 2002). From 1960 until about 1983 the daily estimated energy intake of Americans was constant. However, after 1983 it increased every year significantly (P < 0.001) and in a linear fashion. According to Greg Critzer, author of *Fat Land: How Americans Became the Fattest People in the World* (New York: Houghton Mifflin, 2003), the increasing portion size was driven by the discovery that most individuals will only buy one portion of anything but will pay a lot more for a single gigantic serving of soda, french fries, etc. As Michael Pollan has commented in a review of *Fat Land*, "from a business perspective the fattening of America may have been a necessity" ("You Want Fries with That?" *New York Times Book Review*, January 12, 2003).

153 The leptin story: The actions of the leptin hormone are clear only in treating the severe obesity and sexual immaturity of rare individuals who do not have the leptin-producing gene. Julio Licinio and Ma-Li Wong, senior research scientists at the Neuropsychiatric Institute in Los Angeles, recently studied three cousins from Turkey whose bodies could not produce leptin because of this rare genetic mutation. Ranging in age from their late twenties to 40, these individuals were grossly obese with insatiable appetites. After 10 months of leptin injections, they lost more than half their body weight—over 150 pounds each—and experienced dramatic change in sexual maturity and behavior, which correlated with a measurable change in brain growth.

154 The number of outrageously fraudulent products: Among the fraudulent products are devices that dissolve fat through the principles of acupuncture, such as the fat-be-gone ring worn on the finger, or slimming insoles for your shoes that will trim your hips and thighs by stimulating the nerves of the feet. In the year 2000 Americans spent some $6 billion on such goofy products. See "Fraudulent Marketers Capitalize on Demand for Sweat-Free Diets," by Greg Winter, *New York Times*, October 29, 2000.

154 Children who are overweight: "Energy Expenditure in Lean and Obese Prepubertal Children," by J. P. Delaney, *Obesity Research*, 3: 67–72, 1995. For the commercial response, see "A Plus for Teens: Clothes Companies and Magazines Market to a Growing Number of Overweight Girls," by Sammie Chittum, *New York Post*, August 6, 1998; and "Kids Work Out, Fight Flab at Their Own Health Clubs," by Eleena de Lisser, *Wall Street Journal*, August 4, 1998. American girls now shop for clothes that are roughly two sizes larger than those worn by their mothers ("Big Business: The Obesity Industry, Fat Profits in Fat People," *Economist*, September 27, 2003).

154 Diet books proliferate: *The Zone*, by Barry Sears (New York: Harper-Collins, 1995), has remained a best seller ever since it was published. *Dr. Atkins' New Diet Revolution*, by Robert C. Atkins (New York: Avon Books, 1972), has been continuously in print since 1972 with many revisions. The best-selling author Gwen Shamblin, who runs the Weigh Down Workshop, was profiled in the article "Slim for Him: God Is Watching What You're Eating," by Rebecca Mead, *New Yorker*, January 15, 2001.

155 If activity has disappeared from the routine: There is overwhelming evidence that physical activity coordinates and facilitates many bodily processes that we hardly understand. For a detailed and passionate review, see "Waging War on Physical Inactivity: Using Modern Molecular Ammunition against an Ancient Enemy," by F. W. Booth, M. V. Chakravarthy, S. E. Gordon, and E. E. Spangenburg, *Journal of Applied Physiology*, 93: 3–30, 2002.

Chapter Six: THE TIME TRADE

157 Andrew Carnegie: Quotation is from an essay entitled "Wealth" (*North American Review*, 1899) in which Carnegie, the nineteenth-century American industrialist, sets forth his views on wealth, competition, and survival based on the concepts of social Darwinism, the philosophy of Herbert Spencer (1820–1903). Disillusioned with religion, Carnegie had become a devotee and friend of Spencer's, an English railway engineer and subeditor of the *Economist* who became a philosopher, after Spencer visited America in 1882.

Spencer, together with Thomas Huxley, was responsible for bringing Charles Darwin's theory of evolution to wide public attention. (Spencer coined the term "the survival of the fittest," not Darwin.) In *The Principals of Sociology*, Spencer analyzed the evolutionary process through which successful individuals become differentiated from the group, and in *The Principal of Ethics* he postulated a utilitarian system in which morality and survival are linked.

When Darwin's ideas were rocking the foundations of science, church, and state in England, the industrial barons of America warmly welcomed the tenets of the new evolutionary theory, and Spencer rapidly became the darling of America's affluent society. Darwin's research, through Spencer's interpretation, gave scientific substance to their social practices and justification for the growing economic inequality in a land where all men were considered free and equal. Competition was key. Poverty was a mere by-product of progress. It was through the skill, achievement, and fortune of those who succeeded that human civilization would evolve. In Spencer's theory this would lead to the formation of a new species and—in the American industrialist's mind—to the formulation of a new society. "The American Beauty rose can be produced in splendor and fragrance," pronounced the oil magnate John D. Rockefeller, "only by sacrificing the early buds which grow up around it. This is not an evil tendency of business; this is merely the working out of a law of nature and the law of God." Thus the pressures of poverty had a beneficial effect on the human race and justified the raw competition of the great industrialists of America's Gilded Age, the men whom the poet Walt Whitman saluted in his *Democratic Vistas* (New York: J. S. Redfield; Washington, D.C.: sold by the author, 1871)—"men of extreme business energy and . . . almost maniacal appetite for wealth." *Social Darwinism in American Thought*, by Richard Hofstadter (Boston: Beacon Press, 1944).

158 20 percent of the U.S. workforce: Shift work, especially at night, is the most commonly studied disturbance of sleep in industrial societies. Because of the timing of the work demand, a chronic disruption or misalignment occurs between the body's circadian rhythm and the light-dark cycle in which the person is living. Jet lag is the most common acute example of this phenomenon in our daily lives. Shift workers—those who work outside the standard Monday to Friday, 8:00 A.M. to 6:00 P.M. hours—experience chronic disruption of these circadian systems. Such work schedules have their costs: various studies have reported increased risks for cardiovascular disease, smoking, obesity, reduced fertility, and spontaneous abortion. "Sleep, Waking and Neurobehavioural Performance," by Naomi Rogers, Jillian Dorrian, and David Dinges, *Frontiers in Bioscience*, 8: 1056–1067, 2003. Also "Firms That Never Sleep," *Economist*, January 10, 1998.

158 citizens find themselves tethered to their jobs: See "For the Well Connected All the World's an Office," by Katie Hafner, *New York Times*, March 30, 2000. The leisure industry has also caught on to the trend. One can vacation in Hawaii or a Mexican resort without having to leave the office behind. Luxury hotels frequently provide fax machines, laptops, and cell phones for use while lounging at the pool. Video and telephone conferencing keeps you in the business loop regardless of location. While this phenomenon of "work stress and time starvation" is most obvious in American culture, it is also a growing concern in Britain. A report commissioned by the Salvation Army and published in 1999 by Michael Singer (*The Paradox of Prosperity*) documents the human cost of growing affluence (reported in "Britain in 2010: Rich but Far Too Stressed to Enjoy It," by Kate Watson-Smyth, *Independent*, September 15, 1999).

159 even first graders carrying schedules: "Parents Try to Reclaim Their Children's Time: Rethinking Rush of After-School Activities," by Pam Belluck, *New York Times*, June 13, 2000.

159 National Sleep Foundation: The foundation, based in Washington, D.C., was established in 1990 as an independent nonprofit organization dedicated to improving public health and safety through a better national understanding of sleep and sleep disorder. Its surveys suggest that more than 40 percent of adults experience daytime sleepiness severe enough to interfere with their daily activities, at least a few days each month. It is estimated that in the United States, sleep-related fatigue causes 100,000 police-reported highway crashes each year, resulting in 71,000 injuries and 1,500 deaths (see www.sleepfoundation.org). For discussion of these consequences, and others, of the 24-hour society, see "Catastrophes, Sleep and Public Policy: Consensus Report of a Committee for the Association of Professional Sleep Societies," by M. A. Mitler, M. A. Carskado, C. A. Czeisler, W. Dement, D. F. Dinges, and R. Graeber, *Sleep*, 11: 100–109, 1988; and "An Overview of Sleepiness and Accidents," by D. F. Dinges, *Journal of Sleep Research*, 4 (Supplement 2): 4–14, 1995. Also "Sleepless," by Verlyn Klinkenborg, *New York Times,* January 5, 1997. For a comprehensive handbook on sleep and its disorder written for the general public, I recommend *No More Sleepless Nights*, by Peter Hauri and Shirley Linde (New York: Wiley, 1996).

160 The brain's "biological clocks": The importance of the suprachiasmatic nuclei (SCN) was first recognized in 1972 by two independent investigators, Robert Moore and Irving Zucker, when they reported that destruction of this tiny area in the hypothalamus disrupted sleep and circadian rhythms. Subsequent experiments demonstrated that replacement grafting of the SCN restored the rhythmic function. Circadian variation is an inherent property of cells and is driven by "clock genes," which are present in many species, having been conserved over the course of evolution. For a brief overview, see "The Brain, Circadian Rhythms and Clock Genes," by Michael Hastings, *British Medical Journal*, 317: 1704–1707, 1998.

161 sleep deprivation interacts with the time course: I am indebted to David Dinges, professor in the Department of Psychiatry at the University of Pennsylvania, for information on the subtle effects of sleep deprivation. Dinges has conducted elaborate studies on the effects of a cumulative sleep debt that is in the range of what young healthy American adults commonly experience. In one important study, sleep was restricted by about one-third from the habitual sleep preference. This resulted in approximately 5 hours of sleep each night, which is the length of time that many Americans sleep during the workweek. Subjective fatigue tended to precede objective changes in performance by 1 day. The ability to perform on cognitive and intellectual tasks was impaired the first 2 days, improved a little, and then worsened again on days 6 and 7 of the week-long experiment. The mean time to sleep onset decreased rapidly during the experiment, suggesting that the sleep debt incurred by the shortened sleep period had a dynamic and escalating association with daytime sleepiness. The leveling off of subjective sleepiness between days 2 and 5 of the experiment suggests that there is the capacity to adapt to sleep restriction. But after that the privation begins to take its toll until the ability to stay awake is severely impaired with subjective sleepiness, fatigue, and deficits in intellectual performance. (In the experiment of real life, of course, most people catch up on the sleep deprivation incurred during the week on the weekend.) Dinges's experiments emphasize that sleep deprivation does not eliminate the ability to perform complex functions, but a cumulative sleep debt does make it difficult to maintain a stable performance for more than a few minutes, leading to errors in cognitive performance and irritability in social situations. "Cumulative Sleepiness, Mood Disturbance, and Psychomotor Vigilance: Performance Detriments during a Week of Sleep-Restricted to Four to Five Hours per Night," by D. Dinges, F. Pack, K. Williams, K. A. Gillen, J. W. Powell, G. E. Ott, C. Aptowicz, and A. I. Pack, *Sleep*, 20: 267–277, 1997. See also "Stress, Fatigue, and Behavioral Energy," by D. F. Dinges, *Nutrition Reviews*, 59 (Supplement): 30–32, 2001; "Chronic Partial Sleep Deprivation: Neurobehavioral Response and Sleep Architecture," by H. Van Dongen, G. Maislin, and D. F. Dinges, *Sleep Research Online* (www.sro.org), 2: 735, 1999; and "Differential Effects of Prior Wakefulness and Circadian Phase on Nap Sleep," by D. F. Dinges, *Electroencephalography and Clinical Neurophysiology*, 64: 224–227, 1986.

162 Coffee is particularly effective in reducing sleep inertia: In a study by David Dinges and his colleagues, caffeine eliminated sleep inertia consistently in the face of increasing pressure for sleep, under conditions of sleep deprivation. Not only does sleep inertia intensify with prior sleep loss, but also it is more severe when the individual awakens from deep sleep than from dreaming sleep. The study included 28 normal volunteers who received either low-dose caffeine or a placebo and who were kept awake for approximately 3 days with the opportunity for 2-hour naps interspersed between the sleep deprivation, to simulate under experimental conditions intensive work or battlefield conditions. "Caffeine Eliminates Psychomotor Vigilance Deficits from Sleep Inertia," by H. Van Dongen, N. J. Price, J. M. Mullington, M. P. Szuba, S. C. Kapoor, and D. F. Dinges, *Sleep*, 24: 813–819, 2001.

166 Kim had developed sinusitis: Under chronic challenge, the stress response does not turn off, and the result can be a suppressed immune system prone to infection. Natural killer cells—the specialized immune cells that protect the body from threat by seeking and destroying abnormal cells or virus-infected cells—are good markers of immunity that can be studied in the laboratory. Changes in the number and in the responsiveness of these cells are linked to a number of diseases, including the body's preparedness for viral infection. Stress, social isolation, and difficult relationships can lower the activity of natural killer cells, increasing the vulnerability to infection. While physical challenge and infection are themselves stressors, the most common stressor today—as Kim experienced— is social challenge, particularly in the work environment. Thus social isolation, hostility, and anger increase the risk of chronic stress and of chronic illness.

Although sleep impairment is considered to be harmless, even efficient by many living at the manic edge, there is considerable evidence that this idea is false. In a series of experiments, Karine Spiegel, Eve Van Cauter, and associates measured the impact of sleep debt on metabolic and endocrine function. The study results suggest that sleep is not just for the brain but also necessary for the rest of the body to remain healthy. In a study of young men between 18 and 27 years old in which sleep was curtailed to only 4 hours each day for 6 days within a 16-day period, Spiegel recorded profound effects on body metabolism. The young men were fed carbohydrate-rich meals during the study, similar to those available in fast-food restaurants (62 percent carbohydrate). While glucose and insulin responses were normal in the sleep recovery phase, during the period of sleep debt there was impairment of carbohydrate tolerance. Clearance of glucose from the blood was some 40 percent slower in the sleep debt condition than in the sleep recovery condition. Sleep deprivation and a fast-food diet in combination thus may have implications for the changing pattern of obesity seen in America. ("Impact of Sleep Debt on Metabolic and Endocrine Function," by K. Spiegel, R. Proult, and E. Van Cauter, *Lancet*, 354: 1435–1439, 1999.) Other studies of immune activity after partial sleep deprivation include "Partial Sleep Deprivation Reduces Natural Killer Cell Activity in Humans," by M. Irwin, K. Mascovich, C. Gillin, et al., *Psychosomatic Medicine*, 56: 493–498, 1994; "Neuroimmunologic Aspects of Sleep and Sleep Loss," by M. Rogers, M. S. Szuba, J. P. Staab, D. L. Evans, and D. F. Dinges, *Seminars in Clinical Neuropsychiatry*, 6: 295–307, 2001; "Soluble TNF-Alpha Receptor 1 and IL6 Plasma Levels in Humans Subjected to Sleep Deprivation: Model of Space Flight," by W. T. Scherer, J. M. Reuben, J. M. Mullington, N. J. Price, B. Lee, E. O. Smith, M. P. Szuba, H. P. A. Van Dongen, and D. F. Dinges, *Journal of Allergy and Clinical Immunology*, 107: 165–170, 2001.

166 She had been a young girl: Kim's family had lived in Vungtan, a major military base on the coast south of Saigon, and fled Vietnam in the early summer of 1975 together with some 300,000 others. Half of these individuals, primarily Vietnamese nationals, eventually settled in the United States. The initial wave was composed mainly of well-educated citizenry and those who had served in the armed forces against the North. The refugees went first to Camp Pendleton in California before being dispersed widely across the country, living with host families. However, because they were free to relocate, many individuals eventually returned to southern California.

167 The acute development of panic: Panic disorder takes its name from the Greek God Pan, who in mythology was fond of alarming flocks of animals and humans. What are now distinguished diagnostically by psychiatrists as general anxiety, panic, and agoraphobia comprise a cluster of illnesses together known as the anxiety disorders. Professor Donald Klein of Columbia University in New York has argued that panic lies at the core of these syndromes, with "anticipatory anxiety" preceding panic and agoraphobia driving a fear of places where the panic may recur. The clinical syndromes that psychiatrists distinguish in practice overlap such that over the life cycle, an individual may experience them all. Overlap with symptoms of depression, as in Kim's case, is also commonplace. Occasional minor attacks of panic are widespread in the general population, with some studies estimating the prevalence to be over 40 percent. "False Suffocation Alarms, Spontaneous Panics, and Related Conditions. An Integrative Hypothesis," by D. F. Klein,

Archives of General Psychiatry, 55: 85–86, 1993; "Panic Disorder and Agoraphobia," by James Ballenger, in *The New Oxford Textbook of Psychiatry*, edited by M. G. Gelder, J. J. Lopez-Ibor Jr., and N. C. Andreason (Oxford: Oxford University Press, 2000).

169 In two national epidemiological surveys: In the prevalence figures quoted by Dr. Bystritsky all anxiety disorders are clustered together. *Psychiatric Disorders in America: The Epidemiologic Catchment Area Study*, edited by L. N. Robbins and D. A. Regier (New York: Free Press, 1991); and "Lifetime and 12-Month Prevalence of DSM-III-R Psychiatric Disorders in the United States. Results from the National Comorbidity Survey," by R. C. Kessler, K. A. McGonagle, S. Zhao, C. B. Nelson, M. Hughes, S. Eshleman, H. U. Wittchen, and K. S. Kendler, *Archives of General Psychiatry*, 51: 8–19, 1994.

170 J. Pierpont Morgan: For a lively description of the temperament and competitive practice of the industrial barons of America's Gilded Age, see "Titans at War: The Industrial Legacy of Rockefeller, Carnegie and Morgan," in *America in the Gilded Age*, by Sean Dennis Cashman (New York: New York University Press, 1984), p. 36.

174 the survival equivalent: See "Autonomic Reactivity of Panic Patients during CO2 Inhalation Procedure," by A. Bystritsky, M. Craske, E. Maidenberg, T. Vapnik, and D. Shapiro, *Depression and Anxiety*, 11: 15–26, 2000. The survival mechanisms that serve us throughout life are tuned during childhood and adolescence. Thus Kim's Vietnam experience may have conditioned her toward anxiety when trapped in a fearful business situation. However, that her first episode of depression and anxiety did not occur until she was 39 years old, and only under the circumstances that I describe, makes childhood trauma an incomplete explanation for her illness. "A Developmental Psychopathology Model of Childhood Traumatic Stress: Intersection with Anxiety Disorders," by R. S. Pynoos, A. M. Steinberg, and J. C. Piacentini, *Biological Psychiatry*, 46: 1542–1554, 1999.

175 in a study conducted by the National Institute of Mental Health: The response of 12 individuals with panic disorder to a night of sleep deprivation was compared to that of a matched group of individuals with depression and with normal control subjects. Some 40 percent of those with panic disorder experienced panic attacks in the day following the privation. "Effects of One Night's Sleep Deprivation on Mood and Behavior in Panic Disorder," by P. P. Roy-Byrne, T. W. Uhde, and R. M. Post, *Archives of General Psychiatry*, 43: 895–899, 1986.

175 a capricious and intensively competitive professional environment: Unstable environments, such as Kim experienced after her denouement with her boss, are breeding grounds for stress. Jay Kaplan has investigated the physiological and immune effects of social reorganization and of social group instability in primates, specifically male cynomolgus monkeys. Individual differences (whether the animal was aggressive, fearful, or affiliative) were noted in two experimental groups, one in which social stability reigned for 5 months, and another in which the animals endured the social disruption of new animals being introduced to the group on four separate occasions. Tests of immune system activity, lymphocyte proliferation tests, and natural killer cell cytotoxicity assays were performed before and after the reorganization in both groups. Highly aggressive animals showed lower baseline natural killer cell activity and higher lymphocyte counts than did animals of low aggression. In monkeys having high levels of fear, the reorganization of the social group was associated with increased lymphocyte counts and decreased lymphocyte proliferation in response to blood cell stimulation in the laboratory. Thus affiliation with other animals, particularly in an unstable social environment, seems to be an important element in reducing stress and improving immune competence. ("Effects of Social Reorganization on Cellular Immunity in Male Cynomolgus Monkeys," by S. W. Line, J. Kaplan, E. Heise, J. K. Hilliard, S. Cohen, B. S. Rabin, and S. B. Manuck, *American Journal of Primatology*, 39: 235–249, 1996; "The Relationship of Agonistic and Affiliative Behavior Patterns to Cellular Immune Function in Cynomolgus Monkeys Living in Unstable Social Groups," by J. Kaplan, E. Heise, S. B. Manuck, C. Shively, S. Cohen, B. S. Rabin, and A. L. Kasprowicz, *American Journal of Primatology*, 25: 157–173, 1991; "Chronic Social Stress: Affiliation and Cellular Immune Response in Nonhuman Primates," by S. Cohen, J. Kaplan, and J. Cunnick, *Psychological Science*, 3: 301–304, 1992.

177 As Robert Putnam has detailed: *Bowling Alone: The Collapse and Revival of the American Community*, by Robert D. Putnam (New York: Simon and Schuster, 2000).

178 its cultural contribution is a pseudoreality: While the Internet has been hailed as a technology equivalent in its social force to the telephone, there is some evidence that it increases rather than reduces social isolation. In a study from the Human Computer Interaction Institute of Carnegie Mellon University, Pittsburgh, 169 people in 79 households were studied for 2 years. Greater use of the Internet was associated with declines in participants' communication with family members, declines in the size of their social circle, and increases in depression and loneliness. "Internet Paradox: A Social Technology That Reduces Social Involvement and Psychological Well-being?" by R. Kraut, M. Patterson, V. Lundmark, S. Kiesler, T. Mukopadhyay, and W. Scherlis, *American Psychologist*, 53: 1017–1031, 1998. See also "Sad Lonely World Discovered in Cyberspace," by Amy Harmon, *New York Times*, August 30, 1998.

179 despite winning a national medal in science: The national science prize that Bystritsky won in 1972—a gold medal—was for his study of rat behavior in an open field. "I let the rats run around and then I gave them Valium," he said. "Usually people are content to calculate the mean of such group activity, but I soon realized that I had discovered something more complicated." Looking deeper, he noted that some of the rats were slowing down, as would be expected with Valium, but others—those more anxious that tended to sit in the corners of the open field—started to explore their surroundings. In Bystritsky's words, "the group had established a sameness," and only by looking at the variance of the experiment was the true effect discovered. He then repeated the experiment using amphetamines and found exactly the same effect. Some of the more active rats slowed down, which Bystritsky found reminiscent of attention deficit disorder in children, while those prone to withdrawal speeded up. "I called it the pharmacology of large groups," said Bystritsky, "that extremes are always brought to the mean." It was the beginning of his interest in anxiety and behavior. "Having won the science prize I thought I was destined for the academy and a Ph.D. program," Bystritsky said. "Then my satire got in the way. My reputation had spread. I was forbidden to perform and prevented from pursuing the Ph.D., despite being in the top 1 percent of my class of 750 students. Only with the help of a professor who believed in me was I eventually able to leave Russia, and after some adventures arrived in the U.S. in 1979."

180 SSRI (a selective serotonin reuptake inhibitor): SSRIs block the transport systems in the brain that recycle serotonin at the neuron, thus increasing the levels of this chemical messenger at the synaptic cleft, the gap across which neurons communicate. Because the serotonin system, one of the brain's superhighways, modulates and quiets behavior, these drugs are effective in a wide range of psychiatric disorders, including depression, anxiety, and panic. For details, see "Antidepressants and Other Medications for Mood Disorder, A Glossary and Guide," in *A Mood Apart: The Thinker's Guide to Emotion and Its Disorder*, by Peter C. Whybrow (New York: Harper Perennial, 1998).

PART III
MORE IS NOT ENOUGH:
PROSPERITY RECONSIDERED

183 Alexis de Tocqueville: Quotation from *Democracy in America*, by Alexis de Tocqueville, translated by George Lawrence (New York: Anchor Books, 1969), Vol. I, Part II, Chapter 9, p. 286. In Chapter 9, Tocqueville summarizes the "main causes tending to maintain a democratic republic in the United States." The first of these is the isolation of the country and the "incomparable wealth" of the land. Tocqueville remarks, "One must go to America to understand the power of material prosperity over political behavior, and even over opinions too, though these should be subject to reason alone." In this passage he describes as an example the conversation he had while being entertained one evening at the house of "a rich planter" in "one of the remotest parts of Pennsylvania." Tocqueville describes his host as a Frenchman who had left France decades before and marvels aloud how the New World has changed his opinions. "My host had been a great leveler and an ardent demagogue forty years before, for his name had left a mark on history. It was therefore strange to hear him talk like an economist . . . about the rights of property . . . the necessary hierarchy that wealth establishes . . . the support to order afforded by religious ideas."

Chapter Seven: DREAMS FOR SALE

185 Kevin Starr: From *Americans and the California Dream 1850–1915* by Kevin Starr, page 444 (New York: Oxford University Press, 1973).

186 "The American . . . lives in a land of wonders": From *Democracy in America*, Vol. I, Part II, Chapter 10, p. 404. Here Tocqueville is musing on "some considerations concerning the causes of the commercial greatness of the United States."

188 Europeans have always been mixed: In European eyes, during the 1990s American prestige was enhanced by its fiscal strength. The markets appeared strong, the dollar was strong, and it was the international place to invest, but as the evidence for cronyism and hubris, including deceit and fraud, began to percolate through in the summer of 2002, Europeans stepped back and began to see America's commercial leadership as arrogant rather than prescient. American-European relationships, always testy, soured further with the ascendancy of the neoconservatives of the George W. Bush administration, which demonstrated little interest in international treaties or the deliberations of the United Nations.

Thus by the beginning of the Iraq war, the goodwill toward America provoked by the terrorist attacks of September 2001 had dissipated ("Anti-Americanism: The World out There; Distinctly Unfriendly, and Even More So Than Before," *Economist*, June 7, 2003). The "old" European allies saw America as lacking social concern beyond its own self-protective worldview, giving weight to the French and German position that the European Union should be strengthened as a counterbalance to Washington. (The European Union provides some 65 percent of the world's aid to developing countries; America in proportion to its size gives the smallest percentage of all nations.) President George W. Bush was seen as prototypically American, full of Texas swagger and with little understanding of European democracies but with a mania for self-aggrandizement and self-serving interpretations of the free market. (During the economic downturn, the Bush administration was quick to place tariffs on imported steel.) The opposing American view is that Europe favors international diplomacy for the simple reason that it is weak and America is strong. (*Paradise and Power*, by Robert Kagan (New York: Atlantic Books, 2003).

Any discussion of differences in temperament between the migrants of the New World and the Europeans who stayed behind, first well documented by Tocqueville and increasingly evident as I have set forth here, is remarkable in its absence. (See "A Short History of American Indifference," by Josef Joffe, *New York Times*, April 15, 2001; "Powerless Europe," by Charles Grant, *Prospect*, March 2002; "America the Invulnerable: The World Looks Again," by Steven Erlanger, *New York Times*, July 21, 2002; and "The Great Divide," by Timothy Garton Ash, *Prospect*, March 2003.) In fact, that Europe and America are totally intertwined in almost every other way suggests that such behavioral differences are as important in the ongoing debate as they have been in the past. (See "The Unloved American: Two Centuries of Alienating Europe," by Simon Schama, *New Yorker*, March 10, 2003.) European exports to America totaled some $300 billion in the year 2000 while American exports to Europe were approximately $260 billion. There are a thousand flights a day between America and Europe, and 16 million Americans visit Europe every year. Some 12 million Europeans in turn visit the United States. In its organization the European Union has a 100 million people more than the United States, at 379 million people, but a land mass only a third of the size. America controls 23.9 percent of the world trade, and Europe 18 percent. "Britain and the Great Divide," *Times* (London) May 21, 2002.

189 Poznań, Poland: The details of the history of Poznań are taken from the book *Poznań*, by Konrad Czaplinski and Lech Przeciakowski (Warsaw: Radwan Wano, 1999).

191 Beijing's ancient Forbidden City: Starbucks has an increasing presence in China and around the world. See "Globalization Puts Starbucks into the Forbidden City in Beijing," by Craig S. Smith, *New York Times*, November 25, 2000; and "Planet Starbucks," *Business Week*, September 9, 2002.

191 "In Poland we love all things American": See "Mass Distraction in Poland," *Economist*, February 21, 1998; "In Eastern Europe, a New Generation's Priorities Tilt toward the West," by Donald G. McNeil Jr., *New York Times*, November 21, 1999; and "Central Europe and the United States: We Still Rather Like the Americans," *Economist*, February 1, 2003.

192 a new McDonald's was opening somewhere: The information regarding the growth of the MacDonald's restaurants in Poland is taken from the McDonald's Corporation 1998 annual report.

192 Solidarity used leaflets and books: For a retrospective analysis of the Solidarity movement, see "The Dissidents: A Decade Later: Lech Walesa's Bad Dream and Other Tales of the Revolution," *New York Times Magazine*, November 7, 1999.

192 2 million registered businesses in Poland: "Limping towards Normality: A Survey of Poland," *Economist*, October 27, 2001; and "Crunch Time for Warsaw's Number Cruncher," by David Fairlam with Bogdan Turek, *Business Week*, July 24, 2000.

193 A generation gap has been opened: Stories covering the shifting fortunes of younger and older persons in Eastern Europe, commercial sponsorships, and laissez-faire economics in the first decade of freedom can be found in "Mass

Distraction in Poland," *Economist*, February 21, 1998; and "Eastern Europe: A New Generation's Priorities Tilt toward the West," by Donald G. McNeil Jr., *New York Times*, November 21, 1999.

194 José Bové: Information about Bové is taken from his book *The World Is Not for Sale: Farmers against Junk Food*, written with Francois Dufour (London: Verso Books, 2001), where he is interviewed by the journalist Gilles Luneau. See also "French Unite against U.S. Trade Domination," *Times* (London), September 24, 1999; "The French Farmer's Anti-global Hero," *Economist*, July 8, 2000; and "Putting the Brakes On: Globalization through French Eyes," *Economist*, August 4, 2001.

194 the McDonald's Corporation: Data were gathered from annual reports and "McMissteps," by Mark Tatge and Brandon Copple, *Forbes*, December 10, 2001.

195 Big Mac hamburger as an index of relative value: The Big Mac index or "Mac-currencies" as the *Economist* sometimes calls it, emerges every year or two. See "The Golden Arches Standard: Big Mac-currencies; Some People Read Tea Leaves to Predict the Future, We Prefer Hamburgers," *Economist*, April 29, 2000.

195 "*Le mal bouffe*": Although José Bové's chance of rolling back the commercial juggernaut of McDonald's marketers is slim, the opposition to their exponential growth is gaining momentum in Europe, and the French opposition to American fast food is not unique. The Italian organization Slow-foods, founded in 1986 by Carlo Petrini in response to the McDonald's invasion of Italy, has a similar goal to that of Bové's, supporting local farmers and produce against the homogenizing influence of America's fast-food empire. With its quarterly magazine *Slow*, and a newsletter appropriately titled the *Snail*, Slow-foods has spread rapidly to 35 countries, and now has several supporting chapters in the United States. For an article detailing the increasing interest in slow foods in the United States, see "Tastemakers," by Elizabeth Pochoda, *House & Garden*, September 2000.

195 America's commercial hegemony: While everybody agrees that American pop culture is invading France (and the rest of the world), not everybody agrees on the effects of this invasion. See "Culture Wars," *Economist*, September 12, 1998. The increasing investment in France by U.S. investors is covered in the article "Resisting Those Ugly Americans: Contempt in France for U.S. Funds and Investors," *New York Times*, January 9, 2000. For broader discussion of the growing U.S. hegemony, see "Universal Nation," by Jedediah Purdy, *Prospect*, November 2001; and "Democracy at Risk: American Culture in a Global Culture," by Benjamin R. Barber, *World Policy Journal*, 15 (Summer): 29–42, 1998.

197 "an imperfect substitute": Tocqueville was repeatedly impressed by the practical mind-set of the Americans he met and how they were always looking for "shortcuts" in construction. His speculation was that this approach to life had something to do with a wish to make a cheap product that could be sold to the greatest number. This was in contrast to his experience in Europe, where crafts-men were held to painfully high standards because they were competing to com-mand the attention of the limited number of individuals who could afford their services. See Tocqueville's *Democracy in America*, translated by George Lawrence (New York: Anchor Books, 1969), Vol. II, Part I, Chapters 10–11. (Quotation is from p. 466.)

197 A poll taken in France in the year 2000: Quoted in "Putting the Brakes On: Globalization through French Eyes," *Economist*, August 4, 2001.

197 declared rates of personal happiness: Data from *Francoscopie 2003*, quoted in "France Has Never Had It so Good, or Been So Miserable," by John Litchfield, *Independent*, October 22, 2002.

198 what explains the worldwide appeal of American mass-marketing techniques?: Pop culture is the capitalist culture of self-interest, says Edward Rothstein, in "Damning (Yet Desiring) Mickey and the Big Mac," *New York Times*, March 2, 2002.

199 "soft drinks within an arm's reach of desire": See "Senator, Promot-ing Nutrition, Battles Coca-Cola," *New York Times*, April 26, 1994.

199 McDonald's . . . defends that name with . . . lawyers if neces-sary: See "Today's Burgers, Tomorrow . . . ?" *Economist*, July 15, 2000. "It sounds Mc-crazy," suggests the *Economist*. Perhaps an "arguably unrivaled example of cor-porate paranoia" has led McDonald's to force a tiny health care company based in Switzerland and calling itself "McWellness" to change its name. The article goes on to describe how the prefix "Mc" is aggressively defended around the globe, and this is done in part because "the company admits that its future plans are not lim-ited to food."

199 The consistency of the product denies reality: For discussion of Jean Baudrillard and fast foods, see "The New Means of Consumption: A Post-Modern Analysis," by George Ritzer, in *Illuminating Social Life*, by Peter Kivisto (Thousand Oaks, CA: Sage Publications, Times-Forbes Press, 1997), pp. 261–284; and *America* by Jean Baudrillard (London: Verso Press, 1989).

200 McDonald's and Coca-Cola have close business ties: McDonald's, Coca-Cola, and Disney, the world's three top brands, says the *Economist*, are linked by a hidden web of alliances. For them, as for many others, such alliances offer the best hope of future growth. See "Business: The Science of Alliance," *Economist*, April 4, 1998.

200 Walt Disney remains the unrivaled architect: For a series of articles on Disney as a key symbol of contemporary American culture, including a discus-sion of the influence of Disney's childhood in Missouri on his later designs for his theme parks, see *Designing Disney's Theme Parks: The Architecture of Reassur-ance*, edited by Karal Ann Marling (Paris: Flammarion, 1997). This book accom-panied the exhibition of the same name organized by the Canadian Center for Architecture.

202 the Disney Imagineering Workshop in Glendale: This little publicized enclave of creative artists was profiled in "Connected," *Daily Telegraph Magazine* (London), September 23, 1999.

202 "a new art form in which good is spread throughout the world": See *Designing Disney's Theme Parks: The Architecture of Reassurance*, edited by Karal Ann Marling (Paris: Flammarion, 1997), p. 219.

202 one of the most powerful brand names: In the global marketplace, the role of branding is changing. What began as a form of consumer protection, a guarantee of reliability and quality to the customer, has shifted its ground to represent a way of life or a set of ideas. In a desperate urge to build markets, advertising has moved away from branding as a guarantee of quality that will retain customer loyalty to a promotional strategy exploiting human passion and desire. Thus Coca-Cola sells fun in its fizzy drink, McDonald's is selling happiness, and Nike offers an opportunity to achieve athletic distinction. Spin-offs are tied closely to Hollywood's increasing reliance on the blockbuster film where investment of $100 million in production and $50 million in advertising are now commonplace. The payback comes in merchandising the image: the toys, the clothes, and the games that are associated with Spider Man or Harry Potter. Disney first developed this idea in the branding of Mickey Mouse, when Mickey's image appeared on a pencil case in 1929. Hollywood and Madison Avenue are increasingly interdependent and dependent on "associated merchandising" to make a profit, and an expanding global market is essential to meeting profit goals. Thus the global market for children's TV programs is worth about $2 billion, but the market for licensed toys associated with those programs is $27 billion. For additional information, see "Merchandising and Children's Films: The Spider's Bite," *Economist*, May 11, 2002; and "The Case for Brands," *Economist*, September 8, 2001.

203 Wal-Mart, the American retail giant: See "As Biggest Business, Wal-Mart Propels Changes Elsewhere," by Leslie Kaufman, *New York Times*, October 22, 2000; "Can Wal-Mart Get Any Bigger? (Yes, a Lot Bigger . . . Here's How)," by Bill Saporito, *Time*, January 23, 2003. For data on the community impact of Wal-Mart, see *When Corporations Rule the World*, by David Korten (Hartford, CT: Kumarian Press, 1995), pp. 219–220. Details of merger manias came from "Uneasy Pieces in an Era of Mergers: Who's Afraid Now That Big Is No Longer Bad?" Louis Uchitelle, *New York Times*, November 5, 2000.

204 Giants must become super giants: See "Giant Corporations, Dwarf States," by Ignacio Ramonet, *Le Monde Diplomatique*, June 1998.

204 the continued evolution of the mercantile trading: In using the term *globalization*, it is important to distinguish the early struggles that marked the emergence of a capitalist worldview among European nations in the eighteenth and nineteenth centuries, from globalization as a contemporary political ideology that promotes the ascendancy of laissez-faire economics. The latter, championed by the United States since the Second World War, is of comparatively recent origin, having gathered its present strength since the collapse of the Soviet Union. The United States rose to global supremacy as the European powers declined. Throughout the nineteenth century the global consolidation of labor and trade continued, with Europe's colonies supplying cheap labor and raw materials for domestic industry. However, by the 1930s amid continuing economic and political turmoil, the colonial empires of a weakened Britain and France were disintegrating. Despite fierce military campaigns conducted against "terrorists" during the 1950s and the early 1960s, growing nationalist movements for independence, together with Moscow's challenge, proved overwhelming. The United States, having assumed the role of undisputed superpower, fostered this colonial dismemberment of Europe in the hope of containing communist ideology (although when decolonization intersected with the superpower rivalry—as it did in Vietnam between 1965 and 1973—America quickly took up the challenge).

But the greater global challenge was poverty. America's commercial hegemony of today is rooted in humanitarian concern, in addition to self-interest. In the post–World War II era, as the colonial map was redrawn, the plight of the newly independent nations was apparent to all, including President Harry Truman, who on January 20, 1949, expressed the intent of the American government to solve the problem of global underdevelopment. The intent of the Truman plan was to create the necessary conditions for the developing world to replicate the industrialization of "advanced" societies with the rapid growth of material production, agriculture, and living standards. In Truman's humanitarian vision, the developing countries needed science, financial capital, and technology to jump-start an economic revolution. Hence it was in renewal of America's destiny as the universal nation—self-ordained to foster a new world order of peace and abundance—that the contemporary wave of globalization was initiated.

In practice what distinguishes the mercantile world of today from that of two centuries ago are the changes wrought by information technology. In the last decades of the twentieth century, American capitalism shifted away from a preoccupation with industrial production as the controlling element in profit, to the management of information and the development of international consumer markets. The efficient production of cheaper goods remains important, and has been aided by the globalization of manufacturing. But because an expanding market has become essential to the health of the American economic enterprise, greater effort has been devoted to understanding the habits of consumers as a means of increasing market share. Systems of debt management, in particular the credit card—offering instantly available loans at the mall, the megastore, and now from home for cybershopping—have been key to a relentless expansion of the consumer market in America. From this shift in commercial focus has evolved the ability to channel the behavior of large numbers of people, in ways that seem pleasing to them, while specifically serving the growth requirements of the manufacturer, merchant, and shareholder.

205 the "Davos" culture: See "A Universal Civilization? Modernization and Westernization," in *The Clash of Civilizations and the Remaking of World Order*, by Samuel P. Huntington (New York: Touchstone, 1996). An essay where Huntington outlines his views, "The West Unique, Not Universal," appeared in *Foreign Affairs*, 75 (November-December): 28–47, 1996. For a history of the World Economic Forum, see "One of the Greatest Shows on Earth," *Forbes*, December 2, 1996; and "Swiss Pastry," by Lewis Lapham, *Harper's Magazine*, June 1998.

205 "roughly seventy percent of the world's daily output": Quoted in "Swiss Pastry," by Lewis Lapham, *Harper's Magazine*, June 1998.

206 World Trade Organization and the International Monetary Fund: Globalization didn't just happen but was the brainchild of the Bretton Woods meeting held in 1944 in New Hampshire. With Germany collapsing, the purpose was to build the necessary systems that would enable the international flow of goods and money and accelerate growth through global free trade and deregulation. At the opening session, U.S. Secretary of the Treasury Henry Morgenthau asked participants to embrace the "elementary economic axiom . . . that prosperity has no fixed limits. It is not a finite substance to be diminished by division." (Back to the old ideas of Adam Smith.) At the end of the meeting to facilitate this vision, the World Bank and the International Monetary Fund were founded, and the groundwork was laid for what was to become the General Agreement on Tariffs and Trade (GATT), which is now known as the World Trade Organization. Although the organization was designed to increase the general wealth of the world, many argue that only the most wealthy nations have benefited from the reduction in trade barriers, and that the accelerating gap between rich and poor in America is mirrored worldwide. See "The Limits of the Earth—Paradigms Lost: The Bretton Woods Vision of Endless Growth Is Obsolete," by David C. Korten, *Nation*, July 15, 1996.

206 globalization "tends to *de-link* the fate": From the article "Start Taking the Backlash against Globalization Seriously," by Klaus Schwab and Claude Smadja, *International Herald Tribune*, February 1, 1996.

206 "Only fools believe in the conscience of markets": George Soros as quoted in "Swiss Pastry," by Lewis Lapham, *Harper's Magazine*, June 1998.

207 the trend toward longer working hours: "Snacks Fill Gap Left by Demise of Family Meal," *Financial Times* (London), September 22, 1999; "More Work and Less Pay for Britons," *Daily Telegraph* (London), April 11, 2002; "Britain Isn't Saving," *Economist*, May 25, 2002.

208 "Today money works by itself": From *The World Is Not for Sale: Farmers against Junk Food*, by José Bové and Francois Dufour (London: Verso Books, 2001), p. 146.

Chapter Eight: THE ROOTS OF HAPPINESS

211 Robert Owen: Robert Owen was a British social reformer, the son of a saddler who had little formal education. At the age of 10 he began working in the textile business, and by his early 20s had amassed enough money to become a partner in a successful cotton-manufacturing program in Lanark, Scotland. There he pioneered a model community with good housing, sanitation, nonprofit stores, schools, and excellent working conditions. Owen and the new Lanark experiment were influential in the passage of England's factory reform act in 1819. Owen's conditions of happiness cited here are from *The Invisible Heart: Economics and Family Values*, by Nancy Folbre (New York: New Press, 2001). See Chapter 3, "Measuring Success: The Human Development Index," p. 73.

212 the underpinning for community life: Sharing behavior is the key to community life and is fundamental to market behavior. Sharing important resources, beyond the kinship group, is a core feature of human societies. Other primates indulge in a primitive form of food sharing, but sharing as a method of collective risk reduction when resources are low—that is, during periods of uncertainty and poor food supply—is a uniquely human phenomenon. Another characteristic of human exchange is the sharing of unusual rewards. So, for example, we "treat" our friends when we receive a "windfall," such as winning a prize or some unexpected bonus. In a series of windfall studies, Tatsuya Kameda and associates comparing Japanese and American participants showed that, in general, the Japanese participants shared more readily than the Americans. This may not be greater altruism as much as cultural vigilance on the part of the Japanese—something akin to Adam Smith's impartial spectator—where when a windfall occurs, the Japanese feel more obligated to participate in social sharing, fearing the envy of others and the disrespect that engenders. "Social Sharing and Risk Reduction: Exploring a Computational Algorithm for the Psychology of Windfall Gains," by T. Kameda, M. Takezawa, R. S. Tindale, and C. M. Smith, *Evolution and Human Behavior*, 23: 11–33, 2002.

214 Plainfield, New Hampshire: For a detailed history of the Plainfield township, see *Choice White Pines and Good Land: A History of Plainfield and Meriden, NH*, edited by Phillip Zea and Nancy Norwalk (Portsmouth, NH: Peter E. Randall, 1991).

219 Marco Iacoboni: For details of Iacoboni's original studies, see "Neural Mechanisms of Empathy in Humans: A Relay from Neural Systems for Imitation to Limbic Areas," by L. Carr, M. Iacoboni, M. C. Dubeau, J. C. Mazziotta, and G. L. Lenzi, *Proceedings of the National Academy of Sciences*, 100: 5497–5502, 2003.

219 the rules of social conduct: The use of the term *family values* is an effort to modernize the term *virtue*, which is associated in many people's minds with a rigid Victorian era of double standards. The debate came to a head in America in the early 1990s when then Vice President Dan Quayle bemoaned the declining virtues of the family and the rise in the number of children being born out of wedlock. Indeed, the number of illegitimate births has been rising since the late 1960s in the United States, and by the turn of the century aggregated at around 30 percent; it was this increase that prompted the accusation of declining virtue or *family values*. However, a similar profile of illegitimate births is seen in other industrial countries, particularly Britain, which has about the same illegitimacy rate. Most intriguing, however, is that the rates previously had been flat for about 200 years, at between 5 or 6 percent. For a detailed discussion and historical background to these debates, see *The Demoralization of Society: From Victorian Virtues to Modern Values*, by Gertrude Himmelfarb (New York: Vintage Books, Random House, 1994). That such statistics are viewed by many Americans as evidence of a wider moral problem is underscored by the number of political speeches given ("Rediscovering Our American Values," an address given by House Majority Whip, the Honorable Tom Delay, January 20, 2000, to the Heritage Foundation, as an example) and the number of books published on the subject. One publication is *The Book of Virtues: A Treasury of Great Moral Stories* (New York: Simon and Schuster, 1993), edited by William J. Bennett, who had been secretary of education under President Reagan and director of the Office of National Drug Control Policy under the first President Bush. This heavy compendium went immediately to the top of the best-seller list and stayed there for several months. Unfortunately, even this paragon of public morality was to fall from his pedestal: in 2003 it was revealed that over several years Bennett had squandered $8 million in high-stakes gambling in Las Vegas and Atlantic City ("Vices and Virtues," *Los Angeles Times*, May 9, 2003).

220 These microcultures provide an enriched form of inheritance: For those interested in the complexity of forces that shape human development, I recommend *The Nurture Assumption: Why Children Turn out the Way They Do*, by Judith Rich Harris (New York: Touchstone Books, 1998). The book is unusual in that it breaks away from the idea that parental teaching is the core of childhood learning, and provides evidence that an extended community, particularly peers and the social environment beyond the home, have a major impact on the development of an individual's view of his or her self and of the social responsibilities that he or she has toward others.

222 Between 1987 and 1992, America lost an average of 32,500 farms: These figures are taken from *The Fatal Harvest Reader: The Tragedy of Industrial Agriculture*, edited by Andrew Kimbrell (Sausalito, CA: Island Press in collaboration with the Foundation for Deep Ecology, 2002), p. 17. When Adam Smith was writing about market economies, some 90 percent of all New World residents were involved in farming. In 1994, only 1.4 percent of the American population was farmers. For a precise but comprehensive history of American agriculture, see "A Brief History of Food and Agriculture in America," in *Bitter Harvest*, by Ann Cooper and Lisa M. Holmes (New York: Rutledge Press, 2000).

226 every man is "in some measure a merchant": This quotation comes from Adam Smith's *An Inquiry into the Nature and Causes of the Wealth of Nations*, 8th ed. (London: Strahan and Cadell, 1796), Book I, Chapter IV, p. 35. The full quotation is "Every man thus lives by exchanging, or becomes in some measure a merchant, and the society itself grows to what is properly a commercial society." In his writings Smith was cautious and circumspect when it came to the social consequences of free markets. For a scholarly discussion of the period that influenced Smith in his thinking and his perspective on community, see *Economic Sentiments: Adam Smith, Condorcet, and the Enlightenment*, by Emma Rothschild (Cambridge, MA: Harvard University Press, 2001).

226 "those friendships which are naturally contracted": Quotation from *The Theory of Moral Sentiments*, by Adam Smith (Indianapolis: Liberty Classics Edition, 1969), Part VI, Section II, Chapter 1. This is part of Smith's extensive discussion of the importance to the individual of sustaining the happiness of others in his or her household, and in the community. It was here that Smith believed the origins of dutiful character are to be found. For an excellent analysis, see *Adam Smith in His Time and Ours: Designing the Decent Society*, by Jerry Z. Muller (Princeton, NJ: Princeton University Press, 1993). Chapter 8, "The Impartial Spectator" (p. 100), and Chapter 10, "The Moral Balance Sheet of Commercial Society" (p. 131), are particularly pertinent.

226 "impartial spectator": See "The Impartial Spectator," in *Adam Smith in His Time and Ours: Designing the Decent Society*, by Jerry Z. Muller (Princeton, NJ: Princeton University Press, 1993), p. 100.

228 general health—does *diminish*: In modern industrial and postindustrial societies, social and economic factors are the most powerful determinants not only of happiness but also of general health. While it is generally accepted that poverty fosters disease, it is not as readily recognized that *social inequality* also erodes physical health. Thus among the developed countries, it is the most egalitarian, not the richest, that have the highest life expectancy. In the United States a strong relationship exists between income inequality and death rates across the 50 states and 282 metropolitan areas. See *Mind the Gap: Hierarchies, Health and Human Evolution*, by Richard Wilson (London: Weidenfeld and Nicholson, 2000); and *Social Determinants of Health*, edited by M. Marmot and R. G. Wilkinson (Oxford: Oxford University Press, 1999).

229 *The Loss of Happiness in Market Democracies*: This analysis by Robert E. Lane (New Haven: Yale University Press, 2000) is the most comprehensive available. People tend to be happier in smaller communities than larger ones, and also when they enjoy financial stability and have some say in their political and social destiny. This is clearly reflected in a study of the Swiss cantons, detailed in *Happiness and Economics: How the Economy and Institutions Affect Human Well-Being*, by Bruno S. Frey and Alois Stutzer (Princeton, NJ: Princeton University Press, 2002). However, the plateauing of happiness in market democracies is a worldwide phenomenon, although Americans tend to be rather less happy than many of their affluent neighbors. The size of the nation also makes a difference, with smaller democratic nations having an advantage over larger ones with the same per capita income. For summaries, see the article "Global Happiness," by Robert Wright, *Prospect*, December 2000; and *The Size of Nations*, by Alberto Alesina and Enrico Spolaore (Cambridge, MA: MIT Press, 2003).

229 The widowed and those alone in the world: See "Affective Disorders," by Myrna Weissman and Gerald Klerman, in *Psychiatric Disorders in America: The Epidemiological Catchment Area Study*, edited by Lee N. Robbins and Daryl A. Rieger (New York: Free Press, 1991). For a detailed discussion of emotion and the origins and treatment of mood disorder, see *A Mood Apart: The Thinker's Guide to Emotion and Its Disorder*, by Peter C. Whybrow (New York: HarperPerennial, 1998).

229 some evidence that a lack of companionship: "The Depersonalization of Retailing: Its Impact on the Lonely Consumer," by Andrew M. Forman and Vin Sriram, *Journal of Retailing*, 67: 26–43, 1981.

230 Approximately 1 million legal immigrants: For a survey of recent trends worldwide in migration, including details on migration to the United States, see "The Longest Journey: A Survey of Migration," *Economist*, November 2, 2002. Also "Rethinking Segregation beyond Black and White: Latino and Asian Immigrants Shift the Paradigm," by Janny Scott, *New York Times*, July 29, 2001; and "Trapped: Americans (a) Love, (b) Hate Immigrants," by Eric Schmidt, *New York Times*, January 14, 2001.

231 the average age of a full-time farmer: The material regarding Iowa and the influx of immigrants encouraged by state sponsorship is taken from "Iowa: The Future's Foreign: Immigrants Have Already Been the Salvation of Iowa, They Could Be Again," *Economist*, September 16, 2000.

231 A similar story is being told: See "The Changing Heartland," *Business Week*, September 9, 2002.

232 some see America becoming a nation of two cultures: Gertrude Himmelfarb has suggested that following the cultural revolution of the 1960s, America began to split into two parts: one driven by the hedonistic individualistic interests of the generation that began with the flower people and the other represented by the older generation of individuals who adhere to "traditional" responsibilities of family and church, etc. See *One Nation, Two Cultures: A Searching Examination of American Society in the Aftermath of Our Cultural Revolution*, by Gertrude Himmelfarb (New York: Vintage Books, 1999). While Himmelfarb's analysis may be flawed by political preconception, international surveys do suggest that the United States is traditional in its vision of the church, indeed conservative compared to the secular states of Europe. See "Special Report: American Values—Living with a Superpower," *Economist*, January 4, 2003. Also "One Nation Fairly Divisible under God," *Economist*, January 20, 2001.

232 The worst poverty in America: See "Heartbroken: Is Rural America Really Such a Great Role Model for the Nation?" *Economist*, August 17, 2002.

233 Such an investment is in the great American tradition: America has long seen itself as a nation of individual property owners. The original intent— life, liberty, and the pursuit of property—was well founded in the early experience of the colonists, and this continued as they stretched themselves across the continent. See "Life, Liberty, and Property," by Andro Linklater, *Prospect*, August 2002; and *Fatal Conceit: The Error of Socialism*, by S. A. Hayek (Chicago: University of Chicago Press, 1988).

234 That unregulated capitalist societies carry within themselves: The specific works referred to here are *Capital: A Critique of Political Economy*, Karl Marx, edited by Frederick Engels (New York: Modern Library, 1906); and *Capitalism, Socialism and Democracy*, by Joseph A. Schumpeter (New York: Harper Perennial, 1975). Schumpeter's book was originally published in 1942. The quote from *The Cultural Contradictions of Capitalism*, by Daniel Bell (New York: Basic Books, 1998) is on p. xii of the Foreword of 1978. For a particularly interesting analysis contrasting, from the standpoint of economics and culture, Western democracies focused on individualism with India and China, I recommend *Unintended Consequences, the Impact of Factor Endowments, Culture, and Politics on Long-Run Economic Performance*, by Deepak Lal (Cambridge, MA: MIT Press, 2003).

Chapter Nine: FINDING BALANCE IN THE AGE OF THE MERCHANT

235 William Shakespeare: From *The Merchant of Venice*, Act I, Scene 2. Quoted here are the wise words of Nerissa, maid-in-waiting to the rich heiress Portia.

236 Algonquin Hotel: First opened in 1902, this celebrated New York landmark was home to the "Round Table," a group of newspaper writers, magazine editors, critics, actors, and other hangers-on beginning in the 1920s. Harold Ross, the founder of the *New Yorker* magazine, Dorothy Parker, and James Thurber were among the celebrated literati that brought the hotel to national attention.

236 Brendan Behan, the Irish playwright: Behan first stayed at the Algonquin in 1960, when he was at the height of his fame. Arriving in New York for the opening of his play, *The Hostage*, a story about a British soldier held captive in a Dublin brothel, he became an instant celebrity. Notorious for his love of alcohol and outrageous behavior, he adopted New York as his favorite city, living for a time at the Algonquin until his behavior became so difficult that he was asked to leave. Tom had met him in 1963, the year before Behan died in Dublin at the age of 41.

236 Matilda the Algonquin cat: The Algonquin Hotel has enjoyed a resident cat since Frank Case—the hotel's general manager, and then owner, who encouraged the Round Table of literati—adopted Hamlet, a stray that walked in off the street one day. Since then, all male Algonquin cats have been named Hamlet and the females Matilda. The incumbent (2003) is a 5-year-old Burmese rag doll with her own web site: matildaalgonquincat@destinationhotels.com.

237 "time is money": Benjamin Franklin's famous phrase, "remember time is money," first appeared in his pamphlet "Advice to a Young Tradesman" published in Philadelphia in 1748. At the time Franklin was a printer and an active merchant.

241 "the Rules of TOM," an acronym for "Toward Optimum Mindfulness": Many of Tom's ideas came from his own experience and that of his colleagues. However, they are not alone in their rediscovery of the power of living in the present, an idea that draws heavily on Eastern philosophies. Among the many books available, Tom found the following most helpful: *Zen Mind, Beginner's Mind. Informal Talks on Zen Meditation and Practice*, by Shunryu Suzuki (New York: Weatherhill, 1970); *The Miracle of Mindfulness*, by Thich Nhat Hanh (Boston: Beacon Press, 1975); *Timeshifting: Creating More Time to Enjoy Your Life*, by Stephan Rechtschaffen (New York: Doubleday, 1996); *Slowing down to the Speed of Life*, by Richard Carlson and Joseph Bailey (San Francisco: Harper-Collins, 1997); *The Power of Now: A Guide to Spiritual Enlightenment*, by Eckhart Tolle (Novato, CA: New World Library, 1999); and specifically in the area of appetite and eating, *On Eating: Change Your Eating, Change Your Life*, by Susie Orbach (London: Penguin Books, 2002).

243 over three thousand advertising messages each day: *Data Smog, Surviving the Information Glut*, by David Shenk (New York: HarperCollins, 1997), p. 30.

249 the physiology of all living creatures: A balance in the exchange with the surroundings—or a dynamic balance with the environment, what biologists call *homeostasis*—is the key to understanding the drive and behavior of living things. Living creatures defy thermodynamic law, consuming energy to do so, and the vitality of that autonomy depends on homeostatic regulation. These homeostats are dynamic servo systems—analogous to, but more complex than, a thermostat controlling room temperature—and are organized around a set point. Any challenge that perturbs a dynamic system (causes a deviation from the resting state) will induce a correction (adaptation) designed to reestablish the system's preferred balance. This simple paradigm—of perturbing challenge and adaptive response in the service of homeostatic equilibrium—applies at all levels of human activity, from the molecular and cellular functions of the brain to the complex interaction of individuals and the hierarchical groups that characterize our social behavior. Thus what we call *drives* or *instincts*—emotion, the seeking of reward, sleeping, sex, appetite—reflect the activity of brain systems that are homeostatically controlled. When a stable adaptation is maintained, we speak of coping—implying harmony and balance—and when threatening events perturb the regulatory mechanisms to corrective action, the physiological changes that occur are called *stress*. Adam Smith's concepts of the market behavior may be understood in similar dynamic terms.

252 distrusted large institutions: Smith was troubled by the human frailty for riches as the focus of ambition throughout his life. In the substantial changes Smith made in *The Theory of Moral Sentiments* between the first edition published in 1759 when he was 36 and the seventh edition published just before his death in 1790, he repeatedly returned to this issue. In the last edition Smith ruminates on "the corruption of our moral sentiments" (Part I, Section III, Chapter 3). "We see frequently the vices and the follies of the powerful much less despised than the poverty and the weakness of the innocent. Two different roads are presented to us, equally leading to this so much desired object (respect and admiration); the one, by the study of wisdom and the practice of virtue; the other by the acquisition of wealth and greatness . . . one of proud ambition and ostentatious avidity; the other of humble modesty and equitable justice. Two different models, two different pictures, are held out to us, according to which we may fashion our own character and behavior; the one more gaudy and glittering in its coloring the other more correct and exquisitely beautiful." Clearly Smith hopes for the latter, the cornerstone of his economic balance, but fears the former. And with the test of time that indeed has proved to be the outcome. The "great mob" opts for "wealth and greatness." The learned virtues are no match for instinctual self-interest.

253 individuals carrying the repeat alleles of the DRD4 dopamine receptor gene: See "Nature and Nurture in Novelty Seeking," by L. Keltikangas-Järvien, K. Räikkönen, J. Ekelund, and L. Peltonen, *Molecular Psychiatry*, 9: 308–311, 2004. In this remarkable report, 92 children, derived from a representative population sample of 2,149 healthy young Finns, were studied from childhood to adulthood (a period of over fourteen years) to determine whether the environment of rearing moderated the association between the presence of alleles of the DRD4 gene and novelty-seeking and risk-taking behaviors in adulthood. When the childhood environment was "hostile" (characterized by emotional distance, low tolerance of normal childhood behavior, and strict discipline), individuals carrying alleles DRD2 and DRD5 (DRD7 was not measured) had significantly higher scores on the novelty-seeking scale of Cloninger's Temperament and Character Inventory (see Chapter Three) than did those who also carried the alleles but were reared in a supportive (empathic) environment.

253 America's recent drift toward self-interest: The most detailed analysis of this social shift in America during the last quarter of the twentieth century is found in *Bowling Alone: The Collapse and Revival of the American Community* (New York: Simon and Schuster, 2000), by Robert D. Putnam, who is a professor of public policy at Harvard. With extraordinary detail, Putnam documents the changing behavior of Americans in regards to the social structures of the nation— political parties, church, local community organizations—and how these changes are linked with the changing demographics of the rise of the commercial society and the decline in family values. Complementary to this book is the excellent treatise *An All Consuming Century: Why Commercialism Won in Modern America*, Gary Cross (New York: Columbia University Press, 2000). Cross, a professor of history at Penn State University, follows in detail the rise of consumerism in America, how it has fueled extraordinary economic growth, and how it has changed the way in which we live our lives.

254 a current that now runs broad and deep: For discussion and analysis of executive pay, see "Fat Cats Feeding," *Economist*, October 11, 2003.

254 Richard Grasso: Grasso was not accused of wrongdoing, but his pay package of $188 million during a time of economic constraint and stock-market uncertainty was considered an outrage by the American public. See "The Foxes Are Still Guarding the Henhouse," by John J Sweeney, *Los Angeles Times*, September 19, 2003; and "Would You Like Your Class War Shaken or Stirred, Sir?" *Economist*, September 6, 2003.

254 aligning executive pay with market performance: This practice was proposed first by economists in the 1970s, when corporate performance was stagnant and inflation high. For a concise overview, see "Face Value: How to Pay Bosses," *Economist*, November 16, 2002.

255 a modern form of mercantilism: See "Virtue and Prosperity," by Francis Fukuyama, *National Interest*, 40 (Summer): 21–28, 1995, for a summary of the limitations of "neomercantilism" and the cultural impact of neoclassical economics. A detailed analysis—and a darker set of conclusions—is found in *When Corporations Rule the World*, by David Korten (Hartford, CT: Kumarian Press, 1995).

255 47 percent of the nation's total income: Data from "Sinking Fast? Twenty Years of 'Trickle Down' Policies Have Swamped the US Economy," by Jeff Gates, *Utne*, July-August 2003, p. 59.

256 such as the Seeds of Simplicity movement that is enjoying healthy growth: Established in Los Angeles in the 1990s by Carol Holst, Seeds of Simplicity (www.seedsofsimplicity.org) is a national, nonprofit membership organization of the Center for Religion, Ethics and Social Policy at Cornell University. Through its web site, newsletter, and community support groups (The Simplicity Circles Project directed by Cecile Andrews), this citizen-based effort seeks to build practical alternatives to runaway material consumption and to facilitate habit change for those who seek to simplify their lives. In January 31, 2004, in association with Seeds of Simplicity and Rod Gorney of the Ashley Montagu Institute (www.montagu.org), the UCLA Neuropsychiatric Institute (www.npi.ucla.edu) sponsored the first national conference on mental health and simple living entitled "Countering the Compulsion to Consume." Presentations included distinguishing pleasure from enjoyment, the treatment of addictive clinical disorders arising from material overload, and how through "simplicity circles" individuals can substitute the satisfactions of "enough" for the compulsive frustrations of "more." (See "Seeking Simplicity in Land of Excess," by Steve Lopez, *Los Angeles Times*, January 25, 2004, and "Meeting's Simple Message: Slow Down, Shop Less, Live More," by Steve Hymon, *Los Angeles Times,* February 1, 2004.) To learn more about the simplicity field, see *The High Price of Materialism*, by Tim Kasser (Cambridge, MA: MIT Press, 2002); *The Human Agenda*, by Roderic Gorney (New York: Simon and Schuster, 1972); *Voluntary Simplicity*, by Duane Elgin (New York: William Morrow, 1993); *The Circle of Simplicity*, by Cecile Andrews (New York: HarperCollins, 1997); and *Your Money or Your Life*, by Joe Dominguez and Vicki Robin (New York: Penguin, 1992). In addition, see the PBS television series, "Simple Living with Wanda Urbanska."

257 "use which the Americans make [in civil life] of associations": Quotation from *Democracy in America*, by Alexis de Tocqueville, translated by George Lawrence (New York; Anchor Books, 1969), Vol. II, Part II, Chapter 5, pp. 513–514.

257 our fundamental need for intimacy: I am indebted to Talia Shire for many of these examples of how our need for intimacy is expressed in the media, especially in television.

258 indices of social and behavioral unrest: A baby born in America after 1970 and raised in a big city has a greater chance of being murdered than a World War II GI had of dying in battle. By mid-1989, one out of every four young black males was either in jail or on probation—a larger proportion than in college. A study in 2000 by the U.S. Department of Justice found that almost 1.5 million children had a parent in prison, an increase of 500,000 since 1991. Half the nation's inmates are parents of children under 18 years old. ("Prison Is a Member of Their Family," by Adrian Nicole LeBlanc, *New York Times*, January 12, 2003.) Violence in some inner cities, Los Angeles included, is sufficiently similar to combat that, during the Iraq war, naval trauma teams received final training in the Los Angeles County Hospital Emergency Room before being deployed on active duty at the front. See *The Demoralization of Society: From Victorian Virtues to Modern Values*, by Gertrude Himmelfarb (New York: Vintage Books, 1994); and "Too Many Convicts: America's Tough Crime Policy Is Having Unintended Consequences," *Economist*, August 10, 2002.

259 America has lost sight of the purpose: Commercial success is only one dimension of a civil society. For discussion, see *The Joyless Economy; The Psychology of Human Satisfaction*, by Tibor Scitovsky (New York: Oxford University Press, 1976); and *The Good Society, The Humane Agenda*, by John Kenneth Galbraith (Boston: Houghton Mifflin, 1996). Also *Technopoly, the Surrender of Culture to Technology*, by Neil Postman (New York: Vintage Books, 1993). For one nation's effort at commercial-social integration, see "Model Makers, A Survey of the Netherlands," *Economist*, May 4, 2002.

259 an average annual growth rate: Statistics taken from "Charlemagne, Sclerotic after All These Years. Why Is Europe Growing So Slowly?" *Economist*,

March 15, 2003. In fact, the gross domestic product per capita between 2000 and 2003 grew faster in Europe than in America (5.9 percent in the former compared to 1 percent in the latter). See "Europe Is Strong: Europe's Economies Are Growing Faster Than 'Dynamic' America," by Phillipe Legrain, *Prospect*, September 2003

259 41 million citizens among us: For a thoughtful analysis of America's complex health delivery system and how an understanding of human behavior may be helpful in fixing it, see *The US Health Care Dilemma, Mirrors and Chains*, by Michael McGuire and William Anderson (Westport, CT: Auburn House, 1999).

259 the quality of education a child receives: Even the more than $1 billion spent in federal financial aid for students is distributed in such a way that the lion's share ends up in the coffers of the more expensive private colleges that teach relatively few poor and disadvantaged students. Federal aid per student receiving loans and work study at Ivy League colleges, many of which have endowments in the billions of dollars, is commonly 10 to 20 times the median. See "Richest Colleges Receiving Richest Share of US Aid," by Greg Winter, *New York Times*, November 9, 2003.

259 Ayn Rand's: The Russian-born novelist Ayn Rand came to the United States as a refugee in 1926 at the age of 21. Fiercely concerned with individualism as the route to happiness and self-fulfillment (based in large part from her experiences in the Soviet Union), she is best known for her novels *The Fountainhead* (1943) and *Atlas Shrugged* (1957), both of which explore the relationship between society and the self.

259 tax cuts that largely benefit the wealthy: See "Defining the Rich in the World's Wealthiest Nation," *New York Times*, January 12, 2003.

259 In the interest of commercial gain: Compared to past generations, teenagers living in America have seen greater commercialization than any other age group. Many live frenetic lives, and the use of psychotropic agents to modulate that frenzy is rising rapidly. See "The Prozac Kids," *People*, July 28, 2003.

262 Bill Gates of Microsoft fame: "Creating Small High Schools. Grants Seek to Make Sure NYC Students Don't Get Lost," *New York Times*, September 18, 2003.

263 forging from the affluence of commercial success: The social challenges facing America are clear. The question now is what to do about them. See "America's Choice: And Now, Mr. President," *Economist*, November 4, 2000. For an alternative commercial vision, see *Natural Capitalism, Creating the Next Industrial Revolution*, by Paul Hawken, Amory Lovins, and L. Hunter Lovins (Boston: Little, Brown, 1999); and *The Soul of Capitalism: Opening Paths to a Moral Economy*, by William Greider (New York: Simon and Schuster, 2003).

INDEX

amino acids, 65, 279*n*
Amirkhanov, Hizri, 280*n*
Andreessen, Marc, 112, 287*n*
Andrews, Cecile, 320*n*
angiotensinogen, 152
Anna (businesswoman), 83, 84,
    87–90, 96–97, 99–101, 235
anxiety, 5, 15, 106, 107, 172, 177,
    241
  fear and, 168–69
  Kim's experience with, 165–67,
    173–74, 175, 302*n*–3*n*
Apache Indians, 294*n*
appetite, 241, 244–45
Arizona, 142
Arkansas, 231–32, 233
Art of Eating, The (Fisher), 131,
    292*n*
Arthur Andersen company, 126
Arthur Teacher's Fish and Chips,
    200
Ashley Montagu Institute, 320*n*
associations, 257
Atkins, Robert, 154
Atlas Shrugged (Rand), 322*n*
Australia, 57, 72
Australian aborigines, 139
Australian National University, 277*n*
Australopithecus, 59, 60
automobiles, 108
  dependence on, 132–33
Awash River, 59, 60
axons, 279*n*

Babbage, Charles, 287*n*
baboons, 60, 69
Bank of England, 33
bankruptcies, 43
  of Enron, 124–25
Bantu tribe, 98
Baudrillard, Jean, 199–200
Baywatch (television show), 196
Beaumont, Gustave de, 58, 75, 76

Behan, Brendan, 236, 247, 317*n*
Bell, Alexander, 110
Bell, Daniel, 234
Bell Telephone, 111
Bennett, William J., 314*n*
Bering Sea, 67, 97, 98
Berlin Wall, 127, 189
Berners-Lee, Tim, 287*n*
Bezos, Jeff, 118–19, 122
Bill and Melinda Gates Foundation,
    262
biogenic amines, 279*n*
biological clock, 159, 160–62, 174
Blade Runner (film), 77–78
body mass index (BMI), 134
Bogin, Barry, 293*n*
boldness (novelty seeking), 80–82
Book of Virtues, The (Bennett),
    314*n*
Boston College, 27
Boston Globe, 231
Bové, José, 194, 199, 203, 208, 209,
    213, 252, 308*n*
Bowling Alone (Putnam), 177,
    319*n*–20*n*
Bowman Gray School of Medicine,
    68–69
brain, 5–6, 94
  addictive hijacking of, 71, 93,
    283*n*–84*n*
  anatomy of, 61–62, 278*n*–79*n*
  biological clock in, 160–62, 174
  calories consumed by, 151
  computers and, 114
  economic environment and,
    11–13
  empathetic understanding and,
    219
  intelligence and, 61–62
  meat eating and, 65
  neurotransmitters in, 62–63, 279*n*
  reptilian, 61–63, 80, 168
  sleep and, 159–61